DEVELOPING ACTIVE LEARNING
in the **PRIMARY CLASSROOM**

Education at SAGE

SAGE is a leading international publisher of journals, books, and electronic media for academic, educational, and professional markets.

Our education publishing includes:

- accessible and comprehensive texts for aspiring education professionals and practitioners looking to further their careers through continuing professional development

- inspirational advice and guidance for the classroom

- authoritative state of the art reference from the leading authors in the field

Find out more at: **www.sagepub.co.uk/education**

DEVELOPING
ACTIVE LEARNING
in the PRIMARY CLASSROOM

ANITRA VICKERY

with contributions from Alice Hansen, Katharine Collier,
Rebecca Digby, Mary Briggs, Steve Higgins and others

SAGE

Los Angeles | London | New Delhi
Singapore | Washington DC

Los Angeles | London | New Delhi
Singapore | Washington DC

SAGE Publications Ltd
1 Oliver's Yard
55 City Road
London EC1Y 1SP

SAGE Publications Inc.
2455 Teller Road
Thousand Oaks, California 91320

SAGE Publications India Pvt Ltd
B 1/I 1 Mohan Cooperative Industrial Area
Mathura Road
New Delhi 110 044

SAGE Publications Asia-Pacific Pte Ltd
3 Church Street
#10-04 Samsung Hub
Singapore 049483

Editor: James Clark
Editorial assistant: Rachael Plant
Project manager: Bill Antrobus
Production editor: Thea Watson
Copyeditor: Helen Fairlie
Proofreader: Caroline Stock
Marketing manager: Catherine Slinn
Cover design: Naomi Robinson
Typeset by Kestrel Data, Exeter, Devon
Printed by: Replika Press Pvt Ltd India

First published 2014

Library of Congress Control Number: 2013930308

British Library Cataloguing in Publication data

A catalogue record for this book is available from
the British Library

ISBN 978-1-4462-5546-9
ISBN 978-1-4462-5547-6 (pbk)

CONTENTS

ABOUT THE AUTHOR

Anitra Vickery has been working in teacher education for the last twelve years and is, at present, a Senior Lecturer in Primary Mathematics, Professional Studies Coordinator and a Personal Tutor on the PGCE course at Bath Spa University. Previously she worked with serving teachers in her role as Numeracy Consultant for South Gloucestershire and Swindon LEAs after completing 16 years of teaching in primary schools as class teacher and deputy head. Her area of particular interest is the development of children's thinking and problem solving skills and she has developed a number of teaching and learning materials for publication in this area.

In the field of teacher education her particular interest is the interplay between affective issues and reflective practice. She has built up close working relationships with local Primary Schools, which has enabled her to keep abreast of current practice.

NOTES ON CONTRIBUTORS

Carrie Ansell is Senior Lecturer in Primary and Early Years English, language and literacy at Bath Spa University. Prior to taking up this post, she taught in primary and early years settings, mainly in schools that had multilingual and culturally diverse populations. Her recent research with Deborah Nicholson at Bath Spa University is in the field of literacy and social inclusion. For the past 5 years, she has taught a module entitled 'Learning, Talk and Dialogic Teaching' with her colleague, Kendra McMahon at Bath Spa University.

Keith Ansell has been a primary teacher since 1980, working in Surrey and Bristol where he became an advisory teacher for ICT. Later, as an e-learning consultant with South West Grid for Learning, he supported ICT consultants from Cornwall to Gloucestershire, and represented SWGfL on the Content Committee of the National Educational Network. He has worked as a project manager on a number of online software projects, services and competitions across the South West. He currently works as a senior lecturer on the Primary and Early Years PGCE course at Bath Spa University. Keith is part of the ICT team, and also teaches Design and Technology within the course. He is in his third year as a personal tutor, guiding and supporting PGCE students as they become primary teachers. He has good links with the ICT in education industry and organises the exhibitions at the summer regional ICT conference at UWE.

Chris Collier is Senior Lecturer in Primary Science at Bath Spa University where he is joint coordinator of science on the PGCE Primary and Early Years course. He teaches on a number of courses and modules on the PGCE and undergraduate Education Studies programmes. He is a founder member of the Centre for Research in Early Scientific Learning (CRESL) based at Bath Spa and is heavily involved in the centre's research activity.

Rebecca Digby is Senior Lecturer in Primary and Early Years education. She teaches early years science on the PGCE training programme, is a personal tutor for a group of Bath Spa teachers, and leads the International Perspectives on Early Years education module on the Education Studies undergraduate course. Previously, she taught in schools across the primary and early years phases in both England and Scotland in a number of roles including Advanced Skills Teacher specialising in science and creativity, and deputy headteacher.

Mary ffield worked for a number of years in Primary and Early Years education and care, including as a social worker, a playgroup leader and a teacher. She developed an interest in teacher education while supporting and mentoring student teachers in her classroom, and subsequently worked as a Senior Lecturer and PGCE Programme Leader at Newman University College, Birmingham and at Bath Spa University, where she established a part-time Early Years PGCE course in close collaboration with a local children's centre and a primary school. Her research interests include development and citizenship education, an area in which she has contributed to teaching handbooks, and the early professional experiences of NQTs.

Tor Foster is Senior Lecturer in English on the PGCE Primary course at Bath Spa University. She taught in primary and secondary schools and worked as an advisory teacher before moving into higher education. She was course leader for the postgraduate course in primary education at the University of the West of England. Since moving to Bath Spa University she has been responsible for the English subject knowledge part of the PGCE course. Her research interests are the successful recruitment and retention of male primary teachers, as well as creativity in the English curriculum.

Darren Garside entered the teaching profession in 1999 following a short pre-service career working for academic libraries, political organisations and a management consultancy. He joined Bath Spa University in 2007 after completing a Masters of Teaching on the conversational dynamics of Philosophy for Children (P4C) enquiries. Initially he joined the PGCE English team and is at present a core member of the Education and Childhood Studies degree programme, specialising in the philosophy of education. During his time at BSU he has developed his teaching and research interests into P4C and philosophy of education, and is currently exploring how P4C methodologies can be used to enhance learning at university. He is writing his doctoral thesis on the concept of teachers' pedagogical judgement in the context of the Philosophy for Children movement.

ACKNOWLEDGEMENTS

The authors would like to extend special thanks to the schools, headteachers and teachers, who assisted us in writing the case studies contained within the book, by allowing us to observe and discuss current practice.

Jon Rees, St Anne's Juniors, Bristol

Carol Rusby and Judith Smith, The Orchard Infant School, East Molesey, Surrey

Faye Kitchen and Caroline Harding, Bromley Heath Junior, South Gloucestershire

Keith Ledbury and Theresa Gee, Courtney Primary, South Gloucestershire

Sean Quinn and Janet Dixon, St Anne's C of E Primary, South Gloucestershire

Sam O' Reagan, NQT

James Ridd, trainee teacher

Dan Wilson, St Andrew's C of E Primary, Congresbury, North Somerset

Ian Rockey, Moorland's Infant School, Bath

Johannah Meggs, Acton Turville C of E Primary, South Gloucestershire

Jonathan Hannam, Lead Learner, Fordingbridge Junior School , Hants

Paul Jackson and Lisa Naylor, Gallions Primary School, Beckton, London

Carolyn Banfield and Katherine Morgan, St John's C of E Primary, Midsomer Norton

Many ideas presented here have been developed with others. Individual authors would like to thank them for their support.

Anitra Vickery would like to thank her partner Mike Spooner for his constant support, advice and encouragement, and also Sarah, Pippa and Paul for their motivating interest. Thanks also to James Clarke and Monira Begum at Sage for editorial support.

Keith Ansell would like to thank his colleagues Emma Asprey, Wendy Hanrahan, Carrie Ansell and Deborah Nicholson at Bath Spa University.

Rebecca Digby would like to thank her partner, Iain, and her family for their endless support.

Carrie Ansell and Tor Foster would like to thank Penny Hay, Director of Research for 5x5x5=creativity, and Catherine Lamont Robinson, 5x5x5=creativity artist for the 'Schools without Walls' project at *the egg* theatre, Bath. Thanks also to Deborah Nicholson, English language and literacy lecturer, and Kendra McMahon, module leader with Carrie Ansell on 'Learning, Talk and Dialogic Teaching'.

INTRODUCTION

The overall objective of our book is to provide a synthesis of the factors that contribute to making children active partners in their learning. The book is offered as a hybrid of a practical handbook and an academic text. It sets out to bridge the gap between research-based knowledge and the practical enterprise of teaching by summarising the theoretical foundations and providing models of practical application.

Each chapter uses the same structure; opening with a review of research and published opinion before going on to offer some Try this activities to aid a practical investigation of some of the key ideas. Every chapter also provides a case study and a list of ideas for further reading. It is important to note that the case studies in each chapter, whilst offering a number of vibrant and innovative ideas, have not been chosen to exemplify 'best practice', but rather to illustrate how some schools are responding to the challenge of empowering children to take responsibility for their learning.

All of the contributors to this book are passionate about the development of active learning in the primary classroom. The different chapters they have provided look at active learning from the perspective of different subject disciplines and distinct aspects of pedagogical practice including assessment, questioning and the use of information technology. Chapters 1 and 10 focus on the development of the skills that underpin active learning by discussing Frameworks for Thinking and Philosophy for Children. By bringing together these different perspectives it is possible to identify a number of common themes and appreciate the consistency in the thinking about approaches that lead to the emancipation of the learner.

Recent research into how children learn has resulted in a set of beliefs about pedagogical approaches and curriculum design that is widely shared amongst many schools. These beliefs can be detected within a variety of curriculum 'movements' e.g. creative curriculum, active learning, an enquiry-based approach, personalisation, assessment for learning, the learner-centred curriculum and new areas of activity such as the development of thinking, cross-curricular and learning skills. The key principles of making children active partners in their learning and emphasising the development of learning skills and personal qualities link all of these ideas.

This book seeks to explore these principles and provide trainee and newly qualified teachers with opportunities to explore a range of philosophies and strategies to develop learning.

Time constraints, competing priorities and the other challenges inherent to training courses impact on the opportunities trainees have to make connections between their own experience as learners, their new role as inchoate reflective practitioners and the learning of the children they teach. The book seeks to support trainees in making these connections by bringing together the theoretical basis of key ideas about effective learning, connecting the principles of reflective practice to children's learning, and making practical suggestions for classroom implementation.

CHAPTER 1

FRAMEWORKS FOR THINKING

Anitra Vickery

I cannot teach anybody anything; I can only make them think.

Socrates

Chapter overview

For many years the primary curriculum put an emphasis on passive learning, with the child being considered an empty vessel that needed to be filled with knowledge through a didactic approach. Encouraging children to be active about their own learning and their development of cognition and metacognition requires a very different pedagogy, one which enhances general thinking skills. The explicit development of thinking skills can be offered in different ways; through specifically designed programmes added to the normal curriculum, through targeting thinking and reasoning in specific subjects and by permeating the normal curriculum by identifying and creating opportunities within all lessons. Whichever approach is taken the objective will be to enable children to participate actively in high quality thinking and learning. Efforts to make thinking skills a more central feature of the curriculum have met with resistance. There are competing opinions as to whether thinking skills can be taught, or whether they are best developed through the subject disciplines, and there are questions from some quarters as to whether the teaching of thinking skills is a legitimate curriculum objective.

INTRODUCTION

This chapter will consider the role of thinking skills in the learning process and different approaches to developing thinking skills.

The definition of thinking has occupied academics in a range of fields including psychology, sociology, neuroscience and philosophy from the beginning of time. Each of these fields has influenced the creation of taxonomies, frameworks and definitions of thinking skills. Models that can provide a basis for programmes for the development of thinking skills are available from a number of different sources. These include the ideas of educational thinkers such as Dewey, Feuerstein and Bloom; programmes that focus on implementation (such as the Somerset Thinking Skills courses (Blagg, Ballinger and Gardner, 1988), and Top Ten Thinking Tactics (Lake and Needham, 1993)), programmes that are based on thinking skills in particular subjects (such as Cognitive Acceleration in Science Education (CASE) (Adey, Shayer and Yates, 1989) and Cognitive Acceleration in Mathematics Education (CAME) (Adhami, Johnson and Shayer, 1995)), and movements that seek to add to the traditional curriculum such as Philosophy for Children (see Chapter 10). Reference to the development of thinking skills can also be found in the National Curriculum (DfE website).

The chapter will identify concepts that are common across a range of different frameworks and suggest how these can be incorporated within the curriculum. It will suggest how teachers can integrate thinking skills into their teaching through establishing an effective framework which supports planning, assessment and progression. It will consider the role of:

- the development of metacognition and thinking through pupil presentation;
- assessment for learning, including self and peer assessment;
- collaborative learning and group work;
- discussion.

The chapter concludes with the case study of a primary school practitioner who has been proactive about the development of a greater focus on children's thinking and empowering children as active learners who take responsibility for their own development.

PROGRAMMES FOR THINKING

There has been a surge of interest in the teaching of thinking skills in recent years as a result of an increased understanding about learning and the working of the brain (Fisher, 2005). A number of programmes that claim to help in the development of thinking skills have been developed in the light of this new evidence of brain function.

Dewey (1938) is associated with frameworks for reflection where learners are encouraged to reflect on the process of learning in order to modify and improve it (see Chapter 5). He is also associated with the notion of experiential education (Dewey, 1938). Rebecca Carver was a passionate believer in experiential education and she developed the concept of the ABCs of experiential education (Agency, Belonging, and Competence), to provide meaningful memorable experiences (Carver, 1999). She viewed these as crucial to the development of critical thinkers and life-long learners believing that they enabled growth and deeper critical thinking; characteristics necessary for learners in a complex world. Carver (1999) argued that the 'ABC' elements would support the development of thinking individuals and describes each one as follows:

- **Agency** – represents the development of active learning where children are encouraged to be participants in their own learning. They are encouraged to consider and reflect on their thinking in the problem-solving process, seek and give explanations and be creative and imaginative. This process empowers children to effect changes in their own lives and communities and recognise that they can do so.

- **Belonging** – refers to children recognising themselves as members of a group or community who share the same values and goals. They undertake activities which are meaningful and relevant to all. They feel safe and acknowledge their responsibilities and learn to respect the needs and interest of the members of the group.

- **Competence** – refers to the learning and application of knowledge in different areas, cognitive, physical, artistic, social and technological. The opportunities for application and reflection are provided by the adults and peers with whom the children interact; each adding to the experience of the individual.

One of the most well-known programmes for developing thinking is Feuerstein's Instrumental Enrichment (FIE) (Feuerstein et al., 1980) which was actually developed about 40 years ago. FIE was developed by Reuven Feuerstein, a child psychologist, whilst he was working with holocaust survivors. He believes that intelligence is not fixed and that the cognitive skills of children can be developed if they learn how to think. The FIE programme has been implemented as a curriculum, especially for children with additional support needs, in many countries. The teachers adopt the role of mediators and help the children to think and learn by helping them to filter and interpret the information from set tasks which focus on specific cognitive functions. The tasks which require analytical thinking become increasingly more complex and abstract as the children move through the programme. The sessions are interactive and the children are expected to be active. Those who recommend the programme claim that the children are motivated by the tasks and that they develop problem solving strategies which they can apply in real life. The FIE programme was changed and developed here when Blagg et al. (1988) reported no positive outcome in children's cognitive development in a UK context. The programmes developed as a result were The Somerset Thinking Skills Course (Blagg et al., 1988), a series of generic thinking programmes for secondary-aged children, and Top Ten Thinking Tactics (Lake and Needham, 1993) which is suitable for primary school children. The contents of both were firmly underpinned by Feuerstein's theory. These programmes aim to develop the skills of classification and seriation, focusing on the organisation of ideas and facts and interpreting interrelationships.

Philosophy for children

Philosophy for children (P4C) is used extensively throughout primary classrooms particularly in regard to the development of children's social and moral education. Its use has developed both the quality of questioning and discussion amongst children. It is believed that if children understand their own thinking through thinking about thinking (metacognition) they will improve and develop their ability to think (see Chapter 10).

Bloom's taxonomy

This taxonomy divided learning objectives into three domains – cognitive (thinking, intellectual), affective (feeling, emotional) and psychomotor (doing, practical) – and set out descriptors of progress in each area. The aim was to provide a balance in learning over the three domains and signpost progression in each. In the cognitive domain the objectives range from knowledge and comprehension to the application of skills associated with critical thinking. The taxonomy provides a valuable structure for classifying different types of questions (Bloom et al., 1956) which has been amended and revised by Lorin Anderson, a student of Bloom (Anderson and Krathwohl, 2001) (see Chapter 4 for more detail).

Thinking skills through discrete subjects

Science, mathematics and geography are subjects for which there are well evaluated programmes in which thinking and reasoning are targeted. Cognitive acceleration programmes in maths and science (e.g. Cognitive Acceleration through Science Education, CASE, (see Chapter 9) and Cognitive Acceleration through Mathematics Education, CAME) aim to develop thinking skills by asking questions that facilitate 'guided self-discovery'. These programmes are underpinned by the theories of Piaget and Vygotsky. A major focus is placed on helping children to make the transition from concrete to operational thinking as described by Piaget. The role of the teacher in the programme is defined as operating in what Vygotsky described as the Zone of Proximal Development (ZPD) or the gap between what children can do unaided and what can be achieved with the aid of intervention. The programmes also recognise the importance of discussion between peers and promote the idea of pupils working in groups to solve a problem.

Thinking through Geography (Leat and Higgins, 2002) initiated a movement amongst geography teachers to move away from a knowledge-based curriculum to an approach which focuses on learning. Activities associated with this approach set up rich cognitive challenges and scaffolding for metacognitive analysis. Although designed for secondary students they can be used as a model for primary classrooms.

The infusion approach

Activating Children's Thinking Skills (ACTS) (Dewey and Bento, 2009) was implemented in the Northern Ireland curriculum and initially used with upper Key Stage 2 children to develop thinking skills. It employed an infusion approach in which a teacher's pedagogy is developed alongside making children's thinking explicit. In this programme lessons are designed and planned by teachers across all areas of the curriculum using a framework based on Swartz and Parks' taxonomy of thinking skills. (Swartz and Parks, 1994; McGuinness et al., 1995; McGuinness, 1999; Leat and Higgins, 2002). The programme includes thinking activities for:

- finding patterns;
- considering similarities and differences;
- conjecturing and justifying;
- reasoning;
- considering different perspectives;
- decision making;
- problem solving processes;
- evaluating.

Swartz and Parks (1994) proposed that thinking skills can be taught using a range of strategies including the following.

- Encouraging children to work in collaboration using language that makes their thinking visible.
- Modelling the language through exemplifying the use and extension of prompting probing questions.
- Creating diagrams or mind maps to guide the thinking of both the teacher and the children.
- Making strategies explicit and encouraging children to consider which ones they will use throughout the lesson and then to reflect on the usage at the end. Edward de Bono also advocates the practising of certain strategies for task analysis which enable children to section problems into manageable chunks and become more effective thinkers (de Bono, 1992).

The National Curriculum promotes the development of thinking skills and states in the section entitled 'Learning across the National Curriculum' that: 'By using thinking skills pupils can focus on "knowing how" as well as "knowing what" – learning how to learn.' It sections thinking skills into five key areas that complement the key skills and are embedded in the National Curriculum.

The use of key questions by the child or modelled by the teacher could be used to help develop these skills:

- **Information Processing Skills** enable pupils to sort and collect relevant information, to sequence, compare and contrast, and to analyse part/whole relationships.
  Q. *What is the problem about?*
  Q. *What does it tell me?*
  Q. *How is it similar or different from . . . ?*
  Q. *Can I see a pattern?*

- **Reasoning skills** enable pupils to give reasons for opinions and actions, to draw inferences and make deductions, to use precise language to explain what they think, and to make judgements and decisions informed by reasons or evidence.
  Q. *Can I explain this to a friend?*
  Q. *Can I explain this to my teacher? (more precise language)*
  Q. *If I know that what else do I know?*

- **Enquiry skills** enable pupils to ask relevant questions, to pose and define problems, to plan what to do and how to research, to predict outcomes and anticipate consequences, and to test conclusions and improve ideas.
  Q. *What do I need to do and why?*
  Q. *Where can I start my enquiry?*
  Q. *What do I think will happen?*
  Q. *Can I test this?*

- **Creative thinking skills** enable pupils to generate and extend ideas, to suggest hypotheses, to apply their imagination and to look for alternative innovative outcomes.
  Q. *Is there another way of doing this?*
  Q. *What will happen if I . . . ?*

- **Evaluation skills** enable pupils to evaluate information, to judge the value of what they read, hear and do, to develop criteria for judging the value of their own and others' work or ideas, and to have confidence in their judgements.
  Q. *Could I have approached this in a different/better way?*
  Q. *What could I do to improve it?*

All of these frameworks help to give shape and substance to the idea of any programme that seeks to develop thinking skills. They share many common features and perhaps the aspect that unites them all is the objective that learning should be transferable and equip children for the task of thinking productively throughout life in the twenty-first century.

TEACHING THINKING SKILLS

What does it mean to teach children to think? How can we be explicit about what this means and what it involves?

There are a number of definitions for the term '*thinking skills*' some of which have attracted some controversy. The definition that thinking skills are a set of skills that enable people to think in different ways for different purposes is generally agreed (Fisher, 2010). Thinking skills can be described as techniques and strategies that develop high quality thinking but what exactly does this mean? If children are to learn in a more meaningful way, to develop the strategies outlined in the frameworks referred to above and be more flexible and reasoned in their judgements then they must be shown how to do that. The skills of reasoning or questioning can be taught through modelling and if these are practised sufficiently they become part of a child's 'thinking toolkit' which helps them to make sense of the world.

Designing tasks

Whilst children should be offered a wide variety of learning tasks it is possible to identify certain key ingredients that promote the development of thinking skills. The core ingredients include:

- Tasks that have a degree of uncertainty, open-ended tasks that require children to strive to make sense of the task before selecting a strategy to find a solution.
- Access to any resources that might be used.
- Opportunities to engage in questioning and discussion.
- Structures that allow children to reflect on and explain their process of enquiry.
- Time to present outcomes and process to their peers. This should include a reflection on the efficacy of the process followed and what they would change if they were to repeat the task.

The development of thinking skills relies on being able to make the thinking visible. In order to do this clearly you will need to help children develop a language that can be used to describe their thinking. You can develop language through modelling, through intervening and guiding discussion and by encouraging collaboration and reflection. In this way you will develop the metacognition of all learners. Allow time and create opportunities for children to do this. Build discussion and reflection time into the day so that children are frequently thinking about their thinking.

Children come into school with preconceived ideas about a range of topics including themselves and their ability to learn and contribute meaningfully. You will need to unpick these perceptions through socially constructed dialogue or discussion with peers and other adults as well as constructing new knowledge and understanding through activities and informed teaching. It is important for you to consider how the adults that interact with the children can facilitate thinking and also how they can judge whether the children are thinking and the quality of that thinking. If you present children with cognitive challenge where they are required to think more deeply and systematically you will develop the skills of thinking that will enable them to meet the demands of the uncertain future of the twenty-first century. Everyone worldwide will need these skills to be successful in an increasingly complex world (Fisher, 2010).

THE THINKING ENVIRONMENT

However thinking is taught – whether it is through discrete subjects, across all curriculum areas or through specially designed programmes – it needs to take place in an environment of questioning, discussion and discovery: an environment which has a positive ethos and where the curriculum is suitably challenging and flexible (see Chapter 3).

The environment that is best suited to this is a constructivist environment, where high quality interactions between the teacher and children and amongst children are generated. It should be an environment in which there is an open-minded attitude towards thinking and knowledge where children are prepared to take risks with voicing opinions and reflecting on the opinions of others. In this way children begin to appreciate the process of thinking, both theirs and their peers. The Thinking Together programme (Dawes et al., 2000) has been developed from this premise.

Wallace and Adams (1993) designed a problem-solving wheel called TASC (Thinking Actively in a Social Context) which can be used by children to guide their approach to problem solving. It contains a number of prompts displayed in a circle so that children can be reminded about some of the strategies they can use to solve a problem and note which ones they actually use. They are identified under eight headings, shown below.

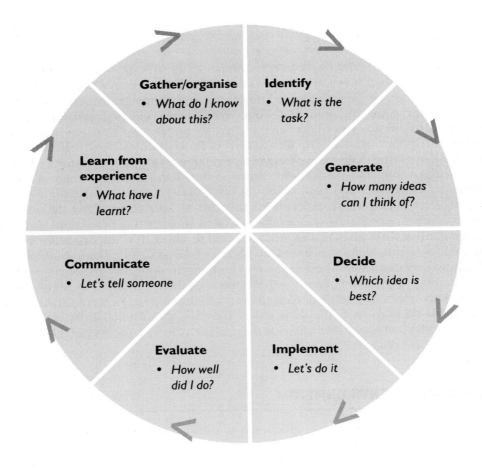

Figure 1.1   Strategies for problem solving

You might feel that it would be more meaningful if the strategies or approaches to problem solving were discussed with and formulated by the children. The process of thinking would be more transparent and could change depending on the topic to be investigated. You could encourage the children to create a mind map or a diagram of their thinking journey which would make their thinking visible and be a vehicle for discussion. It is important to create a dedicated space to display their 'thinking and learning journey'.

Larkin (2002) suggests that this form of analysis would encourage children to ask the questions that would encourage thinking. Devereux (2002) provides a list of key questions for early years children to support this which you might want to use initially to model the thought processes.

- *What will happen if you . . . ?*
- *Have you thought about . . . ?*
- *What is your problem?*
- *How can you find out about . . . ?*
- *What happens when you test?*
- *Why do you think this will happen?*
- *How can you fix this?*

Recent research into the working of the brain informs us that the majority of brain growth occurs before a child is six years old. This has huge implications for the role of parents and teachers and the place of activities that provide cognitive challenge throughout the curriculum.

The role of the adult

The role of the adult in developing thinking is crucial. Dewey (1938) believes that teachers play a very important part in moulding and crafting children's experiences through their interactions with the children. You need to be proactive about developing opportunities for collaborative work where there are appropriate interactions and timely interventions from all adults. Dialogue is essential in the development of thinking skills. It is through dialogue that children begin to be aware of and understand their own and other people's thinking. You can aid this process by consciously planning opportunities for discussion and reflection throughout the day. The adults involved in these opportunities need to know the children well so that an environment of trust can be established; one which promotes discussion, creativity, risk taking and reflection. You should try to impress on your adult helpers that they should use every opportunity to mention the words and phrases associated with thinking such as, learning through thinking, think, 'put your thinking hats on', evaluate your thinking, and reflect on your thinking and learning.

Benefits of an explicit approach to the development of thinking skills

All children regardless of age and attainment will benefit from an education that focuses on the development of thinking skills. This approach will provide opportunities for children to be involved in the planning of their work and be creative and reflective. It should produce learners who are more focused and have an increased awareness of themselves and others as learners as well as developing a disposition for curiosity, perseverance, confidence and reflection.

The framework below sets out the features that underpin the creation of the environment in which thinking skills will flourish. Each time you plan a unit of work or lesson consider each of the three areas illustrated below to ensure that you are addressing all the areas that will promote thinking.

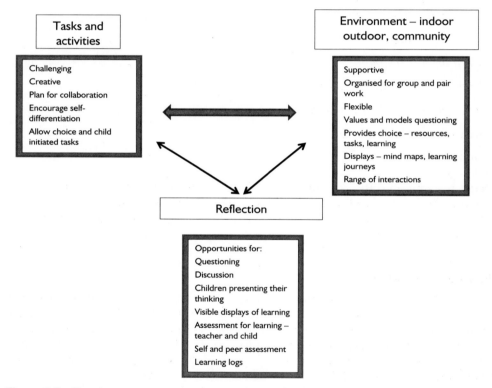

Figure 1.2   Creating an environment that encourages the development of thinking skills.

CASE STUDY

This case study focuses on the work of Jon, deputy headteacher of a city junior school. At the time of the case study Jon had been in post for two years. The school has a mixed demographic with a large majority of pupils of White British heritage. The number of pupils known to be eligible for free school meals is below the national average and the number of pupils with special educational needs and/or disabilities is above average.

The school prospectus outlines a philosophy of teaching and learning and lists aims that take into account the increasingly complex technological environment in which we live. The school has redesigned its curriculum to meet the needs of the twenty-first century recognising that education should be more than just acquiring knowledge. Their skills-based curriculum aims to develop independent effective learners who embrace problem solving.

The deputy head is passionate about enabling children to develop a framework for thinking that will support them in their approach to any problem they may encounter. He firmly believes in equipping children with life-long skills. He has been driven by his personal philosophy and influenced by the research he has conducted into active learning; exploring the ideas of de Bono, Claxton, Pardoe and Wallace's TASC framework. He has also attended workshops on developing active learning. When he was appointed as deputy head to the school he was also made assessment coordinator. This new role further developed his interest in assessment for learning and his belief that children need to know how to assess their own work and take responsibility for developing their own learning. He wanted the children to drive their own learning and for them and the teachers to feel challenged, motivated and equipped to do this.

The school has a policy of using 'I can' statements and a learning wall to make learning visible; however, Jon felt that they were not being used as actively as they could be. He decided to create a framework to encourage the children to become more active about their learning. He wanted to develop perseverance, confidence, teamwork, reflection and creativity amongst the children and to this end he designed a framework called 'Power Learners'. This framework makes visible the characteristics of active learners and suggests how children can develop these to take responsibility for their own learning.

- *Power Learners look for ways to improve.*
  For example: they make use of the success criteria.

- *Power Learners look for creative ways to solve problems.*
  For example: they are brave and try something new.

- *Power Learners give and take ideas.*
  For example: they develop others' ideas to improve them and then make use of them.

- *Power Learners help the team.*
  For example: they help to resolve conflicts.

- *Power Learners take responsibility for their learning.*
  For example: they answer and ask questions.

- *Power Learners talk about their learning.*
  For example: they explain how they found the answer.

- *Power Learners never give up.*
  For example: they never say 'I dunno!' but instead have a go.

The above framework presents the seven 'Power Learner' areas; however, the example underneath each area represents only an illustration of what each includes. He introduced this to the staff, holding meetings to ensure an understanding of both the philosophy and the process and the teachers were enthusiastic. The teachers used Jon's materials and worked with their own classes to develop 'Power Learners'. They appreciated the chance to share the learning with their class and this gave them some ownership. However, by working with the classes during the teachers' Preparation, Planning and Assessment (PPA) Jon was able to see how the programme was developing with children throughout the school.

Each characteristic was introduced separately. Jon created lesson plans and PowerPoints to do this. The first characteristic, 'looking for ways to improve', was introduced through a practical activity with chopsticks. The children were required to move small soft balls from one container to another using the chopsticks. They were then encouraged to discuss ways in which they could improve their performance. This chopstick task was graded at level 3 and the children were asked to suggest how the activity would be different for a lower level, say 1, and a higher level such as 6. The levelling exercise was done in an attempt to help pupils see the whole 'learning journey' so they could see how you can progress in a skill. This particular exercise enabled them to think about how to make progress from one stage or level to the next by looking for improvement.

Each characteristic from the framework has been explored in a similar way using practical problem solving activities as the starting point. The children are extremely enthusiastic about 'Power Learners'. The children's enthusiasm ensures that parents hear a lot about 'Power Learners' and it is also shared on the parents' section of the school's website which states: 'We encourage children to take responsibility for their own learning, to be involved as far as possible in reviewing the way they learn, and to reflect on how they learn'.

The children's understanding of these characteristics is becoming visible across the curriculum not just in the specific 'Power Learning' sessions. For example, when Jon was taking an RE lesson about Moses the children identified that Moses was using the second 'Power Learner' point in that he was being creative and looking for innovative ways of solving problems.

Jon has also devised cards that allocate teamwork roles to develop the effectiveness of group work. These roles have child-friendly names such as 'Captain' for the person who will coordinate the team. The cards have clear suggestions of how the children can fulfil their role. These group role cards are linked closely to the 'Power Learners' framework so that as the children use them they gain a deeper understanding of the associated skills. The relationship between what the children might perceive as 'copying' and collaboration has been examined through discussion.

The 'Power Learning' approach is in its second year now but Jon is no longer responsible for PPA cover so it will be more difficult for him to monitor the programme. Jon ensures that all new members of staff are introduced to the philosophy and practice through the materials he has created. He hopes to continue to develop a more active approach to learning and his ultimate aim is to enable children to deal confidently with any situation that may present itself throughout their lives.

Reflecting on the case study

- What do you think are the strengths of the introduction of the 'Power Learner' programme to
  a)   the children;
  b)   the teachers.

- What would you do to ensure the transferability of 'Power Learner' characteristics across the curriculum?

- Which aspects of the 'Power Learner' programme do you feel are most likely to be effective?

- How does this approach compare to your experience in school?

TRY THIS

Try this 1: Solving problems

Activity 1

Often children can't solve a problem because they don't really understand what they are supposed to find out and have no strategies for a systematic approach. Help children to devise a series of 'prompt questions' to unravel the problem.

- In your own words tell me what you know.
- What don't you know?
- What could we do first?
- Do you think some resources or drawing a picture of the problem might help?

If this procedure is adhered to you may find that more children are prepared to tackle problems by themselves, in groups or pairs, before seeking help from you.

Activity 2

Children can develop their questioning and reasoning through practice and modelling. Work alongside children to solve a problem that requires a systematic approach, modelling each stage clearly. Present them with similar problems and observe their approach.

Are the children able to work systematically through a different range of problems?

Activity 3

Present children with a selection of games that will help them develop their problem-solving strategies. Children seem to be motivated by the idea of a game and particularly if it involves working with a peer or group. There are a number of board games that require a strategic problem-solving approach to play and win and there is a vast selection on the internet. It is important to incorporate these into the curriculum regularly.

Do the children recognise the skills they are developing during these sessions?

Is there a noticeable progression in the approaches the children apply to problem solving as a result of these sessions?

Activity 4

Present children with real-life problems that arise out of the school environment.

- Redesign the school grounds to include a quiet area, a small outdoor theatre, a garden, a ball games area and areas for less boisterous games such as skipping or hopscotch.
- Organise and create appropriate spaces and stalls for a money-raising event.
- Develop strategies to be more environmentally friendly:
    monitoring water use;
    managing the recycling;
    monitoring electricity usage.

Do the children become more aware of environmental issues?

Do the skills of organisation and information processing develop and are they applied in other situations?

Activity 5

Jigsaw puzzles are not just a source of entertainment they help to develop rational thinking. The process of completing a jigsaw also helps with hand–eye coordination and spatial awareness. In order to complete a puzzle children have to consider the shape, compare the size, colour and pattern of each piece and look at how it may connect to another piece. They also use trial and improvement techniques and develop their visual memory. The task may take days to complete and so if this process is shared then the skills of collaboration and discussion will be developed during the process.

Try this 2: Developing discussion

In order to take an active part in any discussion children must be informed about the subject to be discussed, be good listeners, respect the views of others, be prepared to state opinions and reflect on others' points of view before coming to a decision. The extent to which children will be able to do this will depend on their age, the number of times they have taken part in such an activity and their understanding of the rules of engagement. If children are gradually introduced to this process they could become quite sophisticated critical thinkers by upper Key Stage 2.

Activity 1

Ask children to consider a film or television programme and discuss the merits of it under specific headings, such as entertainment value, quality of the acting and so on. Encourage them to develop a less personal bias by presenting facts to support statements and by asking them to comment on opposing viewpoints.

Do children find it difficult to be persuaded from their original viewpoint?

Activity 2

Encourage children to critique educational software programs by first designing questions that would enable them to determine the usefulness of the program and then actually using the program to see how many points are addressed. The merits of the program can then be discussed with their peers.

Do the children gradually become more discerning about the programs they use or does the 'fun' element overcome any reservations about the educational merit?

Activity 3

Read a story that has a moral issue or dilemma and encourage the children to discuss their feelings about it (see Chapter 10 for more ideas). Alternatively present the characters of a fairy story such as 'Little Red Riding Hood' and ask the children to support the actions of those characters and debate which one deserves most sympathy.

Can the children find convincing reasons to support their choice?

Activity 4

Involve the children in a critique of anonymous children's work from across the curriculum. Encourage them to discuss how the child could improve the work and what strategies they would put in place to enable them to do so.

Do the children become more adept at reviewing their own work as well as the work of their peers?

Try this 3: Making children aware of the stages in their learning

Activity 1

Encourage the children to create their own learning objectives for lessons by reviewing what the class learned or were introduced to in the previous lesson. Allow time at the beginning of sessions to discuss this.

How much guidance do you need to give?

Are the children concerned with 'guessing what's in the teacher's head'?

Activity 2

At the end of a topic or unit of work ask the children to predict what the next level or stage of learning might be.

Does this help to secure the 'big picture'?

Are children surprised by the increase in the amount of knowledge or understanding that is required for the next stage?

SUMMARY

Throughout this chapter you have been presented with a number of frameworks, taxonomies and theories about how to develop thinking skills. This provides a range of ideas for creating the right environment and approach to promote thinking skills within your classroom. The importance of developing interactions to increase dialogue and presenting cognitive challenge is emphasised, as is the need for assessment and reflection. There are also suggestions about how the teacher can be proactive at the planning stage to ensure that there are many opportunities to allow the children to be reflective about their learning and the route that learning will take. There is good evidence to suggest that the thinking person, the problem solver, will develop the ability to work successfully as a team member or independently, to be flexible and creative. These skills are highly valued in today's society and will be absolutely necessary in the future world of advanced technology.

FURTHER READING

de Bono, E. (2008) *Six Frames for Thinking about Information.* London: Vermillion.
This book illustrates Edward de Bono's 'six frames' technique in which he presents us with exercises to enable us to direct our attention in a conscious way.

Burton, L. (1989) *Thinking Things Through. Problem Solving in Mathematics*. Oxford: Basil Blackwell Limited.
This is a practical guide to mathematical problem solving that offers advice about the process as well as a range of problem-solving mathematical activities.

Fisher, R. (2005) *Teaching Children to Think*. Cheltenham: Nelson Thornes.
This book provides practical ideas about how to develop the learning and thinking of all children. The author reviews the main findings of research and looks at different ways of teaching thinking skills.

Hooks, B. (2010) *Teaching Critical Thinking Practical Wisdom*. Abingdon: Routledge.
This book addresses some controversial topics facing teachers both inside and outside the classroom. It is an engaging book which contains a series of accessible essays.

Leicester, M. (2010) *Teaching Critical Thinking Skills*. London/New York: Continuum International Publishing Group.
This book explains the essential elements of critical thinking and contains illustrative stories to help the application of abstract ideas such as reasoning and reflection.

Maclure, S. and Davies, P. (eds) (1991) *Learning to Think: Thinking to Learn*. Oxford: Pergamon Press.
This book explores three different beliefs about promoting thinking within the classroom: the skills approach, the infusion model and the belief that the curriculum as it is provides opportunities for developing thinking.

Moseley, D., Baumfield, V., Elliott, J., Gregson, M., Higgins, S., Miller, J., Newton, D. P. (2005) *Frameworks for Thinking. A Handbook for Teaching and Learning*. Cambridge: Cambridge University Press.
This handbook offers practical advice about the use of frameworks for teaching, learning and assessment focusing on thinking processes.

REFERENCES

Adey, P. S., Shayer, M. and Yates, C. (1989) *Thinking Science: Student and Teachers' Materials for the CASE Intervention*. London: Macmillan.

Adhami, M., Johnson, D. C. and Shayer, M. (1995) *Thinking Maths: The Curriculum Materials of the Cognitive Acceleration through Mathematics Education (CAME) Project – Teacher's Guide*. London: CAME Project/King's College.

Anderson, L. W. and Krathwohl, D. R. (eds) (2001) *A Taxonomy for Learning, Teaching and Assessing: A Revision of Bloom's Taxonomy of Educational Objectives* (Complete edition). New York: Longman.

Blagg, N., Ballinger, M. and Gardner, R. (1988) *Somerset Thinking Skills Course Handbook*. Oxford: Basil Blackwell.

Bloom, B. S., Engelhart, M. D., Furst, E. J., Hill, W. H. and Krathwohl, D. R. (1956) *Taxonomy of Educational Objectives: Handbook 1 Cognitive Domain*. New York: David McKay.

Carver, R. L. (1999) Carver's conceptual framework of experiential education. *Ontario Journal of Outdoor Education*, 122: 11–14.

Dawes, L., Mercer, N. and Wegerif, R. (2000) *Thinking Together: A Programme of Activities for Developing Skills in KS2*. Birmingham: Questions Publishing.

de Bono, E. (1992) *Teach Your Child to Think*. London: Penguin.

Devereux, J. (2002) Developing thinking skills through scientific and mathematical experiences in the early years, in L. Miller, R. Drury and R. Campbell, (eds) *Exploring Early Years Education and Care*. London: David Fulton.

Dewey, J. and Bento, J. (2009) Activating children's thinking skills (ACTS): The effects of an infusion approach to teaching thinking in primary schools. *British Journal of Educational Psychology*, 79: 329–51.

Dewey, J. (1938) *Experience and Education*. New York: Macmillan.

Feuerstein, R., Rand, Y., Hoffman, M. B. and Miller, R. (1980) *Instrumental Enrichment: An Instrumental Programme for Cognitive Modifiability*. Baltimore, MD: University Park Press.

Fisher, R. (2010) Thinking skills, in J. Arthur and T. Cremin (eds) *Learning to Teach in the Primary School*, 2nd edn. Abingdon: Routledge.

Fisher, R. (2005) *Teaching Children to Think*, 2nd edn. Cheltenham: Stanley Thornes.

Lake, M. and Needham, M. (1993) *Top Ten Thinking Tactics*. Birmingham: Scholastic.

Larkin, S. (2002) Creating metacognitive experiences for 5 and 6 year old children, in M. Shayer and P. Adey (eds) *Learning Intelligence: Cognitive Acceleration across the Curriculum from 5–15 Years*. Buckingham: Open University Press.

Leat, D. and Higgins, S. (2002) The role of powerful pedagogical strategies in curriculum development. *The Curriculum Journal*, 13(1): 71–85.

McGuinness, C., Wylie, J., Greer, B. and Sheehy, N. A. F. (1995) Developing children's thinking: A tale of three projects. *Irish Journal of Psychology*, 16(4): 378–88.

McGuinness, C. (1999) *From Thinking Skills to Thinking Classrooms: A Review and Evaluation of Approaches for Developing Pupils' Thinking*. Nottingham: DfEE Publications.

Shayer, M. and Adey, P. (eds) (2002) *Learning Intelligence: Cognitive Acceleration across the Curriculum from 5–15 Years*. Buckingham: Open University Press.

Swartz, R. and Parks, D. (1994) *Infusing the Teaching of Critical and Creative Thinking in Elementary Instruction*. Pacific Grove, CA: Critical Thinking Press.

Wallace, B. and Adams, H. B. (1993) *TASC: Thinking Actively in a Social Context*. Oxford: AB Academic Publishers.

WEBSITES

Department for Education: The National Curriculum
www.education.gov.uk/publications

CHAPTER 2

ACTIVE LEARNING IN THE EARLY YEARS

Mary ffield

Why not make schools into places in which children would be allowed,
encouraged and (if and when they ask) helped to explore and make
sense of the world around them . . . in ways that most interested them?

John Holt

Chapter overview

This chapter explores some of the distinctive learning characteristics of young
children. It examines the role of intrinsic motivation in active learning, and the
part that Early Years practitioners play in sustaining children's motivation and
supporting their development, while enabling them to follow their own lines of
interest. It uses a case study to exemplify how schools and teachers can work
creatively with spaces and resources to optimise children's active learning, and
some suggestions for practical strategies are included for practitioners to try in
their own settings. As well as the references, there are suggestions for further
reading to clarify and extend some of the themes explored in the chapter.

INTRODUCTION

The quotation from John Holt which opens this chapter is referenced in Roland
Meighan's *Freethinkers' Guide to the Educational Universe* (1994). The publisher,
Educational Heretics Press, was set up in response to the increasing central control
and standardisation of teaching practices, 'to question the dogmas of education
in general, and schooling in particular' (Meighan, 1994). Many 'freethinking'
educationalists continue to be concerned, but through the questioning, lobbying

and persistence of many Early Years specialists, there has been a shift in Early Years practice over the past 20 years. This chapter will demonstrate how and why, at least in the classrooms of our youngest children, Holt's aspirational model of learning is no longer heretical, but is increasingly shared amongst practitioners and policy makers.

In a book about active learning, the inclusion of a chapter dedicated to learning in the Early Years suggests that there is something distinctive and different about young children as learners. There is. Children start life as learners – powerful, needs driven, exploratory learners, using all their senses, communication tools and cognitive processing to make sense of a whole new world. Nothing is taken for granted or known – everything has to be found out from the start. When young children arrive for the first time in Nursery or Reception settings, they are strong and experienced learners, accustomed to learning through exploring through their senses, asking questions and constructing their own understanding. Early Years teachers have the privilege of working with small people who want to know, want to understand and want to do. This chapter will explore how this powerful competence and motivation can be sustained, what active learning looks like in the Early Years setting, and the role of the Early Years practitioner in supporting active learning.

There are other characteristics of young learners which are vital to recognise if we are to work appropriately with them. They are reliant on limited experience and language skills in seeking for meanings in a complex world. In order to participate fully, they need to extend their active experience, and find ways to express their curiosity so that they can make connections between the known and the not-yet-known. We will review some theories of cognitive and language development, and how these relate to active learning and inform practice for Early Years teachers. We will consider the place of play in active learning, and how the environment contributes to children's learning as they act within it. For the purpose of this chapter, we will consider 'Early Years' to include children up to the end of the Foundation Stage, aged around five years, though this is a somewhat arbitrary cut-off point. The practice of sustaining an Early Years approach to learning for children up to the ages of six and seven, in countries such as Denmark and France (David, 1993), suggests that there are alternatives to the Foundation Stage/Key Stage 1 divide which is the cause of considerable tension in England's primary schools. The recognition that children develop and mature at different rates prompts us to consider the value of 'Early Years' pedagogical approaches to children beyond the age of five years.

SUSTAINING MOTIVATION

It has long been acknowledged that young children are active, enquiring learners. This acknowledgement is recognised in the revised Early Years Foundation Stage document (Department for Education, 2012), which includes, alongside the Areas of Learning, a set of Characteristics for Effective Learning. The characteristics are defined in terms of what children do as they learn, and are named as:

- playing and exploring;

- active learning;

- creating and thinking critically.

They are referenced severally to engagement, motivation and thinking. According to the non-statutory guidance *Development Matters in the EYFS* (Early Education, 2012), active learning, which is related to motivation, is concerned with children being involved at a deep level in the learning activities they undertake, persisting in the face of challenge, and recognising and enjoying success. The very young learner's motivation is expressed with clarity and feeling by Geertz: 'the desire to make sense of self and others, the drive to understand what the devil is going on' (Geertz, 2001: 22). Moyles links motivation, learning activities and theory in describing the child as active learner and meaning-maker:

> That the child learns through making his or her own physical connections with the world, through sensory explorations, personal effort, social experiences and the active seeking of meaning from experiences, has been established in the theories of psychologists and educationalists such as Froebel, Montessori, Isaacs, Steiner, Vygotsky and later Piaget and Bruner. (cited in Collins et al., 2001: 11)

Active learning, therefore, is not concerned only with the 'doing' that we constantly observe in young children, though being physically active is intrinsic to their learning behaviour. It is deeply concerned with children seeking meaning and mastery, struggling to take control of themselves and their world in order to fully participate in it. Consider the child learning to walk. No matter how many times she totters and falls, unless there is some physical impairment to walking, she will eventually succeed, because it is evident to her that walking is a necessary skill. She does not conclude that it is too difficult, or that she is not good at it. Failure is not contemplated.

The combination of intrinsic motivation and self-belief enables children to engage actively as learners with their immediate environment and with new skills and ideas. It is perhaps easier to recognise this potential when working with very young children, before they are immersed in an externally constructed curriculum. Wrigley, in exploring the reasons for some working class children's lack of interest in school learning, comments that 'in the community, learning often resembles an apprenticeship model, where specific skills are acquired in real situations, out of genuine desire and need. School learning normally reverses this' (Wrigley, 2006: 69). Motivation that springs from a 'genuine desire and need' is strong and intrinsic, and is one of the most powerful tools for teachers, if you can recognise its importance and harness the energy it generates.

RECOGNISING POWERFUL LEARNERS

Whether we allow children to benefit from their own positive learning characteristics and attitudes depends on our own beliefs about children and their potential. One of the overarching principles of the revised EYFS document is that 'every child is a unique child, who is constantly learning and can be resilient, capable, confident and self-assured' (DfE, 2012: 3). This image of the child reflects the philosophy and practice of Loris Malaguzzi (Valentine, 2003) the founder of the pre-school system of Reggio Emilia in Italy, which has become a model for good practice in many parts of the UK (Thornton and Brunton, 2010). The Reggio Emilia approach is founded on an image of children as 'rich, strong and powerful . . . They have potential, plasticity, the desire to grow, curiosity, the ability to be amazed and the desire to relate to other people and to communicate' (Edwards, 1998). The belief in children as powerful learners is the cornerstone of practice in which children are trusted and listened to; they build their own curriculum through long-term projects in which they work collaboratively supported by skilled teachers and artists.

Susan Hart (2004) explores the impact on the UK education system of the long-held belief in set intelligence, which informs so much of schools' practice. The notion of set intelligence has led many teachers and schools to define children by ability, and to teach accordingly (Hart et al., 2004). Despite what we know about children's differential pace of development, and different interests (Penn, 2008) and the characteristics of different types of learning (Eaude, 2011, see Chapter 4), many Reception classes are organised into 'ability groups'. Teachers who accept what is often a management strategy as a truth about children's strengths and potential, instead of seeing 'unique children', expect to find 'three levels of ability, normally distributed across the group' (Ball, 1986, cited in Hart et al. 2004: 22). A significant body of research, starting with Rosenthal and Jacobson's study *Pygmalion in the Classroom* (1968), has alerted teachers to the impact of teacher expectations on learners. The research of Meighan (2007) and of Wilkinson and Pickett (2010) has established how vital it is to maintain not only a positive attitude to learners, but a positive perception of what they are and can be. The impact on learners of perceived expectations is known as the 'self-fulfilling prophecy' (Nash 1973, cited in Hart et al. 2004). Learners internalise the messages behind the 'hidden curriculum' and adjust their own expectations accordingly. Their behaviour and attainment rises or falls in line with the perceived expectations of those whom they see to be the 'experts'.

Very quickly young learners can discover that they are perceived to be not good at certain things, that they are slow, or dull. Children's motivation to make sense of and control themselves and their world can be hampered by loss of self-belief. The result can be an increasing reliance on the teacher as expert, not only in terms of how learning takes place, but also in relation to what should be learned. The motivation of 'need to know' is dulled, and children become passive or alienated. On the other hand, practitioners who demonstrably believe that all children are powerful active learners find ways to build on the children's interests and curiosity. They recognise children's needs in terms of knowledge and skills, and support their development through providing relevant activities, appropriately scaffolded.

THEORETICAL PERSPECTIVES

The twentieth century saw a burgeoning of interest in cognition and cognitive development, with notable theorists including Skinner, Pavlov, Vygotsky, Bruner, and Piaget. For a useful summary, see the introduction to David Wood's *How Children Think and Learn* (1988). One of the most influential in directing attention to children as agents of their own learning was Jean Piaget, and in discussing the particular learning characteristics of young children, it is useful to consider the impact on educational practice of the theories of Piaget and his critics (Wood and Attfield, 2005, see Chapter 2). Piaget's model presented cognitive development as innate, progressive, and age-related. Using a series of experiments, he was persuaded that children move in stages from simple to complex concepts and from concrete to abstract modes of thinking. He believed that the movement from one stage to another is dependent on the child's innate 'readiness', linked to specific age bands. He saw children as learners who engaged in learning through linking new experiences to previous knowledge, dealing with increasingly abstract concepts as they matured. His stage theory saw them moving from dependence on working with concrete objects to engaging with symbolic representations and abstract thought.

One element of Piaget's theory of cognitive development that is still widely accepted is that children learn initially through self-directed action, and that their ability to think in the abstract depends on previous concrete experience. At each stage, 'Piaget's theory of cognitive development placed action and self-directed problem-solving at the heart of learning and development' (Wood and Attfield, 2005: 39).

Piaget's theories have been critiqued and refined by, amongst others, Donaldson (1978), Meadows (1993) and Smilansky and Shefataya (1990), whose work has recognised a more open relationship between ages and stages, and the different way children respond to problem solving in different situations. Donaldson (1992) demonstrated the importance of context; that young learners are dependent on working from recognisable, familiar situations in order to make sense of new challenges, and that children's inability to complete a task may not be related to 'readiness' but to whether the task or expectations made sense to the child. Challenging the notion of innate 'readiness' enables Early Years teachers to review their role in children's development. Teachers no longer feel they must wait for children to be 'ready', depending on their age. A Foundation Stage teacher in the case study school commented 'You don't wait for readiness to happen'. If they are no longer 'waiting for readiness to happen', practitioners can be active in creating and building contexts that are meaningful for the learners, and support them appropriately to meet new challenges. Bruner expresses the importance of recognising the child's present and potential stage of development: 'As a teacher, you do not wait for readiness to happen; you foster or scaffold it by deepening the child's powers at the stage where you find him or her now' (Bruner, 1996: 120). A practical, deep, active engagement with new learning at one level, leads the child to engage more easily and deeply with the same domain of learning at the next level.

In order to make sense of their experiences, children need to represent, to themselves and sometimes to others, what they know. Jerome Bruner categorises three ways of representing experience (2006, vol 1: 69), which are developmental but not exclusive. His model describes how children first represent their understanding, or recollection, through actions, as the *enactive mode*. The toddler rocking her arms to represent a baby is communicating but also remembering the baby. The *iconic mode* is representation through visual means. Before they can use language efficiently children can recognise that a picture represents a real object even if they do not know the object's name. Many children are constantly exposed to visual stimuli through television and computers, and may have a wide range of iconic understanding. The *symbolic mode* is the representation of experience through symbols – particularly language both written and spoken. Whilst young learners may use all three modes to demonstrate experience and understanding, some Early Years children, whose use of language is less fluent and whose vocabulary is more limited, will rely more heavily on the enactive mode to recall and represent experience. They will need to be physically active in order to engage with learning.

The development of neuroscience and our growing understanding of how the brain works gives further credence to the observation-based theories of earlier researchers. 'As the architecture of the brain becomes more complex, children progress in how they use their brain power. When learning something new, novice learners use a lot of mental energy in concentration, attention and perception. With practice, children attain increasing levels of mastery, which releases energy for controlling processes and outcomes, and transferring knowledge across contexts' (Wood and Attfield, 2005: 67). Those who work with young children will recognise the picture of the child fully focused on the woodlouse under a log, the wheels on a model car, or the picture book, immersed in a new experience through looking, feeling, listening, and often oblivious to the wider surroundings. The child's brain is active in learning, as his/her senses explore.

THE PLACE OF LANGUAGE

We are very reliant on language for sharing understanding and information. Language enables us to be social, to express our needs and wishes, to have our views heard, and to understand the lives of other people. Language also plays a key role in cognitive processes. Even as experienced learners, we sometimes speak aloud to remember instructions or to sort out complex problems. Vygotsky considered language an 'essential psychological tool' for thinking and learning (Wood and Attfield, 2005). Vygotsky's model of language and cognitive development presents language as originating through social interaction, whilst thought originates from direct sensory experience. He suggests that at about the age of two years, the two aspects of development merge and a new linguistic model of cognition begins to emerge, as speech becomes internalised and thought becomes verbal. Vygotsky proposed that the child is able to direct and control their own thinking through the use of language. Other theorists, such as Piaget and Wells, see a different relationship between the development of language and cognition, but there is general agreement that language and thinking are closely allied and that language is a vital tool for learning.

Besides the use of language to enable and support thinking, in order to communicate in the class or setting, teachers and learners are heavily reliant on talking, explaining, describing, instructing, questioning, as well as reading and writing in all its forms. In the Early Years context, there is usually a wide diversity of language competence, which is significant for teachers who are facilitating children to think and communicate. Many four and five year-olds are still novice learners of language, as well as users of language for learning. A key objective for Early Years teachers is to develop children's communication and language skills, but alongside this, they are also working to enable children to progress across all areas of learning, whatever their level of language competence or confidence. Children who have been supported and encouraged at home to talk and listen are often at an advantage, and it is important to recognise that this may not correlate with social class – beware of stereotyping and the self-fulfilling prophecy (Tizard and Hughes, 2002; Feiler, 2005), but few at this stage have developed the subtleties of inference, or can articulate their thought processes in words. Those who come to their first educational setting with less experience of using language, or of using a language other than that of the classroom, need particular support in order that their participation in learning is not hampered by their more limited vocabulary and semantic knowledge.

When children are physically active in their learning, they are able to represent their understanding in ways that are less reliant on language, for example by enacting, by drawing, by making or building. This documentation of their learning by the children (Edwards, 1998) enables them to evidence, review and extend their learning. Practitioners who work alongside them are able to observe their understandings and uncertainties without the same dependence on language. Talking and listening, reading and writing are part of active learning, but there other powerful representations which are necessary tools in the Early Years.

THE ACTIVE ENVIRONMENT

The learning environment, both indoor and outdoor, has received a lot of attention particularly since the Early Years Foundation Stage (DCSF, 2008) identified the 'enabling environment' as a core theme of early years practice. In the non-statutory material supporting the revised EYFS, *Development Matters in the EYFS* (Early Education, 2012), the enabling environment, alongside the other themes, is linked to the Characteristics for Effective Learning. Amongst the statements describing what practitioners should provide in relation to the environment (pp. 6, 7), some are particularly relevant to children being active learners:

- Arrange flexible indoor and outdoor space where children can explore, build, move and role play.

- Plan first-hand experiences and challenges appropriate to the children.

- Notice what arouses children's curiosity, looking for signs of deep involvement to identify learning that is intrinsically motivated.

- Ensure children have time and freedom to become deeply involved in activities.

- Build in opportunities for children to play with materials before using them in planned tasks.

- Establish the enabling conditions for rich play: space, time, flexible resources, choice, control, warm and supportive relationships.

The school in the case study in this chapter demonstrated how you can use the learning spaces creatively in order to provide many of the above features of an enabling environment. The children benefited from the flexibility of approach and the commitment of the practitioners to learners' deep involvement, frequent opportunities for children to be active, and substantial periods of choice and freedom. This was balanced by a sense of security generated by routines and familiarity, and by the positive relationships between practitioners and children (see below). Children started each day knowing what they had to do and where to find resources to do it. The initial task was part of the daily routine, and the children settled comfortably to it, chatting to each other about the activity and other things. This freedom within a routine gave them some control, whilst establishing the safety of familiarity, and also enabled the teacher to greet parents and children at the start of the day.

Active learning and Play

The Tickell report on the EYFS (Tickell, 2011), which resulted in the revisions to the EYFS in 2012, draws heavily on the work of Evangelou et al. (2009), describing play as the process in which children actively construct knowledge and understanding, and the importance of play as 'a context for children to bring together their current understandings, flexibly combining, refining and exploring their ideas in imaginative ways. Representing experiences through imaginative play supports development of narrative thought, the ability to see from other perspectives, and symbolic thinking' (Evangelou et al., 2009: 78).

Play has been a by-word in Early Years learning for many years, its place in pedagogy founded on the work of pioneers such as Dewey, Froebel and Steiner, and developed and supported by the work of Moyles (2005), Fisher (2002), Macintyre (2011), and Chazan (2002), amongst many others. The place and nature of play is not, however, uncontroversial, and with increased scrutiny of outcomes in Early Years settings, there is a developing focus on the balance between child-initiated and adult-led activities (Sylva, 2010), and the contribution that free-flow play makes to the overall learning experience of children. Grieshaber and McArdle (2010) and Wood and Attfield (2005) engage with other significant questions raised about, for instance, the fairness and naturalness of play, access to play, and play as work. This is not the place to pursue these issues at length. Instead, acknowledging that a definition of play is problematic, we will consider the value to children of having freedom to choose, to walk and run and climb, to pretend and imagine, to make and draw, to use tools and other resources, to talk and sing and sometimes shout. These are some of the things that children do as they play, and they are all part of being active in their learning.

The key words in discussing play in relation to active learning are choice, ownership and control. Play activities are those which are generally chosen and managed by the children themselves, and children control the process and outcomes. The autonomy experienced during these activities enables children to follow their own lines of enquiry, to practise skills linked to their own experience, at their own pace, and to seek their own solutions to problems. The benefits to children of taking responsibility for decisions, solving problems, and evaluating their actions are highlighted in the longitudinal study of the High/Scope approach in the US (Weikart, 1978). The study showed that adults who had had experience of this pre-school approach, appeared, against a number of criteria, to become more socially competent adults than their peers.

Children as they play can be observed engaging in all areas of learning, rather than 'working to the curriculum'. An example of this is described in the case study, where children together act out the story they have been writing, developing aspects of collaboration, turn-taking and empathy (personal social and emotional development), climbing and running (physical development), recounting, describing and discussing (communication and language).

What does active learning look like?

Early Years children, in the Nursery or Reception class, are thrust into a plethora of experiences and expectations which they have to explore, make sense of and master. The child who, when the teacher asks the class to 'make a circle', puts out his arms and starts to spin, is following the instruction based on his previous experience. His arrival in a formal educational setting presents him with a new culture and language, and in order to function well within it, he must initially explore it as he has explored the whole of his world – through using his senses, and through using previous experience to interpret the new.

As children make connections between experiences, they can start to generalise and, as expressed by McShane (1991) can begin to put 'chunks of learning into large wholes', enabling them to order and manage what they have learned. The child who 'spins' a circle, watches, listens, and discovers that certain instructions (make a line, put your hand up, make a circle, find your place) are context-specific and mean a particular form of activity in the classroom, but also relate in a particular way to his previous knowledge of the world. The effective practitioner, observing the initial 'mistaken' interpretation, notes that the child knows what a circle is, draws the child's attention to what other children are doing, and encourages the child to look at or even walk around the circle to recognise it in this different form. The active perception of the circle in this different form extends the child's understanding of the 'circleness' of a circle, and the child can participate more fully and independently in the life of the classroom. Learning is reinforced and motivation is sustained.

The role of the practitioner in active learning

An important part of the practitioner's role is to stimulate ideas and make connections in children's learning as they work alongside them, through asking questions, providing resources and making suggestions in response to children's ideas. This type of engagement requires the practitioner to be observant and reactive, following the child's lead and being a 'co-researcher' (Edwards, 1998). 'A model that perceives children as having a central role in their own learning also has to acknowledge teachers as learners themselves, rather than as general purveyors of existing knowledge' (Collins, Insley and Soler, 2001: 19). The research study of Sylva et al., the Effective Pre-school and Primary Education project (Sylva, 2010), highlighted the importance of engaging children in sustained shared thinking. As well as planning for this during adult-led teaching, as practitioners engage alongside children in their play they sustain and share in children's thinking by following children's lead in conversation, modelling curiosity in formulating questions, suggesting additional or alternative resources. Practitioners need to be alert to indicators of children's lines of thinking, through listening, observing, and being attentive.

This is not to say that teachers do not have a role in leading and directing learning (Sylva, 2010). The Foundation Stage leader in the school of the following case study expressed clearly her commitment to developing children's skills and strategies so that they could use those skills and strategies for themselves. She was observed leading a whole-group session doing jigsaw puzzles. It was clear that this was a teacher-led activity, but it went beyond showing the children how to do the puzzles. The teaching and learning strategies included selecting puzzles of interest, questioning, feeling for the edges of the pieces, guidance in looking for 'the next piece' in the picture, laughter, modelling and discussing strategies. It enabled her to work with individual children who had different levels of experience of solving jigsaws, supporting them with teaching strategies appropriate to each, and facilitating their active involvement, both physical and cognitive, in the activity.

This is an example of what Bruner described as 'scaffolding' learners – giving them the appropriate level and type of support to enable them to work independently with a task. The teacher intervened to a different degree and in different ways with different children, depending on their interaction with the task. Eaude (2011) cites Greenfield's view that 'scaffolding . . . does not involve simplifying the task. Instead it holds the task constant while simplifying the learner's role through the graduated intervention of the teacher'. Following this fifteen-minute session, several children chose to stay with the jigsaws, and worked playfully together to solve increasingly complex puzzles, using the strategies they had been developing alongside the teacher.

Vygotsky (1978) identified the point where the learner is nearly ready to work autonomously but needs some support, as the 'zone of proximal development', and it is in this zone that teachers can work most effectively with learners. Learners can then move forward to work independently, 'scaffolding' their own and each other's learning until the new learning is internalised. What is also vital is that teachers, through the style of their scaffolding, enable and encourage children to continue to take responsibility for their own learning (Dweck and Leggett, 1988). Ownership of learning happens only with deep learning, which depends on actively constructing understanding.

An overarching principle of the EYFS is that children learn to be strong and independent through positive relationships (Early Education, 2012). Relationships between children and practitioners are significant contributors to children's security and sense of well-being, particularly as young children move out from the circle of home and family. Developments in neurology have given insights into how changes in emotional state impact on parts of the brain which affect learning. When we feel threatened or helpless the hormone cortisol inhibits memory and thinking. The chemical dopamine, which is released in the brain when we feel confident, secure and happy, supports memory, attention and problem-solving (Wilkinson and Pickett, 2010: 115).

The personal, social and emotional area of learning has been identified as one of the 'prime areas that are particularly crucial for igniting children's curiosity and enthusiasm for learning, for building their capacity to learn, and to form relationships and thrive' (Early Education, 2012). The main way in which children learn to build effective relationships, to understand their own feelings and the feelings of others, to collaborate and share, is through the relationships they have with those around them. The actions and attitudes of adults are the models of interaction from which children build their understanding of their own value and place in the world.

CASE STUDY

The Orchard Infant school is a three-form entry school in Surrey. The Foundation Stage Unit, made up of 90 Reception children, three teachers and three teaching assistants, is based in a fairly small internal space, arranged as three classrooms all leading off a central area, and a large outdoor area accessible to all three classrooms. The nature of the 'geographical space' is important to the way learning happens, as it has generated creative thinking by the teaching staff about how the environment might be used. Choices have been made about organisation of space and time, which reflect the strong Early Years philosophy of active learning held by the school and staff team.

The school's Foundation Stage Policy includes as 'principles of learning': *'the development of independence, through challenge, consolidation, praise and encouragement; purposeful, practical activities which stimulate all (the children's) senses; child-initiated activities where children can learn from each other and explore ideas and interests in depth; creative use of the indoor and outdoor learning environment'*. The complementary 'principles of teaching', include *'interacting with and supporting children in a way that positively affects their attitudes to . . . their learning; teaching of strategies to help children learn to investigate, explore and solve problems; direct teaching of skills to enable children to become creative thinkers and risk-takers'*.

In order to maximise opportunities for children to develop as active learners, the Early Years indoor area has been developed as a shared space, with four 'bays', each housing resources and stimuli for an area of learning. The three classrooms house CLL, PSRN and KUW, while the central area is focused on creative development. The children, in groups of 30, have a 'home' classroom and their own class teacher, but for most of the day they are organised and managed in groups of 15, with Teaching Assistants taking a strong role alongside the teachers in leading or following children's learning in the different bays or in the outside area. In each designated bay, adult-led learning activities are led by a teacher or TA, with a particular focus on the areas of learning: Communication Language and Literacy; Problem Solving, Reasoning and Numeracy; Knowledge and Understanding of the World; Creative Development. Meanwhile, when not engaged in adult-led activities, the children have free choice, during which time they move freely between the bays and the outside area, where a range of resources are available to them, some of them on-going, some linked to current themes, and their activity and learning are supported by the remaining two adults. The outdoor area has been made weather-proof through carpeting the grassy slopes with astro-turf, the creation of flexible-use covered areas, and availability of several small huts which the children can adapt to their own purposes.

The organisation and use of the learning spaces evokes the Reggio Emilia approach to Early Years learning (Edwards, 1998), with the atelier as a central resource which the children can access freely to express, extend and document their learning. In each bay the teaching and resources support children's learning development in that area, and the children are free to access the learning resources of their choice. The Early Years team leader expresses a strong commitment to 'developing children's skills and strategies, so that they can *use* them', and this principle is evident in practice in all aspects of learning, with children actively linking new knowledge and skills as they move through the day. The following examples indicate how children are making these connections.

- Children had been learning about 3D shapes. Outside later, Child A picked a leaf and curled it 'I've made a cone for the ice cream'. She collected sellotape from the CD bay to secure the cone.

- Children had been story-writing with the teacher in the CLL Bay. Outside later, Child B used the dressing-up clothes and the climbing equipment to re-enact the story with his friend.

- Children had been working on doubling numbers. Later, in the CD Bay, Child C made a fishing net, then added a net on the other end of the pole. 'I've made a double net. I can catch double fishes'.

- Children had set up and observed an experiment to find out what plants need in order to grow. Later, outside in the nature garden, Child D rolled a small log looking for insects, and observed a pale plant. 'Hmm, not enough light in here. Why are the ants black then?' She asked a nearby adult, leading to discussion about ants'/plants' ability to move about.

Despite the apparent complexity of organisation, the children are evidently confident in using the routines and systems which enable them to access the whole Early Years area for their learning. This confidence appears to derive partly from familiarity with routines, and partly from the ethos of independent enquiry on which practice is built. For example:

- In the KUW Bay, at the start of the day children were encouraged to review progress on their on-going experiments, and to discuss this with each other and the adults.

- Children chose how they would record their results, the teacher showing them some examples of recording.

- Children collected their own writing resources, and helped each other with their attempts at letter writing – Child A, 'I can't do a proper n.' Child B, 'Go down up first'.

- During 'Choosing time', children in the CD Bay were observed independently drawing plans for their models and reviewing the models against the plans.

Practitioners frequently prompted children to consider 'How will you do that?', and 'How will you know?' The Foundation Stage practitioners recognise the potential and ability of young children to think about their own learning. They offer the freedom for children to make their own connections and have created an ethos and environment that build confident active learners.

Reflecting on the case study

- What do you think about the use of physical space in the Foundation Stage area?
- Is there a 'hidden curriculum' in how the space is used?
- What attitudes and principles from the policy are reflected in practice?
- What might be the challenges of working in this way across three classes of children?
- What elements of practice do you think would contribute most effectively to active learning?

 TRY THIS

The EYFS non-statutory guidance, *Development Matters in the EYFS* (Early Education, 2012) contains a great number of valuable practical suggestions, relating to the characteristics for effective learning and appropriate to stages of development, under the following headings.

- observing what a child is doing;
- what adults could do;
- what adults could provide.

The suggestions below begin to build on these, in areas that have been addressed in the chapter.

Try this 1: Sustaining motivation

Activity 1

Alongside your individual records of activity and attainment, note down each child's interests and preferred activities. When planning, use these as starting points or contexts for adult-led activities.

Do children other than those whose interests you planned from respond to the activity?

Do some children have a much wider range of interests and preferences than others?

Activity 2

Observe a group of children playing together. Identify what skills or knowledge would help them to increase their involvement. Plan a time to scaffold the 'next steps', and tell the children how it is linked to their earlier activity.

Do children use and practise the new skill?

Do they return to the previous context, or do they use it in a new context?

Might it have been better to intervene immediately, or not?

Try this 2: Recognising powerful learners

Activity 1

Set up a routine for children to choose, plan and review their activities. In reviewing, support children in recalling the process as well as the product.

Do all children stay with their plan?

What do you do about the practical issue of too many children choosing the same activity or resource?

For those children who keep returning to the same activity or resource, can you add or change anything to extend their learning? Should you?

Activity 2

Make spaces in the setting where 'work in progress' can be kept. If it is not movable, consider leaving it in situ for an agreed period of time. At review time, support children in planning the next steps.

How much flexibility can you provide, so that children can complete an activity in their own time?

Does this have any impact on the quality of the process or product?

Activity 3

For some activities, pair children to help each other. Make sure the same individuals are not always the helped or the helper. Children are inclined to 'do it' for each other, so demonstrate the process of modelling.

Was your pairing successful?

What is the impact on the self-esteem of the helped and the helper?

Are different children good at different things?

What skills did the children use in scaffolding each other?

Try this 3: Language and cognitive development

Activity 1

Develop a set of signs that you and the children use to support communication about learning, e.g. facial expressions for 'I'm thinking', 'I don't understand', body language for 'I have an idea', 'I remember', 'I have forgotten', 'let's do it again'.

Do children use the signs more readily than the language?

Does it make you more aware of the children's thought processes?

What is the impact of this on the pace of interaction?

Activity 2

Provide children with a set of picture cards of resources they might want to use, or enable them to make their own. Each time they use the cards, you use the relevant word within a complete sentence.

Do children start to use sentences or are they dependent on the cards?

How can you develop this starting point into a dialogue?

Activity 3

Check that externally introduced words are familiar and meaningful to the children, e.g. words from phonics schemes. Use pictures and actions to establish meaning.

How does this impact on children's interest?

Do the children use the new words in other contexts?

Try this 4: Play

Activity 1

Observe children engaged in free play for a morning. Note down all the areas of learning they are engaged in, and how many decisions they make.

If free play is confined to the afternoon in your setting, why is this? What does it say about attitudes to play?

Are some areas of the setting, such as the outside area, more conducive to play-based active learning?

Are some children more inclined to take the decisions than others? What might you do about this?

Activity 2

Plan in advance what you will do whilst children are playing. Practise some strategies for scaffolding their learning.

How do you decide when to intervene?

Does your intervention alter the children's play?

Do some interventions work better than others?

Activity 3

Play alongside a child, following his/her lead.

Did you see or hear anything unexpected?

Did this have any impact on your relationship with the child?

Was the child eager or unwilling to have you as a playmate?

Try this 5: The enabling environment

Activity 1

As well as resources which are readily available, put out new stimuli linked to ideas you have heard from the children, or linked to adult-led learning. Draw the children's attention to these without directing too closely how they might be used.

How did the children use them? Did they make their own connections with other learning?

Did the new stimuli get used alongside existing resources?

Might they be part of on-going resources?

Activity 2

Make sure resources are available to the children, that they know where and how to access them and put them away. Get children to label the containers (pictures as well as words). Add photographs of children using them.

Which resources are most popular with which groups of children? Do you know why?

Does the location of a resource affect its use?

Do children use a mix of resources in a single activity? What does this tell you about their learning?

Activity 3

During a fine week, plan to do everything outside. Observe the impact on children's engagement and learning behaviour. Use your observations to adjust how you spread the activity of a normal week across the indoor and outdoor area.

Are children and /or adults constrained by traditional views of indoor and outdoor environments?

What are the constraints in your setting on doing certain activities indoors or outdoors?

How do you feel at the end of the week?

Try this 6: Active teaching for active learning

Activity 1

Be curious, asking questions rather than giving answers. Bring into the class something you genuinely don't know about, and ask the children what they think it is, what it might be for, how does it work etc.

Did any children offer suggestions who don't usually do so?

How did it feel not to know the answers?

Does this support children's curiosity?

Activity 2

Describe what you are doing as you work on a problem.

How did the children participate in the problem solving?

How do you ensure your language is meaningful to the children? If it isn't, can they fully participate in the problem solving?

Activity 3

Make up a story about the children in the class, based around things you have observed them doing.

Were the children interested? Did they add to the story? How might you use the story as a starting point for literacy or other activities?

SUMMARY

Young children are instinctively active both physically and cognitively, as they work to make sense of the world around them so that they can participate fully in it. They are powerful learners, intrinsically motivated to learn, provided their self-belief is sustained and they feel safe to act in the learning environment. Children learn best through a combination of child-initiated and adult-led activities, where connections are made between previous learning and new ideas. Children gradually become better able to deal with abstract ideas, as they can organise their thinking through symbolic representation, but in the Early Years of formal education, learners need practical, concrete, hands-on activity to enable them to explore and express ideas. Many young children do not have sufficient mastery of language to rely on it as a tool for communication and thinking, so they choose to use a range of strategies and representations to learn effectively. Early Years practitioners have a vital role to play in sustaining children's motivation, providing opportunities for children to explore ideas and practise new skills, and scaffolding their learning through appropriate interventions and sustained shared thinking.

FURTHER READING

Craft, A. (2003) Creative thinking in the early years of education, *Early Years*, 23(2): 143–54.
  Makes a case for children and adults working creatively within the constraints of the classroom, to enable children to free up their thinking.

Drake, J. (2009) *Planning Children's Play and Learning in the Foundation Stage*, 3rd edn. London: David Fulton Publishers.
  Some practical ideas for taking children's learning forward through play.

Foot, M., Brown, T., and Holt, P. (2001) *Let Our Children Learn*. Nottingham: Education Now Publishing Co-operative.
  An inspiring story of children pursuing a project, and teachers and children learning together.

Hirst, K. and Nutbrown, N. (2005) *Perspectives on Early Childhood Education*. Stoke-on-Trent: Trentham Books.
  Part 2 explores some issues about how gender affects children's choice of activity.

Johnston, H., and Halocha, J. (2010) *Early Childhood and Primary Education*. Maidenhead: Open University Press.
  A valuable overview of theories of different aspects of development, and some prompts for reflection about the place of play.

REFERENCES

Bruner, J. S. (1996) *The Culture of Education*. Cambridge MA: Harvard University Press.
Bruner, J. S. (2006) *In Search of Pedagogy: The Selected Work of Jerome S. Bruner*. London: Routledge.
Chazan, M. (2002) *Profiles of Play*. London: Jessica Kingsley.

Collins, J., Insley, K. and Soler, J. (eds) (2001) *Developing Pedagogy, Researching Practice.* London: Paul Chapman Publishing.

David, T. (ed.) (1993) *Educational Provision for our Youngest Children: European Perspectives.* London: Paul Chapman Publishing.

DfE (2012) *Early Years Foundation Stage.* London: Department of Education.

DCSF (2008) *Early Years Foundation Stage.* London: Department for Children Schools and Families.

Donaldson, M. (1978) *Children's Minds.* Glasgow: Fontana.

Donaldson, M. (1992) *Human Minds: An Exploration.* London: Allen Lane.

Dweck, C. and Leggett, E. (1988) A social-cognitive approach to motivation and personality. *Psychological Review,* 95 (2).

Early Education (2012) *Development Matters in the Early Years Foundation Stage.* London: Early Education.

Eaude, T. (2011) *Thinking through Pedagogy for Primary and Early Years.* Exeter: Learning Matters.

Edwards, C. (1998) *The Hundred Languages of Children,* 2nd edn. Westport CT: Ablex Publishing.

Evangelou, M., Sylva, K., Wild, M. and Glenny, G. (2009) *Literature Review for the Early Years Foundation Stage.* DCSF: London.

Feiler, A. (2005) Linking home and school literacy in an inner city reception class. *Journal of Early Childhood Literacy,* 5(2): 131–49.

Fisher, J. (2002) *Starting from the Child: Teaching and Learning from 3 to 8,* 2nd edn. Maidenhead: Open University Press.

Geertz, C. (2001) Imbalancing act: Jerome Bruner's cultural psychology, in D. Bakhurst and S. G. Shanker (eds) *Jerome Bruner: Language, Culture, Self.* London: Sage.

Grieshaber, S. and McArdle, F. (2010) *The Trouble with Play.* Maidenhead: Open University Press.

Hart, S., Dixon, A., Drummond, M. J. and McIntyre, D. (2004) *Learning without Limit.* Maidenhead: Open University Press.

Macintyre, C. (2011) *Enhancing Learning through Play: A Developmental Perspective for Early Years Settings,* 2nd edn. London: Routledge.

McShane, J. (1991) *Cognitive Development: An Information Processing Approach.* Oxford: Blackwell.

Meadows, S. (1993) *The Child As Thinker: The Development and Acquisition of Cognition in Childhood.* London: Routledge.

Meighan, R. (1994) *The Freethinkers' Guide to the Educational Universe.* Nottingham: Educational Heretics Press.

Meighan, R. (ed.) (2007) *A Sociology of Educating,* 5th edn. London: Continuum.

Moyles, J. (2005) *The Excellence of Play,* 2nd edn. Maidenhead: Open University Press.

Penn, H. (2008) *Understanding Early Childhood: Issues and Controversies,* 2nd edn. Maidenhead: McGraw Hill Education.

Rosenthal, R. and Jacobson, L. (1968) *Pygmalion in the Classroom.* London: Holt Rinehart and Winston.

Smilansky, S. and Shefataya, S. (1990) *Facilitating Play: A Medium for Promoting Cognitive, Socio-emotional and Academic Development in Young Children.* Gaithersberg: MD: Psychosocial and Educational Publications.

Sylva, K. (2010) *Early Childhood Matters: Evidence from the Effective Pre-school and Primary Education Project.* London: Routledge.

Thornton, L. and Brunton, P. (2010) *Bringing the Reggio Approach to your Early Years Practice.* Abingdon: Routledge.

Tickell, C. (2011) *The Early Years: Foundations for Life Health and Learning.* London: DfE.

Tizard, B. and Hughes, M. (2002) *Young Children Learning,* 2nd edn. Oxford: Blackwell Publishing.

Valentine, M. (2003) *The Reggio Emilia Approach to Early Years Education.* Learning and Teaching Scotland.

Vygotsky L. S. (1978) *Mind in Society.* Cambridge, MA: Harvard University Press.

Weikart, D. (1978) *The Ypsilanti Preschool Curriculum Demonstration Project: Preschool Years and Longitudinal Results.* Ypsilanti, MI: High/Scope Educational Research Foundation.

Wells, G. (2009) *The Meaning Makers: Learning to Talk and Talking to Learn,* 2nd edn. Bristol: Multilingual Matters.

Wilkinson, R. and Pickett, K. (2010) *The Spirit Level: Why Equality is Better for Everyone.* London: Penguin.

Wood, D. (1988) *How Children Think and Learn.* Oxford: Blackwell Publishers.

Wood, E. and Attfield, J. (2005) *Learning and the Early Childhood Curriculum,* 2nd edn. London: Paul Chapman Publishing.

Wrigley, T. (2006) *Another School is Possible.* London: Bookmarks.

CHAPTER 3

CREATING A CULTURE OF ENQUIRY

Anitra Vickery

*You can teach a student a lesson for a day; but if you can
teach him to learn by creating curiosity, he will
continue the learning process as long as he lives.*

Clay P Bedford

Chapter overview

This chapter examines the way that education can best prepare children for
an unknown future. It explores ways of developing active learners through
a consideration of classroom ethos, different models of and approaches to
learning, relationships within the classroom and the physical environment. It
shares ideas of how to place children at the centre of their learning. Activities
provide opportunities to explore some of the issues raised at first hand. A case
study features a school that has taken on the challenge of equipping children to
become critical thinkers. The chapter concludes with references and suggestions
for further reading that will enable the reader to gain further insight into
recommended approaches and access further activities that can be used in the
classroom.

INTRODUCTION

The term 'culture of enquiry' in this chapter means a learning environment which
is designed to develop children's curiosity, creativity and critical thought. It is an
environment that offers children the opportunities to learn through exploration,
questioning and conjecture where the teacher provides well-timed, considered

interventions to guide learning and encourage quality interactions and discussion. It is an environment that encourages children's independence and resilience; an environment in which children feel supported to investigate, make mistakes, refine approaches and ideas, and fundamentally one that equips them for life in the twenty-first century. The term learning environment includes the outdoor space within the school and the community, and the virtual space created through technology. 'Learning must not be limited to the classroom, however meaningful and active that classroom might be' (Hart et al., 2004: 232).

This chapter follows the structure used throughout the book. It opens with a brief discussion about how the teaching and learning that takes place in schools today will equip children for the future. The next section explores how to create a culture of enquiry by considering different factors that provide the foundations for active learning in the classroom including:

- putting children at the centre of decisions about their learning;
- modelling learning and sharing enthusiasm;
- the physical space;
- active learning across the curriculum;
- facilitating collaborative enquiry;
- teacher/child relationship;
- language and discussion;
- effective groupings;
- developing a supportive environment.

This is followed by a selection of activities which have been designed to give you opportunities to explore some of the issues discussed. A case study illustrates some of the strategies being employed in one school to enrich and extend the learning environment. The chapter concludes with a summary and some suggestions for further reading and study.

CONTEXT

As long ago as 1856 educational reformer Joseph Payne voiced concerns about the frequent testing of children's knowledge and advocated an education that 'trained' the child to form habits of thinking (Claxton, 2008). This sentiment is still being expressed today by advocates for educational change. Robinson (2010) believes that the development of thinking in its broadest sense is not incorporated in the majority of teaching and that in recent years there has been a rather superficial response to including thinking in the curriculum.

Our education system needs to respond to the challenge posed by the technological advances by preparing the children of today for the uncertain future that awaits them. If technology continues to advance, even at the same rate as in the last ten years, when children who are currently in reception classes complete their school lives they will be living in a very different world. The children of today will have to face unknown challenges using technologies that have still to be created (Claxton, 2008).

The findings of The Delphi Report, a major international survey that sought to define critical thinking (Facione, 1990), suggested that the growth in interest in thinking skills within the education community was related to the realisation that the traditional curriculum did not suit the needs of a rapidly changing society. The report also gave an account of the opinion of 46 experts within the field who explored the term thinking skills. The consensus of opinion was that thinking skills are holistic in nature and that it is important to develop the right social context and attitude to acquire these skills. If we accept this conclusion it would be advisable to develop thinking skills through a cross-curricular approach.

More recently thinking skills have been catered for through specific subjects such as the CASE programme for science (Adey et al., 1995) or in Philosophy for Children (Lipman, 2003) but do not appear to be embedded across the curriculum or underpin the teaching and learning approach.

Centralised curriculum development in England has not resulted in increasing the prominence of the development of transferable skills such as those related to thinking. When the National Curriculum first appeared in 1988 there was a heavy emphasis on the acquisition of knowledge even though several attainment targets across the curriculum referred to process skills and the application of knowledge. In those early days the application of learning was often conceived as a discrete area of study with some schools introducing weekly sessions of investigations to help children to learn to apply facts.

Many would argue that the content of the National Curriculum tests has had a disproportionate effect on how teaching time is used and in turn created concern amongst teachers about the amount of time that can be allocated to teaching thinking skills (Jones, 2008). Will an approach which is dominated by preparation for tests equip the children of the twenty-first century for the future that lies ahead? Claxton (2008) urges a different focus for our schools. He uses the term 'epistemic apprenticeship', advocating that schools focus on ways of developing critical thinkers; an apprenticeship in learning, thinking and knowing.

CREATING THE LEARNING ENVIRONMENT

What is learning? The Merriam Webster's dictionary defines learning as follows:

- to gain knowledge or skill by studying, practising, being taught, or experiencing something; to cause (something) to be in your memory by studying it;
- to hear or be told (something);
- to find out (something);
- to become able to understand (something) through experience.

So what makes the difference between learning and effective life-long learning? Shirley Clarke (2008) states that children need a stimulating environment and the skills to develop and control their own learning. The environment should provide frameworks and scaffolding so that all children can acquire 'learning to learn' skills (Wallace, 2001). If we accept that intelligence is not fixed (Feuerstein et al., 1980) and that children's learning ability can be enhanced through appropriate interventions within an empowering environment then it is important to get those features right.

'All children are born with a gift for learning, with a natural curiosity and a drive to find things out for themselves . . .' (Wallace, 2001: 1) If that is true then our task is to recreate that sense of curiosity within and for all learning. In the discussion that follows we look at factors that can be considered the key ingredients of creating an environment that celebrates and develops active learners.

Putting children at the centre of decisions about their learning

Diana Pardoe (2009) recommends that the teacher discusses with the children the learning and the learning environment which the class want, and to establish a framework for developing that. The children are also asked to decide what would develop or restrict their engagement with the learning process and also what are their expectations of their teacher. These ideas are recorded and reflected upon so that the children can create their learning environment and become responsible for its success. Active learning becomes a reality when children can be involved in the planning and evaluation of their learning. If children are actively involved in making suggestions about what they should study, based on their interests from both the real world and an imaginary world, they are more likely to be motivated and engaged. Ideally this should take place across all areas of the curriculum and that would ultimately result in a richer curriculum. The Curriculum of Excellence in Scotland (2007) advocates this approach. They maintain that through active learning the children can develop as successful learners, confident individuals, responsible citizens and effective contributors.

Modelling learning and sharing enthusiasm

The teacher who demonstrates great interest and enthusiasm for a topic will usually imbue the children with that enthusiasm (Day, 2004). The passionate teacher tries to instil a love of learning as well as an enthusiasm for the content. She demonstrates care and illustrates how she also is learning too, if not necessarily about the content then about the children and their responses to learning (Hattie, 2012). Whatever you do in the classroom and the way you react to situations will be observed and noted by the children (Wright, 2006). Obviously a teacher cannot be highly enthusiastic about everything – they would be exhausted by the end of the week – but introducing 'specialists' from the community who can share things that they are enthusiastic about and asking children to do the same will generate interest and motivation within the class. A visit from a 'specialist' has the added bonus of giving children further insight into real life and also helps them to refine and focus their questioning. Public service organisations are usually very willing to work with schools on a range of diverse topics from police to ambulance personnel. Also many businesses often volunteer to be involved with schools; use the opportunities to enhance the curriculum and bring learning alive. Children are much more likely to learn if they are engaged and motivated. This happens when the learning is contextualised (Wright, 2006). In the absence of a real specialist it might be productive to adopt the approach advocated by Heathcote and Bolton (1996), where the class become an imagined group of specialists. The planned tasks enable the children to develop their learning through assuming the same kind of challenges and responsibilities that the experts face.

The physical space

The arrangement of the physical environment of the classroom can play a very important part in facilitating effective learning and improving the learning environment (Dryden and Vos, 2005). The design of the classroom can significantly affect engagement and learning (Hastings and Wood, 2002). The classroom should be arranged to reflect the diverse needs and interests of the children and obviously be an environment that has been designed for the specific children within that room. As such it should take account of preferred learning styles and conditions, and be as stimulating as possible. Both three- and two-dimensional display areas that celebrate achievement and reflect the learning ethos of the classrooms can enhance learning subliminally and promote engagement through content and colour (Garnett, 2005).

The Reggio Emilia system places great emphasis on the classroom environment because they consider it to be 'another teacher' in the way it can motivate and develop curiosity and learning (Kinney and Wharton, 2008). Some teachers delegate different areas of the classroom to different types of activity. So there are areas for quiet study, discussion and collaborative work, practical work, computer areas etc. as well as clear storage to facilitate easy access for children thus developing independence and avoiding queues.

Furniture and use of space

The design of the classroom is a statement of what teachers value and the space provided should be arranged in such a way to enable the intended learning to happen. The teacher can be creative about the physical space even if the classroom is old and stems from an era when little consideration or acknowledgement was given to the potential impact that the environment for learning could have on motivation and development of learning. The physical space should reflect the teacher as a learner as well as considering the learning of the children. It is always helpful to reflect on your own experience of areas of space that have motivated you but have also made you feel confident and safe, and try to replicate some of these in your classroom. Also give it a personal touch through the colours, objects or plants you include. Start with an audit of the physical layout, the furniture and its arrangement, storage areas and display boards. Creating an empowering environment takes time and consideration and experimentation (Cullingford, 1995).

Consideration must be given to the furniture in the room and the way it is arranged to enable different activities and styles of learning and teaching. All classrooms seem to contain desks but some now also contain sofas and soft cushions and allow children to choose where and how they want to sit. These different arrangements are vital in enabling different forms of learning and also relaying essential messages about the ethos of the classroom (Dudek, 2005). The children's awareness of the purpose and learning gained from different activities can become more heightened when they recognise that they might require different arrangements of space within the classroom (Hastings and Wood, 2002). There will be times through the day when children will learn individually, in groups and as a whole class. There will be times when a lot of space is required for presentations and large group activity and spaces that allow children to move around. Arrange the classroom so that these different configurations of furniture can be changed smoothly. Ensure that the storage area is clearly labelled and accessible and that because it could be a congested area, is located away from spaces of learning activity. The important element about the classroom space is that everything isn't predetermined but there is flexibility within units of time to rearrange the environment to suit the learning and enable creativity (Dudek, 2005). This frequent rearranging of the physical space will be a novelty for the children which in itself should make the classroom a more exciting place (Garnett, 2005).

Colour

The psychological and physiological impact of different colours can have significant impact on learning. Colour is used effectively with mind maps to aid memory and recall (Smith et al., 2003) and different colours are associated with calm or stimulating environments (Garnett, 2005).

Temperature, lighting and noise levels

Studies suggest that when children's preferred conditions for learning are catered for then they tend to be more engaged and successful (Jensen, 2000). Factors that need to be taken into account to facilitate this include temperature, lighting, and noise level. Try varying the lighting areas in the classroom – natural light, bright artificial light and dim light – and allow children to sit where they feel most comfortable. Children who are excited are often found to calm down and focus better when the lighting is dim (Kelly, 2005). The temperature will also affect the children's readiness to learn. We know from our own experience whether we find it difficult to concentrate if the temperature is too hot or too cold. Encourage children to consider their clothing and where they sit to help with this (Maslow, in Wright, 2006).

Some children prefer to work in silence when they are working individually and others with some background noise. It is thought that music can be used positively to promote learning and develop an atmosphere conducive to concentration (Campbell, 1983). Create stations with headphones to deal with this. Children who learn in this type of environment soon learn to appreciate that different learners have different needs and develop respect for each other.

Active learning across the curriculum

Some subject areas within the primary curriculum, e.g. science and the investigations element of mathematics, have a stronger tradition of association with an enquiry approach. Much of the current debate about the curriculum has centred on the unhelpful polarisation of content versus process. Many educationalists are very concerned that the curriculum is in danger of becoming content driven and as such will not prepare our children to be confident, well equipped citizens of the twenty-first century. The quest therefore is to seamlessly combine the development of thinking skills and the acquisition of knowledge (Joyce et al., 2009).

Three questions particularly relevant to this topic are taken from the Cambridge Review (2006):

- What kinds of curriculum experience will best serve children's varying needs during the next few decades?

- Do notions like 'basics' and 'core curriculum' have continuing validity, and if so of what should twenty-first century basics and cores for the primary phase be constituted?

- What constitutes a meaningful, balanced and relevant primary curriculum?

This review discussed the National Curriculum, which is statutory, and the Primary National Strategies, which were non-statutory but obligatory and came to dominate the curriculum for a number of years (MacGilchrist and Buttress, 2005). Application and enquiry was considered to permeate the National Strategies. No explicit reference to an enquiry approach was made within Strategy documents or the training that introduced them and the emphasis on this element of experience of the subjects was, to a great extent, lost during the initial years of implementation. The success of the investigative directive of the National Curriculum had been eroded with the introduction of the Strategies and primary science was a major casualty. Science should present children with the opportunity to explore, enquire, investigate and reason; however, the introduction and demands of SATs meant that content became all-important and was valued more than scientific enquiry and understanding. Science teaching and learning should provide children with opportunities to work with their peers to investigate issues that are highly relevant to their lives; global issues such as sustainability and health being just two of them.

Papert (1993) suggests that rather than teach children something about mathematics we should be teaching them to behave as mathematicians. In all subjects if children are encouraged to think like a specialist they develop an interest in enquiry and consequently their questioning skills. Claxton (2008) cites an exchange between a teacher and her pupils where she asks them to think of the questions a scientist would ask on observing the behaviour of magnets. In this way she was developing the children's questioning skills to a high level.

The idea of getting inside the subject by behaving as the specialist can work across the curriculum. Children can become writers, geographers, designers, artists and musicians. History and English are inherently enquiry subjects; so much discussion and investigation can ensue from the study of literature and periods of history. For example, the book *Teaching Thinking Skills with Fairy Tales and Fantasy* (see further reading) contains ideas and activities for developing skills such as deductive thinking and reasoning using fairy tales. Also consider how much historical enquiry could result from a visit to the local cemetery or even from a walk around a well-established village.

The word investigate is not usually associated with the study of art which is often perceived as an aesthetic subject that encourages a passive appreciation rather than investigative engagement. It could be much more exciting to investigate the influences on artists' styles, the development of art movements and the effects of experiments with colour and different media, rather than replicating a painting in the style of a well-known artist.

All subjects can be approached through active enquiry if the approach is valued, encouraged and facilitated by the teacher. It is important that the children are engaged with the process of learning and recognise that the content can be the vehicle for the exploration and not just facts to be absorbed (Hart et al., 2004). The focus should be on the style of learning rather than the subject (Cullingford, 1995).

Traditionally the core subjects are taught in the morning. It's important to recognise the unintentional message that is being relayed to the children about the value attributed to particular subjects by the place you give them in the day. Children should be aware that the curriculum is not just a series of facts to be learnt and performance to be measured by complying with what they perceive the teacher wants. We want children to be encouraged to share their innate curiosity and love of learning openly (MacGilchrist and Buttress, 2005).

Facilitating collaborative enquiry

The objective of all teaching should be to develop an independent enquiry approach to learning which will equip children with the life-long skills of resilience and critical thinking (Joyce et al., 2009). The ultimate goal should be to create autonomous learners; that is children who are open minded, who can think for themselves and relate that thinking to their experiences (Kelly, 2005). In order to do this the teacher will need to decide, develop and facilitate the culture of the classroom that best develops the learning of her children. The classroom environment impacts on a child's self-esteem, achievement and participation so it is essential to get it right. This can be negotiated so that the idea of learning to learn is at the centre of the curriculum and children are actively involved in their own learning.

One model designed to achieve this is the creation of a constructivist classroom which creates learning opportunities for children to acquire both knowledge and thinking skills. Children can be grouped to pursue collaborative learning through enquiry and in that way they can actively learn from and scaffold one another. The resulting understanding is greater than if it had been undertaken by an individual child (Kelly, 2005). Successful collaborative work also results in mutual respect and a development in personal and social growth (Joyce et al., 2009). In addition, when children collaborate to achieve a goal they will begin to develop cooperation and an appreciation of different children's strengths. Ultimately this leads to a greater interest in the intrinsic rather than the extrinsic reward of learning. They begin to enjoy learning for its own sake and this quality will equip them for life (Sharan, 1990).

The teacher will need to design opportunities for collaborative enquiry, whilst actively involving children in the planning, that are appropriate to the children's abilities (Dryden and Vos, 2005). To maximise the learning, opportunities should be planned for that use the local and extended environment in which the children live. In this way it will be easy to identify what are the missing features and factors of their lives. Visits can then be arranged to address these factors so that the children's experiences can be richer providing them with a more balanced curriculum (Davies, 2006).

A constructivist classroom doesn't mean that all learning is pursued in groups. It is absolutely vital that individual differences and interests are taken into account and all individuals are given the opportunity to generate their own enquiries. Allowing the child to actively make choices about their learning and to question and discuss throughout the learning activity confirms the interest and expectation of the teacher for each child (Muijs and Reynolds, 2011). This is a great motivator for children and helps to develop greater self-esteem which is vital for learning (Joyce et al., 2009).

Teacher/child relationship

There are a number of models of learning operating in schools today but it is important to realise that it is the relationship between the child and the teacher that underpins the success of the learning (Joyce et al., 2009). Really knowing a child enables the teacher to deal sensitively and appropriately with any incident that occurs (Hart et al., 2004). This will mean getting to know the interests, culture, background, preferred learning styles for different elements of the curriculum as well as their attainment at different stages. The support of a caring and able teacher is of paramount importance (Dryden and Vos, 2005). Humour is an essential part of a teacher's tool kit; it develops a more personal relationship with the child and can negate potential negative feelings. It adds to the child's security (MacGilchrist and Buttress, 2005). Trust is established when children believe in the teacher's interest and that they are learning together.

During the last twenty years there have been extensive studies about brain function and as a result educators know that every child has a 'unique learning and psychological profile' (Garnett, 2005: 41). Consequently multisensory approaches to learning have been advocated so that teachers can actively recognise, support and celebrate children's differences (Wright, 2006). It is the responsibility of the teacher to encourage children both to approach and present learning in the way that enables them and to ensure that physical resources and the availability of space facilitate this. Technology is very much a part of the culture of society and should be used to support learning through integrating it into enquiry (Joyce et al., 2009). The teacher will play a vital role in teaching the children to use this all pervasive technology wisely. Children should be helped to recognise and comprehend the potential bias and moral implications presented through technology (Smith et al., 2003).

Language and discussion

'Pupils who have been actively involved in learning through discussion, interactive teaching, independent research or experiments, have been found to be more likely to transfer their knowledge to other situations' (Muijs and Reynolds, 2011: 160).

A limited language is a barrier to learning (Cullingford, 1995). Language and thought are interconnected (Alexander, 2006); however, communication is more difficult if a child does not have the necessary 'language of school' and therefore thinking can be unexpressed or stultified. A child may not be familiar with the terminology of school and not have the necessary practice, exposure or interaction with language within the home environment. This needs to be taken into consideration in developing discursive activities. Discussion is about learning to extend ideas and sustain thought and is therefore essential in the development of thinking skills. It is about sharing ideas and respecting others. All children will benefit from the chance to be involved in dialogue and discussion: talking, listening and responding; generating active learning in the constructivist fashion and reaching agreement when required through negotiation (Luxford and Smart, 2009). These skills need to be learnt; it is not enough for the teacher to encourage discussion or dialogue without creating some rules of engagement and modelling. Conversation needs a framework that enables extended conversations and good listening skills for both the teacher and the child thus giving the child a voice (Best and Thomas, 2007). It is important to consider what questions to use to develop sustained conversation because if not chosen carefully they can close down a conversation rather than extend it (Cullingford, 1995). If the teacher dominates the question posing, questions become associated with particular responses and the child is inhibited. Questions need to be authentic and useful, not a guessing game about what is in the teacher's head (Dawes, 2011) otherwise conversations will be short and closed. The teacher's role is crucial (Alexander, 2006) and much of this can be taught through modelling and reflecting on the amount of encouragement you are giving to children to ask their own questions. Responding to wrong answers or negative points in a way that opens up discussion is a useful strategy. 'Errors need to be welcomed' (Hattie, 2012: 124). (See Chapter 4, Developing teacher and learner questioning skills.)

Effective groupings

There are many advantages to grouping children, both pragmatic and philosophical; however, despite the extensive literature, that exists on the benefits of group work e.g. Wallace et al. (2004) and Wegerif (2003), it is still not common practice to place children in a group to develop collaboration but rather to counteract the constraints of the classroom design, the limitation of materials, to facilitate good behaviour or to make differentiated teaching easier (Blatchford and Baines, 2002).

Advocates of group work have argued that as members of a group, which is required to discuss and share ideas in order to solve a problem, children will be exposed to different views, including some that they may not have realised in other situations. Also that as they will need to explain their approach and reasoning this will not only clarify their own thinking and develop metacognition but will aid the concept development of all the members of the group (Hattie, 2012). Furthermore, a collaborative approach used across the curriculum would transfer the ownership and control of learning to the children themselves as they would share the responsibility for the learning that took place. This approach could have a major impact on children's learning by improving and increasing children's motivation and engagement (Blatchford and Baines, 2002).

Ogden (2000) investigated the conditions under which cooperation and collaboration might be developed and the importance of age and context in the development of these skills. She believes that children's ability to interact, share ideas and contribute cooperatively and collaboratively is dependent on a number of factors. The findings from naturalistic studies inform her that the context in which children interact has a great bearing on their degree of collaboration and cooperation. Previous research suggests that children do not have the ability to appreciate that others may have different beliefs or reasoning approaches until they have reached the age of six or seven. However, the familiarity of the home environment and the personalities within the home setting result in an ability to cooperate, which is not realised in the early years in a school setting. This research suggests that if teachers create the opportunities within a supportive environment that encourages interaction this will lead to the development of cooperation and collaboration. Cohen (1994) recommends that team-building activities are implemented in the classroom before cooperative, collaborative work takes place so that children can begin to develop the necessary social skills. He also states that for group work to be successful the children must first be taught to listen, to respond to an idea and to present ideas without aggression or by dominating.

If children are arranged in groups where collaboration is expected they can share resources, scaffold each other's learning through discussion and learn to cooperate. The seating arrangement must support collaboration so the space needs to be arranged so that the children can easily make eye contact with each other and each child is positioned so that they can listen to and discuss with the other members of the group easily (Hastings and Wood, 2002). If children are placed in groups the tasks and composition of the group needs to be considered carefully. It is generally considered that different compositions, such as attainment groups, gender groups or friendship groups, all have a place depending on the task but that the task must be one that lends itself to collaboration where each member of the group has both an individual and collective role (Cullingford, 1995). Small groups of two or three children might be a good idea to start with if the children are not used to discussion, cooperation or collaboration (Joyce, 2009). A group of four usually works well – larger groups tend to be unmanageable and some children can feel excluded. It is vital, however, that the composition of the groups should change regularly depending on the tasks, interests and strengths of the individuals as this will enable children to learn alongside different classmates with different talents and dispositions.

Developing a supportive environment

Feeling confident is an important prerequisite for engagement (Hart et al., 2004). Children need to feel safe (Cullingford in Webb, 2006). All children need to feel valued members of the class. If the ethos of the classroom is such that each child is encouraged to develop self-belief and that their contribution to planning and learning is valued then a common purpose about learning develops (Joyce et al.,

2009). Children's thoughts and ideas need to be listened to and respected so that the child is understood by other children and the teacher. Friendship groups can change frequently throughout the school and children who are excluded at any point can feel insecure and miserable. This ultimately impacts on their learning.

One model of active learning which is presented in *Learning without Limits* (Hart et al., 2004) describes how the teacher allows the children to self-differentiate by choosing the task or level of task that they feel comfortable with. This is essential if children are to feel confident about their task but obviously it needs to be monitored so that children are encouraged to challenge themselves in a safe environment.

The emotional security of each child is paramount if they are to engage as a team member and given opportunities to take control of their own learning. A supportive environment should embrace the social, emotional and intellectual activities of learning, recognising that children are sometimes reluctant to take risks in their learning. Who they think they are and how they are perceived by their peers can impact significantly on how much contribution children are prepared to make (Kelly, 2005). If children believe that their contributions are valued and important they feel secure to voice them (Rosenthal and Jacobson, 1968).

Children with high self-esteem are generally secure. If children believe that they 'aren't good' at something they generally dislike it. However, if they believe that they have something to contribute to the study of a subject the reverse is true (Wright, 2006). Using closed questions to which there is either a right or a wrong answer could expose a child to insecurity; however, if the reaction of the teacher was valued despite the answer being wrong then the experience could be positive. Open questions present less fear and they can always be answered by reference to another person or persons. A classroom where being stuck is acceptable feels safe, and this phenomenon can often lead to interesting discourse or areas of investigation (Hattie, 2012). Ultimately it is the values that the teacher models and projects that dictate the ethos of the classroom and create a safe environment (Crick, 2006). Being told that everyone has something valuable to contribute is a powerful motivator (Hart et al., 2004). Damasio (1999) confirmed the belief that there is a direct link between attitude and motivation. His neuro-biological research revealed the close link between emotion and cognition, thus stressing that one's self-esteem has a great impact on one's ability and desire to learn. Self-esteem needs a safe environment in which to grow.

CASE STUDY

This case study looks at a school that believes strongly in personalised learning and in the portrayal of learning as an exciting adventure. The approach, content and experience received by the children sets out to make them independent and aspirational risk takers.

The school is a junior school in a semi-rural, predominantly white and fairly affluent area. The focus of the School Development Plan is to increase the children's engagement with other communities and make them collaborative learners. One of the teachers has been appointed Community Cohesion Leader and in this role strives to ensure that the children experience situations that their local community might not be able to provide, as well as becoming as involved as they can with different elements of the local community. In other words, the school is keen to address gaps in the children's experience, making them better prepared for life in the twenty-first century. An example of this was where Black and Asian members of the police service were invited to run a series of workshops with the children to gauge and positively influence their understanding and empathy with multi-ethnic groups. These workshops were followed by a visit to a mosque, a Sikh temple, an Islamic school and an Asian Day Centre.

The school also engaged in a project with a local residential home for the elderly. The children consulted with the elderly people about an art installation which their gifted and talented artists led and they also planted time capsules for both generations. There are plans to become involved with international communities with the aim of developing respect for differences amongst people and their cultures.

The school have invested in SEAL (social emotional aspects of learning) activities that focus on the children questioning themselves and others, and also on the development of reasoning and thinking in the belief that this approach will develop empathetic reasoning individuals. They also use de Bono's 'Six Thinking Hats' programme (de Bono, 2000) to facilitate effective discussion through creativity and collaboration.

The teachers feel supported through regular observation. Peer observation doesn't happen automatically but it would be welcomed if requested. There is a close relationship amongst the teachers and the children see and appreciate the interaction and the humour that permeates. Staff meetings tend to focus on developing learning and consist of sharing ideas and information. For example, following LA input on the development of questioning in mathematics, the staff decided to ask their TAs to monitor the frequency of didactic teaching as opposed to teaching through questioning. The results were subsequently discussed and improvement in questioning made through collaboration.

The school wants to create a trusting environment. The word trust is used and appears frequently during learning. The children are actively taught not to abuse trust and that good learning requires trust.

The classroom space clearly mirrors the school's approach to learning. Classrooms are set up with different furniture for group work or independent individual work, and provide comfortable areas as well as different arrangements of desks. Lighting, noise and temperature levels are monitored and chosen. Displays encourage a learning journey and the children's individual understanding is elicited at the start of a topic so that their learning is focused and relevant. The school believes that the children's attitude to learning is helped by their obvious recognition of different learning styles and the fact that each child is allowed to be an individual. The children are encouraged to learn with different people although initially this may be directed. During the first week of term the children are encouraged to think about the characteristics of a good learner and how during particular learning experiences children may encounter individuals whom they could class as 'movers' or 'blockers.' A 'mover' is someone who enables the child to learn. It's used to describe a child who is focused on the task and is prepared to work collaboratively. A 'blocker' prevents learning either by being disruptive or failing to concentrate on the task and preventing their peers from focusing. Children are asked to make sensible choices about whom they work with and where they sit. In these circumstances they can remove themselves from 'blockers.' The children discuss what they need to do to be a successful learner using a model and guide supplied through a workshop about successful learning by consultant Diana Pardoe (Pardoe, 2009). The 'pirate' wheel (a staged approach to problem solving which is cyclical) is used to guide different stages of problem solving and concludes with a reflection of the activity and process.

The vocabulary for successful learning is a shared vocabulary throughout the school. It is displayed in the classrooms and promoted verbally and visually in the celebration assembly, where success is not linked with ability. The children and teachers are encouraged to have high expectations of themselves and others. Marking is productive and positive. It is focused on moving on and closing the gap, as are all the interactions about learning. The approach of this primary school has been constructed in the belief that it will promote the development of independent confident children who will be equipped with the resilience needed to cope with the uncertain future of the twenty-first century.

Reflecting on the case study

- What is this school doing to develop a culture of enquiry?
- Which aspects do you feel are most likely to be effective?
- What do you feel is missing?
- How does this compare to your experience in school?
- Describe and discuss the classroom layout of schools in your experience.
- Is the layout important?
- Can classroom displays encourage independent learning? How?

 TRY THIS

Try this 1: Putting children at the centre of decisions about their learning

Activity 1

Present an area of study to the children and elicit their knowledge base through elicitation exercises. Generate discussion groups to share interest and knowledge and to create areas of enquiry. This way you listen to the children and give them a voice in their learning.

Does the fact that the learning pursues the interest of the children make them more motivated and engaged?

Activity 2

Audit the local environment and encourage the children to suggest an idea for a project that will improve a facility or territory, for example the local shopping area. Create groups to research different areas, for example parking facilities, range of shops, demography of shoppers and disabled facilities, ask them to suggest improvements.

Does the local community show interest in the project?

How difficult is the project to arrange?

Activity 3

Use question, research and celebration format e.g. 'How different is the life of a child in the twenty-first century from that of a child in the nineteenth century?' Allow groups to choose the topics to explore with some intervention and guidance from the teacher.

Does this approach motivate all children?

Try this 2: The physical space

Activity 1

Rearrange the furniture in the classroom to provide areas with different lighting and seating arrangements. Through discussion encourage the children to choose appropriately.

Does this require a level of maturity from the children that they can develop through discussion or does the teacher have to dictate?

Activity 2

Allocate specific display areas to the children and give them time to create.

Do the children develop a sense of responsibility and a more organised approach?

Encourage collaborative displays that illustrate learning as well as some to showcase interests and hobbies.

Do children develop greater pride and responsibility in and for their work?

Do you all become more informed about the children in the class?

Activity 3

Change the arrangement of furniture in the classroom fairly frequently to enable different types of activity to take place.

Do the children look forward to the differences?

Does it demand too much organisation and is it therefore disruptive?

Does it make the classroom a more exciting, empowering environment?

Try this 3: Active learning across the curriculum

Activity 1

Create opportunities for children to work with local artists, writers, engineers, etc.

Do children learn to look at things from different perspectives?

Activity 2

Create the idea of children becoming 'specialists' and ask them to embrace the idea for different subjects.

Does the level of questioning become deeper and more focused?

Activity 3

Encourage children to become engaged in authentic enquiries, such as developing an allotment researching types of crops, soil and costs.

Is it possible to engage all children if the enquiry is chosen for them?

Activity 4

Simulate an archaeological find by displaying artefacts relating to a specific period in history and encourage the children to investigate in teams to discover the period and the relevance of the artefacts.

How much intervention is necessary to facilitate the investigation and the resulting learning?

Activity 5

Present children with a coded unknown language to decode to explore a 'lost civilisation'. Encourage them to compare it with a known ancient civilisation.

How sustained is the enquiry?

Is it possible to allocate large periods of time to allow complete investigations?

Try this 4: Language and discussion

Activity 1

Use role play to model how discussions move past the contradicting and challenging stage, where no common decision is agreed, to one where agreement is reached.

Ask the children to evaluate the process and suggest they create rules of engagement where each child is given a voice and an agreement is reached through collaboration.

Monitor the effectiveness of this and decide whether or not this process needs frequent modelling.

Does rearranging the groups help to avoid dominance by some children?

Activity 2

Video the children taking part in discussions and analyse.

Does this make the children reflect on their interactions and adjust their participation?

Activity 3

Create the role of observer in each discussion group to feed back on the group's success with enabling:

- participation;
- collaboration;
- respect;
- extended thinking.

Do the children reflect on the information and subsequently develop the quality of the dialogue?

Activity 4

Try to avoid the 'ping pong' effect of question and answer by including other children in the elaboration of ideas.

Do children exhibit more sustained discussion?

Try this 5: Developing a supportive environment

Activity 1

Transfer control over some content to the children. Allow children to investigate topics that interest them.

Are the children more engaged with learning?

Does this approach develop self-esteem?

Activity 2

Share your lack of knowledge of a particular topic and model creating a list of things you would like to find out. Encourage children to do this for themselves thus creating genuine investigation.

Are children more prepared and confident about saying that they don't know or are stuck?

Activity 3

Create the tradition of children asking other children to answer a question that they aren't sure of (phone a friend).

Do more children want to be engaged or do they feel as if they could be intimidated?

Activity 4

Focus on praising the learning rather than the ability.

Do children recognise that effort and process are more important than result?

Activity 5

Try to engage parents fully in their child's development of thinking by using a comment book to facilitate discussion about an enquiry based in the home environment, e.g. how might we measure the amount of water the family uses during Sunday morning?

Monitor the parents' reaction and engagement.

Try to involve parents more by asking them to suggest topics for investigation.

SUMMARY

Teachers need to prepare the children of today for a very different future from that of their parents. To that end children will need to become independent, empathetic, creative thinkers. Those qualities can be developed by immersing children in an environment which values those characteristics. The environment needs to motivate and challenge as well as engender feelings of security. Working collaboratively alongside the teacher and other children, where there is an expectation of shared responsibility for learning provides a good starting point. Add to that the expectation and realisation of trust, sensitivity and tolerance and the teacher has a very good chance of developing responsible citizens of the twenty-first century.

FURTHER READING

Clarke, S. (2008) *Active Learning Through Formative Assessment*. London: Hodder Education.
    Chapter 3, 'The ideal learning culture', focuses on the work of Carol Dweck and the development of a growth mind-set.

Cohen, D. (2002) *How the Child's Mind Develops*. Abingdon: Routledge.
    This is an interesting, entertaining and accessible book which summarises many issues in cognitive development.

Dawes, L. (2011) *Creating a Speaking and Listening Classroom*. Abingdon: Routledge.
    This book presents lots of practical ideas for developing speaking and listening within the classroom.

Polette, N. (2005) *Teaching Thinking Skills with Fairy Tales and Fantasy*. Westport, CT: Teacher Ideas Press.
    Exploring and developing thinking through fairy stories.

Staricoff, M. and Rees, A. (2006) *Start Thinking: Daily Starter to Inspire Thinking in the Primary Classroom*. Birmingham: Imaginative Minds.
    A range of short starters that could be used during registration time to encourage thinking skills.

The Scottish Government (2010) *A Curriculum for Excellence: Building the Curriculum 2 – Active Learning: A Guide to Professional Development*. Edinburgh: The Scottish Government.

Wallace, B. (ed.) (2001) *Teaching Thinking Skills Across the Primary Curriculum. A Practical Approach for All Abilities*. London: David Fulton.
    A collection of activities linked to the National Curriculum which will systematically develop children's problem-solving skills.

Warren, C. (2004) *Bright Ideas: Speaking and Listening Games*. Leamington Spa: Scholastic.
    Lots of good ideas for games covering all aspects of speaking and listening.

REFERENCES

Adey, P. S., Shayer, M. and Yates, C. (1995) *Thinking Science: The Curriculum Materials of the CASE Project*. London: Thomas Nelson and Sons.

Alexander, R. J. (2006) *Towards Dialogic Teaching: Rethinking Classroom Talk*. York: Dialogos.

Best, B. and Thomas, W. (2007) E*verything you Need to Know about Teaching. But are too Busy to Ask*. London: Continuum International Publishing Group.

Blatchford, P. and Baines, E. (2002) 'The SPRinG Project: The case for group work in schools' [online]. Institute of Education, University of London. Available at: www.spring-project.org.uk/ (accessed 20 April 2012).

Campbell, D. G. (1983) *Introduction to the Musical Brain*, 2nd edn. St Louis, MO: MMB Music Inc.

Clarke, S. (2008) *Active Learning Through Formative Assessment*. London: Hodder Education.

Claxton, G. (2008) *What's the Point of School?* Oxford: Oneworld Publications.

Cohen, E. (1994) Productive small groups. *Review of Educational Research*, 64(1): 1–36.

Crick, R. (2006) *Learning Power in Action: A Guide for Teachers*. London: Paul Chapman.

Cullingford, C. (1995) *The Effective Teacher*. London: Cassell.

Damasio, A. (1999) *The Feeling of What Happens: Body and Emotion in the Making of Consciousness*. New York: Harcourt Brace Jovanovich.

Davies, S. (2006) *The Essential Guide to Teaching*. Harlow: Pearson Education Limited.

Dawes, L. (2011) *Creating a Speaking and Listening Classroom*. Abingdon: Routledge.

Day, C. (2004) *A Passion for Teaching*. London: Routledge.

de Bono, E. (2000) *Six Thinking Hats*. London: Penguin Books Ltd.

Dryden, G. and Vos, J. (2005) *The New Learning Revolution: How Britain can Lead the World in Learning, Education and Schooling*. Stafford: Network Educational Press Ltd.

Dudek, M. (2005) *Children's Spaces*. Oxford: Architectural Press.

Facione, P. A (1990) *Critical Thinking: A Statement of Expert Consensus for Purposes of Educational Assessment and Instruction*. San Jose, CA: The California Academic Press.

Feuerstein, R., Rand, Y., Hoffman, M. B. and Miller, R. (1980/2004) *Instrumental Enrichment: An Intervention Programme for Cognitive Modifiability*. Baltimore, MD: University Park Press.

Garnett, S. (2005) *Using Brainpower in the Classroom 5 Steps to Accelerate Learning*. London: Routledge.

Hart, S., Dixon, A., Drummond, M. J. and McIntyre, D. (2004) *Learning without Limits*. Maidenhead: McGraw Hill.

Hastings, N. and Wood, K. C. (2002) *Reorganising Primary Classroom Learning*. Buckingham: Open University Press.

Hattie, J. (2012) *Visible Learning for Teachers. Maximising Impact on Learning*. Abingdon: Routledge.

Heathcote, D. and Bolton, G. M. (1996) *Mantle of the Expert Approach to Education*. Harlow: Heinemann.

Jensen, E. (2000) *Brain-Based Learning The New Science of Teaching and Training*. London: Corwin Press.

Jones, H. (2008) Thoughts on teaching thinking: Perceptions of practitioners with a shared culture of thinking skills education. *Curriculum Journal*, 19(4): 309–24.

Joyce, B., Calhoun, E. and Hopkins, D. (2009) *Models of Learning Tools for Teaching*, 3rd edn. Maidenhead: Open University Press.

Kelly, P. (2005) *Using Thinking Skills in the Primary Classroom*. London: Paul Chapman Publications.

Kinney, L. and Wharton, P. (2008) *An Encounter with Reggio Emilia. Children's Early Learning Made Visible*. Abingdon: Routledge.

Lipman, M. (2003) *Thinking in Education*, 2nd edn. Cambridge: Cambridge University Press.

Luxford, H. and Smart, L. (2009) *Learning through Talk*. London: Routledge.

MacGilchrist, B. and Buttress, M. (2005) *Transforming Learning and Teaching*. London: Paul Chapman Publishing.

Muijs, D. and Reynolds, D. (2011) *Effective Teaching. Evidence and Practice*, 3rd edn. London: Sage.

Ogden, L. (2000) Collaborative tasks, collaborative children: An analysis of reciprocity during peer interaction at Key Stage 1. *British Educational Research Journal*, 26(2): 211–26.

Papert, S. (1993) *Mindstorms: Children, Computers and Powerful Ideas*, 2nd edn. New York: Basic Books.

Pardoe, D. (2009) *Towards Successful Learning: Furthering the Development of Successful Learning and Teaching in Schools*, 2nd edn. London and New York: Network Continuum.

Rosenthal, R. and Jacobson, L. (1968) *Pygmalion in the Classroom*. London: Holt Rinehart and Winston.

Robinson, K. (2010) TED Talks: Ken Robinson: Changing Education Paradigms. Available at: www.ted.com/talks/ken_robinson_changing_education_paradigms.html (accessed 23 March 2012).

Sharan, S. (1990) *Cooperative Learning: Theory and Research*. New York: Praeger.

Smith, A., Lovatt, M. and Wise, D. (2003) *Accelerated Learning. A User's Guide*. Stafford: Network Educational Press Ltd.

Webb, R. (ed.) (2006) *Changing Teaching and Learning in the Primary School*. Maidenhead: McGraw Hill.

Wallace, B., Maker, J., Cave, D. and Chandler, S. (2004) *Thinking Skills and Problem-Solving: An Inclusive Approach*. London: David Fulton.

Wallace, B. (2001) *Teaching Thinking Skills Across the Primary School*. London: David Fulton Publishers Ltd.

Wegerif, R. (2003) *Literature Review in Thinking Skills, Technology and Learning*. Bristol: NestaFuturelab/Open University.

Wright, D. (2006) *Classroom Karma: Positive Teaching, Positive Behaviour, Positive Learning*. Abingdon: Routledge.

CHAPTER 4

DEVELOPING TEACHER AND LEARNER QUESTIONING SKILLS

Anitra Vickery

> *. . . The art of proposing a question must be held of higher value than solving it.*
>
> *George Cantor*

Chapter overview

This chapter explores the role of questioning in developing active learning. Throughout the chapter we consider the development of the art of questioning for both teachers and learners by discussing factors that, according to research and published opinion, influence the effectiveness of questioning. Factors examined include: types of questions, developing children as questioners, affective issues, and teachers' skills and strategies. The reader is encouraged to try out and reflect on different approaches and techniques. A short case study describes the approach one school is following to develop its use of effective questioning. The chapter concludes with a summary, suggestions for further reading and references.

INTRODUCTION

This chapter follows the structure used throughout the book. It opens with a brief discussion of how questioning contributes to the overall aim of promoting active learning. This is followed by a review of research and thinking about factors which affect the effectiveness of questioning and a brief discussion of how a curriculum can be based around questioning. The chapter also contains suggested activities to try out that will give you opportunities to explore some of the issues discussed. The chapter concludes with a case study from a school that is working on the development of questioning skills, a summary and some suggestions for further reading and study.

WHY IS QUESTIONING IMPORTANT?

The acquisition of the skill of effective questioning can be of significant value in a child's education and life. The development of questioning skills will enable children to effectively investigate physical, social and moral elements of the world around them and it is a skill that once acquired will transfer to adulthood (Duffy, 2003). The ability to pose effective questions will undoubtedly help teachers and children to improve the quality of learning and is an important element of problem solving (de Bono, 1992). The act of posing or answering questions sends a clear message to the children that we want them to be active participants in their own learning. Children need to make questioning a large part of their lives (Claxton, 2008).

   People ask questions if they really want to learn something. Therefore it follows that teaching and learning should involve both the teacher and pupil talking and asking questions. The quality of these interactions and their impact on learning will depend on the quality and effectiveness of the questions and the interest level of the pupil. It is vitally important to capture the natural curiosity of the child and be aware of ways in which this can be developed especially if, for whatever reason, it has been stifled. Children will not be motivated to ask questions or take part in investigations if they are not curious (Johnston, 2005). The results of studies have established that high attainment is not solely dependent on the style of questioning; however, many studies show that increasing the number of higher order questions impacts significantly on pupil achievement. Effective questioning can raise achievement (Askew et al., 1997); however, it is very important that teachers vary their approach to questioning using a range of formats and types of questions to encourage the engagement of the children (Best and Thomas, 2007).

REVIEWING THE RESEARCH

In the pursuit of the development of questioning we are going to consider factors that we know to be influential. In each case there is research that has given insight into the issues that arise. We will be looking at the following issues:

- Classifying questions:
   - typology of questions;
   - the role of different types of questions.

- Developing successful questioners:
   - modelling;
   - reflective teachers – reflective children;
   - affective issues – establishing a supportive classroom culture.

- Teacher skills and strategies:
  - effective intervention;
  - planning for questioning;
  - wait-time;
  - alternative questioning strategies.

Classifying questions: A typology of questions

In order to develop the use of questions in the classroom it is necessary to be able to monitor and reflect upon how they are being used. The following characteristics are often used to classify questions:

- higher or lower order;

- open or closed;

- managerial or thought-provoking.

Each pair of terms can be seen as the opposite ends of a spectrum. Each spectrum can be used to gauge the likely impact of questions and form a question to match a specific purpose.

Higher and lower order questions

Consider the progression of types of questions as implied by Bloom (Bloom et al., 1956) in his taxonomy of educational objectives (see Figure 4.1). This structure was designed to help teachers to classify their aims and targets. His taxonomy relies on the idea that not all learning objectives and outcomes have equal merit. If teachers are conversant with this taxonomy they will be able to ensure a balance of learning through choosing objectives that will enable all levels of the taxonomy to be addressed. Although Bloom's ideas have not met with universal approval, his taxonomy has been used and adapted by many educationalists.

During the 1990s, a former student of Bloom's, Lorin Anderson, was instrumental in revising the taxonomy so that it would be more suitable for students and teachers of the twenty-first century.

The new terms are defined as:

- **Remembering**: Retrieving, recognizing, and recalling relevant knowledge from long-term memory.

- **Understanding**: Constructing meaning from oral, written, and graphic messages through interpreting, exemplifying, classifying, summarizing, inferring, comparing, and explaining.

- **Applying**: Carrying out or using a procedure through executing, or implementing.

- **Analyzing**: Breaking material into constituent parts, determining how the parts relate to one another and to an overall structure or purpose through differentiating, organizing, and attributing.

- **Evaluating**: Making judgments based on criteria and standards through checking and critiquing.

- **Creating**: Putting elements together to form a coherent or functional whole; reorganizing elements into a new pattern or structure through generating, planning, or producing. (Anderson and Krathwohl, 2001: pp. 67–8)

- Knowledge – this lowest level is the straightforward memory recall consisting of remembering previously learned material.

- Comprehension – requires interpretation of information and the ability to explain. 'How' and 'why' words are often used at this level and they begin to open up enquiry.

- Application – ability to use information in a different context to solve a problem.

- Analysis – inference with evidence to support the inference. Dealing with the complexities of materials by splitting them into parts.

- Synthesis – reassembling parts to create new structures building on previous knowledge and structures. We need to give children freedom here to enable them to trial new ideas and approaches.

- Evaluation – this is where judgements are made and the validity of the work is checked.

Figure 4.1 Bloom's taxonomy

The National Curriculum of the late 1990s contained a list of five core thinking skills to be embedded across the curriculum: information-processing skills, reasoning skills, enquiry skills, creative thinking skills and evaluation skills. The ability to question lies at the heart of all these. (See Try this 1: Menu for creating higher order questions, p. 72.)

The higher levels of the taxonomies include all of the cognitive skills and employ higher level questioning skills. Children who are encouraged to become engaged and successful with the higher levels of the taxonomies are usually those who are able to adapt quite easily to new situations.

There is a tendency to think of the taxonomies as being hierarchical and/or sequential. This perception may stem from the ideas of Piaget (Piaget, 1928) who believed that young children didn't develop the skill of abstract thinking until they were older (Wilks, 2005). If thinking were viewed as a process rather than a product it might enable teachers to consider it as a creative, critical process which combines the questioning of oneself with the questioning of others (Lipman, 2003). It simply isn't the case that young children develop and should only be exposed to lower-level questioning skills. Or that older children move from these to develop higher-level skills. Open and closed, lower and higher order questions can and should be used with all children.

All young children have the ability to think and reason. However, the extent to which they are able to verbalise their thinking varies. We should not assume that they are unable to reason because they do not have the language. For some children thinking can be primarily internal. We should not assume that because the child appears not to be curious that she is not analysing or investigating. Young children can ask an enormous number of questions during the day but it is thought that young children tend to ask questions to communicate not necessarily to learn the answer. So as language and curiosity develops and the child is encouraged to try to make sense of the world through the use of exploratory, enquiry questions they need to be encouraged to talk through their perceptions.

The role of lower order questions

Higher order questions are essential to develop thought and reason (Askew et al., 1997), however, the term lower order as opposed to higher order sounds almost pejorative. Higher order questions are not superior to lower order they just serve different purposes. It is important to recognise that both should be used. Lower order questions, where children are required to demonstrate what they have remembered, are a necessary and desirable part of assessment. If a teacher asks lower order questions to elicit the starting point for an activity then she will be prepared to engage the children at the right level and also be aware of the possible misconceptions or gaps in knowledge that exist (see Try this 2: Mapping knowledge, p. 73).

Lower order questions are easy to ask during a lesson and this process often helps to move the lesson forward, whereas asking higher order questions where children are required to think and reason may take longer and may interrupt the flow of the lesson. Higher order questions need to be planned for and therefore it is not surprising that these feature much less in a lesson than those that are simply judging recall and absorption of facts.

Open and closed questions

Some children believe that all questions are closed questions. This is because when some teachers ask a question, whether it is closed or open, they have a specific answer in their heads and no other answer that a child supplies will be correct. This can often result in children becoming disengaged with the process because they believe that they have little chance in 'guessing' the required answer, or it can result in them developing insecurity about understanding or knowledge that they previously were confident about. An example of practice that was reported to me confused the children so much that they believed that what had been thought correct one day was certainly disputed the next. A teacher asked the class to give her two numbers that added up to ten. Different children supplied answers such as 8+2, 6+4, 7+3, and each one was told no that's the wrong answer because it wasn't the one she wanted. She wanted a low attaining child to give her the answer of 5+5 and when he did she stated that that was correct. That exercise made a number of children insecure about their knowledge. They also began to form the misconception that mathematical answers can be correct one day but incorrect the next.

Managerial and thought provoking questions

Hastings (2003) states that teachers ask two questions every minute; up to four hundred a day. However, these tend to be procedural questions linked to the management of the classroom. The Leverhulme Primary Project undertook research into teacher questioning and reported that the 1000 questions asked by the sample of teachers could be categorised into managerial (57 per cent), lower order (35 per cent) and higher order (8 per cent). This suggests that unless teachers monitor the range and format of their questioning, they could be under the misconception that they use questioning effectively to promote learning, when in effect the majority of the questions add little to the quality of discourse in their classroom.

Developing successful questioners

Modelling

Effective questioning needs to be modelled. If this happens, and probing and higher order questions are part of a teacher's repertoire, then there is every probability that children will be stimulated to do likewise when they are presented with any problem. Vygotsky writes that by using an approach that combines demonstration and learner support teachers can help children develop higher levels of thinking through effective questioning (Lee and Smagormsky, 2000). The skill of the teacher in modelling questioning by engaging in dialogue, and extending that dialogue as appropriate with children, is significant and cannot be underestimated. It is no mean task for a teacher to develop or change a weak question from a pupil into one that is effective for the development of thought (Petty, 2009). It requires extended carefully constructed dialogue to refine the thought. The interactions between the teacher and the child need to be challenging and sustained rather than perfunctory and routine.

Reflective teachers – reflective children

The ability to reflect meaningfully is a desirable skill for any practitioner as this enables them to develop and refine their professional practice. The process of reflection requires systematic thought and questioning. Reflecting on your role as a questioner requires the knowledge and transparency of what it is you are trying to achieve and the processes that will enable you to be successful.

One strategy which may help you reflect on your use of questions could be to create a mind map for questions that would aid knowledge and development of understanding in each topic you are going to teach. This could be quite minimal to begin with. It might include:

- elicitation exercises to assess knowledge – generally closed questions;
- elicitation exercises to assess understanding – open and probing questions (these key questions should be constructed and noted);
- targeted questions to aid differentiation – broad range of questions.

This could then progress to teachers constructing key questions to challenge ideas and thinking. In order to reflect fully on the amount and nature of the questioning that a teacher engages in she could actively monitor the usage of different types of questions reflecting on the impact they have on children's learning. It may be useful to ask adult support that you have working with you in the classroom to do this.

Similarly, if children are to become active learners they also need to reflect on how, why and to what level they have engaged with the learning and where they want it to lead. They need to make judgements about their learning and the learning of others if they are required to self or peer assess. Creating success criteria will aid this process; however, those skills need a firm foundation of questioning. The skill of using appropriate probing questions is something that needs to be taught and this is best achieved through frequent modelling and usage.

Affective issues – establishing a supportive classroom culture

Questioning should be part of a child's everyday experience; however, research suggests that this can create great anxiety for some children (Anderson, 2000). Children who are insecure fear being asked a question that they can't answer because it might expose them to the ridicule of others, thus reducing their self-esteem further. This can be further exacerbated by a well-meaning teacher who moves on too quickly for fear of embarrassing the child. Children adopt all sorts of avoidance strategies during whole-class teaching when questions are asked. For example, some delay the raising of their hand until they are sure that the teacher has targeted someone else; some sit on the fence half raising their hand and others drop their hand because they become bored with waiting (Measor and Woods, 1984). It is vitally important to remove or at least minimise the stress associated with asking and answering questions. Strategies such as enabling children to discuss as a pair or group before answering or providing them with a personal resource such as a mini whiteboard on which to record an answer appear to reduce anxiety. Another observation from the Leverhulme Project was that questions were mainly directed to individuals rather than groups (Dunne and Wragg, 1994).

Group problem solving develops security for the participants because they can refer to each other. It also promotes discussion through the challenge presented by the searching questions that develop through the pursuit of problem solving. Collaborative group work, which is facilitated, allows children to interact with each other and take some control over their learning. The participants learn from and support each other and the interaction with the teacher then tends to be higher order as opposed to managerial.

If children are forewarned that they will be required to ask a question during a session they begin to realise and accept the value placed on questioning. This could be achieved by giving them a picture of a large question mark at the beginning of the session. They can then devise a question to be asked at the end either through consultation with others or independently. This strategy helps to engage children in the lesson and ensures that they are active rather than passive learners and also recognises the contributions of the reluctant questioners.

Some schools take a quite extreme view of how children indicate that they are prepared to answer a question and ban a hands-up approach (Best and Thomas, 2007). It would seem that a variety of approaches is desirable and also that the environment of the classroom plays a significant role. If the children feel secure in their environment and mistakes are viewed positively as a starting point for discussions and investigations then most children will view question and answer sessions as a normal part of the teaching and learning process. It is helpful if the teacher monitors who they pose questions to and how those questions are differentiated to ensure that they are appropriately pitched for the development of individuals. One strategy that is in common usage, which is used to aid this process, is the use of lollipop sticks. The children's names are written on sticks of different colours with specific colours being reserved for girls or boys, so that the teacher can consider the gender element. Choosing a stick then appears apparently random and children accept that this is going to happen. The advantage of this approach is that the teacher will try to ask the same number of questions to both boys and girls. Also if the children know this approach is going to be used it reminds them that they really need to focus on the lesson content in case they are asked questions about it. It also requires the teacher to consider differentiation and target the questions so that each child's attainment and needs are considered. The disadvantage of using this strategy all the time is that there might be an imbalance because of its randomness and some children might not be asked any questions or very few during the course of a week. Teachers would have to note which children had not had an opportunity to answer and redress the balance by ensuring that other approaches were used.

Dealing with the misconceptions that you become aware of through questioning or marking can be difficult with an insecure child. Identifying children who have made mistakes can engender such negative emotions in some children that they are unable to engage with the process of relearning (Koshy, 2000). One strategy to address this is of using the device of the 'unknown' child which enables the children to become the teacher and use the 'unknown' children's errors as a starting point for a discussion about errors and solutions (Spooner, 2002). See Try this 3: Creating a culture within the classroom which encourages and values questions for more strategies to explore the development of a classroom environment in which children are encouraged to ask and answer questions.

Teacher skills and strategies

Effective intervention

There is a much greater emphasis on learning through play and the development of speaking and listening skills now than there has been in the past. This enables teachers to take advantage of the opportunities to develop the enthusiasm and natural curiosity of young learners. All teachers have opportunities to display Socratic ignorance (communicating a genuine need and desire for an explanation) (Fisher, 2008) by questioning/commenting on children's pursuits and interactions in a way which actively encourages children to think about their actions. This not only enables them to develop thinking and learning but gives them opportunities to learn independently. The skill in this approach depends on the timing and degree of intervention by the teacher. Posing a considered question at the right time and giving the child time and space to contemplate it is an art worth cultivating.

Planning for questioning

The creation of higher order questions or enquiry questions needs careful consideration. Some teachers address this by devising what are sometimes called 'extension activities' which tend to involve some kind of problem solving. These provide opportunities for children to apply their understanding and develop reasoning, but the disadvantages are that only certain children reach this stage of the lesson and that children miss out on the modelling and discursive elements. Teachers should build this into the planning stage by posing a series of key questions to themselves. This is an art which when mastered is a very important part of a 'teacher's toolkit' (Best and Thomas, 2007). Firstly what can the children gain from the teaching of this topic? How can they take that further and encourage a development in reasoning and reflection on process and learning? What prompts and questions could be included to develop real learning and reasoning?

Wait-time

The time that a teacher waits after posing a question, before moving on or supplying a hint, is vitally important because it can significantly impact on the number and quality of the responses. It is known that many teachers' average wait-time is less than one second (Black and Wiliam, 1998). If it's too short then there will be a limit to the number who can respond and if it's too long then one risks children opting out because they are bored with the wait. Teachers should judge the wait-time based on the type of question but also be aware of the anxiety that quick-fire question and answer scenarios can create. As mentioned above it is important to create a safe environment within the classroom where the asking of questions is valued as much as the answering and 'wrong' answers are used productively. Lower order questions that simply require recall of a fact that is either known or not would not benefit from an extended wait-time but higher order questions where time to think or discuss is needed would require a longer wait-time. Higher order questions will be less threatening if they are pursued by a group or set at the end of a lesson or day so that children have the time and opportunity to consider options and discuss with others.

Alternative questioning strategies – Provocative statements

Statements, as opposed to higher level questions, can also be successful in encouraging and developing reasoning. James Dillon (1988) suggests that thought and reason can be developed more effectively by posing provocative statements. He believes that children who engage in a discussion centred on a provocative statement, may display greater involvement and participation resulting in deeper, richer thought and connection. For example consider the statements: '*The perimeters of all rectangles have a different numerical value from the area*' or '*Any object that weighs less than 5g will float in water*'. The children will have to research and challenge these statements. This process will automatically stimulate discussion, thought and reasoning. The practice of explaining their approach and findings allows children to consider their thinking and thus develops metacognition.

A curriculum based around questioning?

Following the perceived restrictions of the government's numeracy and literacy initiatives many schools are now adopting a more creative approach to the curriculum. Schools are introducing 'creative curricula' which they believe will make learning a process that develops creativity, curiosity and enquiry. The approach used to apply to the curriculum, rather than the content of the curriculum, will affect the learning that takes place and whether or not that learning is sustained. If a curriculum is engaging, promoting thinking and reasoning, it should contribute to producing active, problem-solving citizens of the future. It is in a teacher's power to enhance and enrich learning opportunities by creating enquiry-based classrooms where good questioning is modelled and utilised to develop creativity. Inspiring teachers create inspired learners. One well-posed question can increase the extent to which learners are motivated and actively involved in their own learning. I have witnessed stimulating lessons where the majority of the content is questions. Nowadays the curriculum of some schools is designed around questions (see, for example, Lighting up Learning at www.lightinguplearning.com). Learning cycles, that replace topic plans or schemes of work, are based around an enquiry question and are developed in a way that addresses the acquisition of desirable skills. Some creative curricula start with a question that is explored and culminate with a celebration which recognises the result of the investigation. In designing the provocation the teachers take into account the skills that will be necessary to engage with the investigation. Sometimes these skills are taught separately and sometimes they are developed alongside. This approach gives credibility to the acquisition of skills and a clear purpose to the resulting dialogue. It is usually a group enquiry which includes the teacher and so she is on hand to direct through the posing of effective questions. This modelling is vital and often enriches the level and power of the questioning of the children involved in the project. This development in curriculum design in England may have been inspired by the Reggio Emilia approach in Italy. This approach has almost certainly been the inspiration for some Early Years settings in Tyneside. In Reggio Emilia the learning journeys of the children arise from the germ of an idea that comes from observations of children's interests. The projects or learning cycles that are then created aim to encourage and sustain the children's enquiry through posing questions to groups of children. The aim is to enable the children as questioners and allow them to express their ideas. Their ideas often dictate the direction of the enquiry. The journey culminates with a celebration of the learning that has taken place. The role of the teacher is vital as through questioning and observation they are able to intervene with prompts or questions in order to maximise the interest and the subsequent learning. 'Excellent questioning skills are underestimated in how we implement the curriculum' (Ewan McIntosh, SW ICT conference, 2011).

CASE STUDY

This case study looks at a school that has been proactive about developing questioning skills amongst the staff. It charts the development from the initial catalyst through the difficulties of implementation to the resulting situation to date and concludes with the school's future aspirations.

The school is a semi-rural primary where language acquisition is a problem for a number of children. The school's mission statement is headed 'Learning Together We Can Achieve Great Things'. It emphasises a belief that children's education should be a partnership and concerned with life-long learning in academic, social and practical contexts. There is a big emphasis on life-long, active learning as illustrated by the following selection of aims for each child:

- Develops a level of knowledge, skills and attitudes that prepares them for life in a changing, diverse world.

- Develops an enquiring mind through a spirit of enthusiasm for learning.

- Is able to be an active participant in their own learning.

- Can extend their individual skills of reflection to work out problems.

The school is committed to developing effective teachers and observes practitioners regularly, to identify needs, in a supportive environment. The OfSTED report of 2008 highlighted that the more able children in the school weren't being stretched. As a result of this and observations of staff, the senior management decided that they needed to review the use of questioning throughout the school.

A staff meeting focusing on the need to increase higher order questioning involved the modelling and analysis of Bloom's taxonomy to share knowledge about different levels of questioning and to encourage staff to consider the range and purpose of the questions. The school development plan was focusing on assessment for learning and they received input from the LA and 'best practice' training to support this. Questioning features heavily in assessment and so the staff have been encouraged to incorporate questioning into their planning. The whole school focus centred on developing teachers' subject knowledge with a view to modelling desirable technical vocabulary for literacy, numeracy and ICT. The teachers were asked to record the key questions that they considered would help to raise achievement.

The school stresses the importance of modelling and valuing children asking questions. As a result of an idea shared during 'best practice' training, one member of staff has purchased a set of dinosaurs and named them according to the learning behaviour she feels is desirable. One is called 'Askaraptor' and the child who asks the highest number of well-considered questions over a specific period is allowed to 'take care' of the 'raptor'. This has been very well received by the children and children's questions have increased significantly. The teachers are very aware of the need to use 'wait-time' and encourage the children to discuss the question in pairs before answering. They have no set policy about the use of hands or otherwise to indicate a desire to answer, but use a variety of approaches believing that if the environment is supportive children will not be worried about being asked directly to answer a question.

Speaking and listening is very much on the agenda because of the language difficulties of many of the children and so the deputy head conducts a pupil conference with each class which allows and encourages children to talk about how and what they are learning.

The school is increasing the focus on questioning and some of the things they hope to include in the next stages are:

- developing discussion in children;

- encouraging peer observation to monitor the use, application and success of questioning;

- joint planning for questioning amongst teachers;

- children creating their own success criteria as they become more articulate;

- including a question in the marking of work and giving children time to respond;

- improving the children's self-assessment through modelling focused questions.

There is some evidence of increased language and questioning skills amongst the children but it is slow. The staff will continue to monitor the output.

Reflecting on the case study

- What is this school doing to develop the use and range of questions?

- Which aspects do you feel are most likely to be effective?

- What do you feel is missing?

- How does this approach compare to your experience in school?

- Discuss the potential benefits or drawbacks to a no-hands approach in questioning.

- How might a teacher be proactive about improving her questioning skills?

- Have you ever audited the frequency with which you ask questions or the range of questions that you ask? Is this important? Why?

TRY THIS

Try this 1: Menu for creating higher order questions

Higher order questions can be posed with relatively simple language and should consist of more than who, what, where and when.

The questions need to be:

- targeted;
- prompting;
- probing;
- open.

The questions/prompts should:

- Challenge assumptions and conclusions. *How can we be sure . . . ?*
- Prompt children to ask their own. *If this is the answer what might the question be?*
- Test generalisations and hypotheses. *Is it always . . . ?*
- Suggest attack strategies which develop starting points for enquiry. *Can you break down the problem?*
- Address errors and misconceptions. *Are you able to demonstrate your thinking?*
- Gauge what they know, what they have learned and what they need to practise further. *Tell me what this means to you.*
- Promote reflection. *Could you have approached this in a different way?*
- Stimulate and provide support for new learning. *I'm unsure about this, shall we look at it together?*
- Challenge ideas. *Convince me. What would happen if we changed something?*
- Promote discussion/encourage the verbalisation of ideas. *Let's discuss this in a group of four. 'How would you explain this to a friend?'* encourage both verbal and written responses.
- Encourage reporting. *'Talk me through what you did'*; *'Tell me how you did this'*; *'Talk to me about something that you did today'.*
- Extend the task and the thinking. *'What if?'*

These questions are open and personalised thus linking the cognitive and the affective. Kissock and Iyortsuun (1982) believe that this combination leads to more effective questioning. You will also notice that some of the above are prompts rather than questions. Prompts invite a child to say, do or suggest something. These can be starting points for modelling enquiry or promoting sustained quality discussion.

Try this 2: Mapping knowledge

Responses to a group of lower order questions focusing on recall can be recorded on a mind map. Then if the process is repeated at the end of the topic and the information recorded in a different colour on the mind map the teacher will have a clear idea about which children have remembered what and how much learning has taken place. This summative assessment can then be used formatively to inform future teaching and learning. Lower order questions are vital in establishing what knowledge the children have acquired.

Does this enable you to be more focused in your planning and assessment?

Does it allow you to encourage the children to be more active in their learning if you ask them to suggest what they want to find out during the investigation of different topics?

Try this 3: Creating a culture within the classroom which encourages and values questions

Monitor whether reluctant questioners become more confident as they become more secure in this environment.

Activity 1

Give children the opportunity to 'post' questions into a box and use them to generate enquiry. You don't have to know the answer to the question.

The process of finding out the answer allows the children to see that you are curious and like to question and investigate in order to find answers. Johnston et al. (2007) state how the teacher is a very important role model for questioning behaviours.

Does this impinge too much on the reality of teaching the school curriculum?

Does the fact that you know you won't be able to be the 'all-knowing adult' create a tension?

Activity 2

Set up interactive displays and create a stimulating environment which encourages children to pose questions. Build displays around a question that children genuinely want the answer to.

Does posing a question to the whole class encourage more children to contribute with suggestions?

Activity 3

Encourage the children to take charge of an area of the classroom to create a museum of curiosity.

Are the children excited by 'unknown' artefacts and if so is the amount of conjecture and questioning increased?

Activity 4

Create a set of large cards that display a brightly coloured question mark. Give them to reluctant questioners at the start of the day and challenge them to think of an important question at some point during the morning or afternoon.

Did you see an increase in confidence in these children or the reverse?

Activity 5

Allow time for group discussion and support to answer higher order questions at the end point of sessions.

How realistic is this? Were you able to make time to have extensive dialogue?

Activity 6

Encourage children to pose their own questions about a written text. Move from those that test comprehension to those that explore 'what if' possibilities.

Can you involve the children orally in this way through guided reading and the class story?

Activity 7

Allow reluctant questioners to see and discuss written texts before being required to answer questions.

Does displaying questions around the room encourage more discussion and engagement?

Activity 8

Prepare children to discuss. Children need to be taught the language of discussion. Fruitful discussion will not necessarily take place because children are placed in groups and told to discuss. Consider giving children different roles to facilitate this.

Does teacher modelling and intervention help to facilitate and increase the quality of discussion?

Activity 9

Play games such as . . . *The answer is . . . What might the question be?*

Would it be useful to have one displayed each morning as the children come into class then release the responsibility to designated children?

Activity 10

Prepare a bank of higher order questions to use during the lesson.

Were these useful in probing and developing understanding?

Did they slow the pace of the lesson too much?

Were there management issues with the range of answers?

Were you aware of a shift in the balance of lower and higher order questions that you ask?

SUMMARY

The skills of questioning of both teachers and learners provide the bedrock for active learning. This chapter identifies and explores a number of factors that affect the effectiveness of questioning and provides opportunities to investigate some of these at first hand. The case study and the example of the Emilia Reggio approach illustrate how the art of questioning can provide a starting point for whole curriculum development.

Research into how and when questioning can be incorporated into teaching and learning has provided useful models with which to classify questions. This understanding allows teachers to construct questions to suit distinct purposes and to ensure that they use a range of different types of questions in the pursuit of learning. The research alerts teachers to the need to consider the affective issues related to question/answer exchanges and suggests how developing an awareness of strategies such as wait-time and collaborative answers can minimise potential anxiety.

FURTHER READING

Wragg, E. C. and Brown, G. A. (2001) *Questioning in the Primary School*. London: Routledge Falmer.

A workbook developed from the Leverhulme Primary Project that offers a range of useful practical exercises to enable both experienced and trainee teachers to improve their own and their colleagues' questioning skills.

Godinho, S. and Wilson, J. (2004) *How to Succeed With Questioning. Little Books of Big Ideas.* Melbourne: Curriculum Corporation.
Compact handbook full of interesting ideas on questioning to try in the classroom.

WEBSITES

Geographical Association: www.geography.org.uk/gtip/thinkpieces/questioning/
An alternative discussion of the issues covered in the chapter.

http://teachertools.londongt.org/?page=questioningTechniques
Guy Claxton, Professor in Education and Director of CLIO Development, University of Bristol, presents this slide show about the role that questioning can play in developing the cognition of gifted and talented learners.

http://bit.ly/HU4FaJ
A downloadable paper offering lots of ideas about planning the questioning approach and preparing the level of questioning. A range of strategies for engaging the children in the process, such as 'phone a friend' and sustaining and extending thinking are also supplied. de Bono's 'Thinking Hats' are explained clearly as is Bloom's taxonomy.

http://teachingcenter.wustl.edu/asking-questions-improve-learning
An American view of how questions can be used develop learning.

REFERENCES

Anderson, J. A. (2000) Teacher questioning and pupil anxiety in the primary classroom. British Educational Research Association Conference, Cardiff University, September 2000.
Anderson, L. W. and Krathwohl, D. R. (eds) (2001) *A Taxonomy for Learning, Teaching and Assessing: A Revision of Bloom's Taxonomy of Educational Objectives*, complete edition. New York: Longman.
Askew, M., Brown, M., Rhodes, V., Wiliam, D. and Johnson, D. (1997) *Effective Teachers of Numeracy: Report of a Study Carried out for the Teacher Training Agency.* London: King's College, University of London.
Best, B. and Thomas, W. (2007*) Everything You Need to Know About Teaching – But are too Busy to Ask.* London: Continuum International Publishing Group.
Black, P. and Wiliam, D. (1998) *Inside the Black Box.* Assessment Reform Group.
Bloom, B. S., Engelhart, M. D., Furst, E. J., Hill, W. H. and Krathwohl, D. R. (1956) *Taxonomy of Educational Objectives: Handbook 1 Cognitive Domain.* New York: David McKay.
Claxton, G. (2008) *What's the Point of School?* Oxford: Oneworld Publications.
de Bono, E. (1992) *Serious Creativity.* London: Harper Collins.
Dillon, J. T. (1998) *Questioning and Teaching: A Manual of Practice.* Beckenham: Croom Helm Ltd.
Duffy, Gerald G. (2003) *Explaining Reading: A Resource for Teaching Concepts, Skills, and Strategies.* New York: Guilford Press.
Dunne, R. and Wragg, T. (1994) *Effective Teaching (Leverhulme Primary Project).* London: Routledge.
Fisher, R. (2008) *Teaching Thinking: Philosophical Enquiry in the Classroom.* London: Continuum International Publishing Group Ltd.
Hastings, S. (2003) Questioning. Available at: www.tes.co.uk/article.aspx?storycode=381755 (accessed 19 January 2012).

Harris, D (2005) Questioning strategies in the early years science activity and discourse. Paper presented at the British Educational Research Association Annual Conference, University of Glamorgan. Available at: www.leeds.ac.uk/educol/documents/156393.doc (accessed 19 January 2012).

Johnston, J. (2005) *Early Exploration in Science*, 2nd edn. Buckingham: Open University Press.

Johnston, J., Halocha, J. and Chater, M. (2007) *Developing Teaching Skills in the Primary School*. Maidenhead: Open University Press.

Kissock, C. and Iyortsuun, P. (1982) *A Guide to Questioning: Classroom Procedures for Teachers*. London: Macmillan.

Koshy, V. (2000) Children's mistakes and misconceptions, in V. Koshy, P. Ernest and R. Casey (eds) *Mathematics for Primary Teachers*. London: Routledge.

Lee, C. L. and Smagormsky, P. (2000) *Vygotskian Perspectives on Literacy Research: Constructing Meaning through Collaborative Inquiry Learning in Doing: Social, Cognitive and Computational Perspectives*. Cambridge: Cambridge University Press.

Lipman, M. (2003) *Thinking in Education*, 2nd edn. Cambridge: Cambridge University Press.

Measor, L. and Woods, P. (1984) *Changing Schools: Pupil Perspectives on Transfer to a Comprehensive*. Milton Keynes: Open University Press.

Piaget, J. (1928) *Judgement and Reasoning in the Child* (reprint 1959). New Jersey: Littleford, Adams and Company.

Petty, G. (2009) *Evidence Based Teaching: A Practical Approach*. Cheltenham: Nelson Thornes.

Spooner, M. (2002) *Errors and Misconceptions in Maths at Key Stage 2*. London: David Fulton.

Wilks, S. (ed.) (2005) *Designing a Thinking Curriculum*. Melbourne: The Australian Academy of Arts.

CHAPTER 5

REFLECTIVE TEACHERS, REFLECTIVE CHILDREN

Anitra Vickery

Be the change you want to see in the world.
Mahatma Ghandi

Chapter overview

This chapter examines the way in which teachers can develop a reflective
practice that will be personally motivating and enhancing and in turn will
impact positively on the quality of the educational experience that they are
able to provide for children. It provides information about established reflective
frameworks and suggests ways in which teachers might focus their reflection.
It explores ways of helping children to become reflective so that they can
become more active about the development of their learning. Activities provide
opportunities for reflection on both pedagogy and children's learning and
engagement. Case study cameos cite how PGCE students used the reflective
process to unravel concerns and dilemmas and also demonstrate how the
process might change and develop during a first year in teaching.

INTRODUCTION

This chapter begins by introducing the reader to theoretical perspectives on
professional reflection. It will outline the nature of reflective practice and explain
how it is much more than just thinking about what has happened in the classroom.
The skills and attitudes on which effective reflection is founded – observation,
open-mindedness, reasoning and analysis, and the links to problem solving – will
be explored and the possible parallels in children's development of higher order
thinking will be considered. A discussion about the comparative inexperience of

the trainee teacher and the benefits of engaging with a more experienced other will highlight the potential affective issues associated with the analysis of practice. This in turn will lead to a discussion of the benefits of collaboration and discussion for both teachers and children.

The chapter makes reference to the two tiers of professional reflection and considers the resulting effects of firstly improving practice and then reflection which explores the moral aspects of understanding and critiquing educational change in the wider society. The development of a supportive framework will help achieve a balance between development through reflection and managing the practical demands of the initial years of teaching. This will be illustrated by some accounts supplied by newly qualified teachers (NQTs). The chapter will conclude with practical suggestions of how to develop the reflection of both the teacher and the learner followed by suggestions for further reading, and references.

WHAT IS REFLECTION?

Reflection is an intellectual and affective activity where people explore their experiences in order to understand and appreciate them in new light (Boud et al., 1985). Refection in its simplest terms is thinking about something that has happened in order to make sense of it (Race, 2002). Reflective practice, however, is rather more than simply thinking about what you're doing. It involves a proactive analysis of experience, and drawing on a repertoire of skills and experiences in order to learn and develop from that experience. This is the reflective practice that we recommend for both teachers and children because these reflective insights allow them to grow and learn from their experiences by identifying and creating the changes that are needed to best support and develop learning (Pollard et al., 2008).

There are a number of proponents of reflective teaching, most notably Dewey (cited in Pollard, 2002), Schön (1983) and Pollard et al. (2005). These authorities have suggested 'frameworks' or 'models of learning' to guide the reflective process (Ghaye, 2011).

John Dewey is credited with being proactive about introducing the notion of reflective practice into the field of education (Larrivee, 2009). Dewey believed that reflection is a rational and purposeful act. He talked about routine action and reflective action as two processes. Routine action is action that is not normally consciously debated by the individual teacher and very much linked to the intuitive process. Routine action may be dictated by tradition, internal and external authorities, circumstances and situations. The danger for all practising teachers is that they accept situations because 'that's the way it's done': similarly as a trainee teacher you may feel that as you are a guest in the host school you must concur with all decisions made about the content and approach in teaching and not question the philosophy or values promoted by the school. Brookfield (1995) suggests that the assumptions that we hold about teaching are heavily influenced by the hegemony within the education system, created by authority structures within the school and the policies of central government. To counteract this he suggests that teachers should consider their practice through four lenses:

- the experience that has made us who we are;
- the children we are working with;
- the other professionals that we work with;
- the knowledge, research and theory we absorb.

The reflective process you engage in will be unique to you because of the individuality of your classroom, your personality, the assumptions you bring to the job and the nature of the dilemmas you face at any particular time.

Reflective action can be triggered by the need to solve a problem and involves 'the active, persistent and careful consideration of any belief or supposed form of knowledge in the light of the grounds that support it' (Dewey, cited in Pollard, 2002). Dewey suggests that practitioners need to develop the qualities of 'open mindedness, responsibility and wholeheartedness' in order to be flexible and rigorous with their analysis (Warwick, 2007).

Schön developed the idea of a teacher as a reflective practitioner in the early 1980s. Some critics suggests that his framework focuses on the individual and fails to appreciate the positive impact that peer support and discussion can have on one's development. For that reason, even though many of the suggestions are applicable to teachers, it tends to be adopted primarily by other professions and businesses (Larrivee, 2009). Peer support and discussion is also particularly important for children. Nisbet and Shucksmith (1986), through their programme of meta-cognitive training for primary school children, produced strong evidence that discussion enables children to become more reflective about their own processes. Discussion tasks, if designed carefully, lead to interactions that are purposeful and result in increased understanding for the participants (Scardamalia and Bereiter, 1994). Reflection is essentially a social activity (Soloman, 1987 cited in Warwick, 2007).

Schön talks about reflection *in* action and reflection *on* action. In action is essentially thinking on your feet and changing what needs to be changed there and then. On action means considering what happened after an event and planning a change by result of the analysis. Schön also proposes re-framing practice – by this he means looking at practice from different perspectives. These different perspectives in teaching could be from the point of view of the child, the student, the parent or carer and other colleagues (Ghaye, 2011).

Another desirable element of Schön's framework is that he is concerned with the wider societal and ethical implications of what happens in the classroom, thus taking the understanding of reflection to a deeper level (Cole and Knowles, 2000). Pollard's framework, developed from the work of both Dewey and Schön, comprises seven characteristics to aid the process of reflection (Pollard et al., 2005). He encourages teachers to develop the reflective process through a series of actions presented in a cycle. These actions involve monitoring what happens in the process of teaching and learning, evaluating the outcomes and then making adjustments as a result of reflection. This systematic process of monitoring and reflecting on actions should enable teachers to refine their practice in order to develop learning.

As teachers become involved in their first job they are inevitably immersed in the culture of an organisation that has its own unique dynamic. The task of being

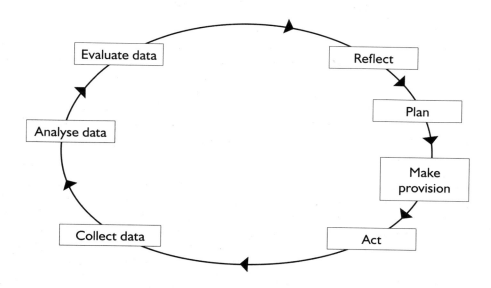

Figure 5.1 Pollard's Framework

responsible for a class of children whilst coming to terms with the expectations of the school and the parents as well as developing expertise in all the topics pursued in a primary school will seem quite overwhelming. This sense of being overwhelmed often results in negative emotional responses. This negativity could be exacerbated by the reflective process, as insecurity can mean that the affective aspects overwhelm the intellectual analysis (Zimmerman, 2009). Boud and Walker (1998) fervently believe that the reflective process should involve a subjective approach to make it more credible and effective; however, reflection by its very nature could be quite demoralising. It is important that the reflective process is founded on the recognition of positive aspects. Ghaye's (2011) model addresses this point. He suggests that practitioners should focus on the strengths of their practice and his model provides lots of opportunities to focus on positive experiences and use them to move forward. This is also supported by the Department for Education (2001) who state that reflective practitioners need to focus on their strengths and reflect on how and what they could share with colleagues in the process of identifying their needs.

THE SKILLS AND VALUES ASSOCIATED WITH REFLECTIVE PRACTICE

Teachers

Reflection will take place at many different times and at different levels because of the nature of teaching. Some reflection will just happen during the course of the school day and a lot of reflection will also happen at the end of the day, when you consider the outcomes of that day so that you can plan for the next stages of the teaching programme. An early stage of reflection will be concerned with the everyday occurrences within the classroom and its constantly changing dynamic because the classroom environment is unpredictable.

Reflective practice is likely to be a significant part of the course of many training teachers. You will be encouraged to become familiar with the most significant reflective frameworks and critically analyse suggested approaches. You will be encouraged to log your developing reflection through reflecting on problems you encounter in your practice as well as being asked to question and reflect on issues of teaching and learning and the impact on wider society. This worthwhile practice, however, could be short lived and not taken forward into your teaching career if the process isn't encouraged overtly.

Consider this scenario: A newly qualified teacher is concerned about the behaviour of the children in her class. The teacher identified the problem and knows that she needs to do something about it because her classroom is not supporting learning. She may feel a 'sense of failure' because her thoughts (reflection) tell her that this shouldn't be happening and so it must be her fault. She is at this stage engaging in surface reflection (Larrivee, 2009). She has introduced emotion into the scenario and doesn't reflect further because it might be threatening or demoralising. She closes down and reacts by acting without consultation or deeper thinking. She may try to increase her 'discipline' by becoming severe or developing different behaviour for learning strategies at random. She may try to separate out the children who she believes are disruptive. Her emotional state doesn't allow her to discuss the problem with a colleague.

In order to move forward with her practice she needs to develop a procedure which becomes habit and minimises the affective issues of reflection. Engaging with other colleagues may enable her to reflect at a deeper level and be objective about what is happening. The discussion should enable her to view the problem as a problem rather than as evidence of professional inadequacy on her part. This discussion might trigger a deeper consideration about what is happening as regards learning in the classroom. If the teacher recognises that the children aren't really engaged with their work she might then connect the two and take the reflection deeper, thereby engaging in pedagogical reflection. This might lead her to consider how and what she can do to change things by focusing on the learning context. She might be encouraged to consider accessibility of content for all children, structure of groups, discussions and rules of engagement as well as looking at the teacher child relationship and the values and expectations she projects through her voice and body language.

The above paragraphs contain lots of conditional words – may, might, if, could – because there is such an element of chance. The amount and quality of reflection that occurs will be dependent on the environment in which she is teaching. A supportive school environment is considered to be one in which it is the norm for all teachers to share elements of practice and where colleagues listen to any problems that are being experienced by a colleague. Together they try to find solutions. As helpful and laudable as this is it is not, in itself, indicative of genuine reflective practice. If there is no forum to enable reflective practice then it won't exceed the level of problem solving. A truly reflective practitioner will question practice whether or not a problem is evident. A school that sets aside time for their staff to meet together to discuss not only problems in learning but questions about learning will enable meaningful reflection which will contribute to the smooth running and success of the school. Regular focused meetings will enable the staff to engage with reflection at an even deeper level – sometimes referred to as critical reflection. They will consider how they can encourage the children to become responsible, independent and respectful and retain those qualities for life (Larrivee, 2009). This form of reflection examines the individual's personal and professional belief system. Sometimes there is a dissonance between the individual's beliefs and those promoted by school or government policy. A reflective practitioner needs to realise that who she is has been formed by experience which is embedded in her culture and it is therefore essential to develop the quality of open-mindedness, as promoted by Dewey, so that it is possible to engage in professional analysis that is free from the effects of preconceptions.

Children

New knowledge or skills that arise from learning that is active and reflective tends to become embedded in our development (Freire, 1973). Moon (1999) suggests that learning without reflection is only transitory or superficial. This is a clear message which suggests that the key to successful learning is reflection; however, when children are asked to reflect on their learning or their actions they often fail to engage meaningfully with the process because the term reflection in an educational sense hasn't been defined or modelled clearly. A teacher who encourages and promotes reflection will ensure that time and space is allocated to the process and that it is facilitated in a supportive context and environment. Providing space where children can reflect individually or with others transmits an important message about the value attached to reflection (Jensen, 2005).

Pollard's approach to reflective teaching and his belief in the resulting improvement in practice can be transferred to reflective learning (Hayes, 2006). The principles apply equally. Children's learning can be subconscious and they often don't realise the developmental characteristics of learning.

There are many demands on a teacher during the day and setting aside time for reflection may seem just another hoop to jump through; however, because of its obvious importance in the development of open-minded, responsible attitudes to learning it is worth incorporating into different parts of the day regularly so that it becomes second nature. Providing different experiences and structures to allow children opportunities to reflect should be an important part of the planning process. The plenary or end of the lesson is the ideal time to encourage children to reflect on and discuss the content of the session and the perceived learning for each individual; however careful management to counteract time pressures will be essential. Reflection on learning can best be achieved through guided discussion. The interaction with the ideas and thoughts of other children will present a range of perspectives to be considered. This will result in opportunities to make meaning of the teaching and learning and also to develop higher order thinking skills through the analysis, synthesis and evaluation of their learning. In order to do this successfully children should be guided to share their ideas and feelings honestly so that a true understanding of learning can be elicited. For example, at some point during the learning the teacher might encourage the children to think about the things they find easy to remember as opposed to those that are short lived. In this way she is drawing attention to the way that individuals learn. Each child will then be able to reflect on what is the most effective method of learning for them and also be aware of others' preferred learning approaches. In turn the discussion will inform the teacher about the most effective experiences she can give her children in order to further learning. If the teacher scaffolds reflective discussions so that children can share their thinking out loud then teaching and learning become more focused and productive and enable children to take ownership of the learning process by making their thinking process explicit.

Children need to feel safe if they are required to share any insecurity, but once a safe environment is created and reflection becomes an automatic part of learning the whole process of learning moves to a deeper level. Children need to feel comfortable that they can share their ideas openly and that what they express about their learning is not just a set response to the acquisition of the learning objective for the session but an honest appraisal of their individual learning in a non-threatening environment. Valuing honesty over attainment in an environment of trust where everyone is a learner will ultimately develop active independent learners.

Children who can appreciate what they do or don't know and what they do or don't feel are able to take some responsibility for their own learning journey. Teachers should interrupt the day to encourage the children to take notice. They could ask questions to develop the vocabulary for noticing learning.

- What are you doing and why?
- What helped you to access and achieve the learning?
- How do you feel about it?
- Are you prepared to persevere?
- Why are you doing it?
- Where will it lead?

Opportunities for reflection that take place before new topics or activities will enable children to consider their starting point and be able to assess what and how they need to develop. There are a number of schemes available that provide a series of questions at different levels to enable children to determine their starting level; their entry and exit point for the topic. Some teachers use the Assessing Pupil Progress (APP) DfE (archived 2011) statements to facilitate this approach. This analysis would primarily be an individual activity but could be discussed in pairs. In order to facilitate this analysis of learning the teacher should model an open-ended questioning technique using questions such as:

- What do you think you have learnt?
- Why do you believe that?
- How has your understanding or knowledge changed?

These enquiry questions should enable children to articulate and make sense of their learning thus participating in their own learning.

Some children will benefit from using a flow chart or diagram for reflection like the one in Figure 5.2. This can be an individual or shared response either written or oral.

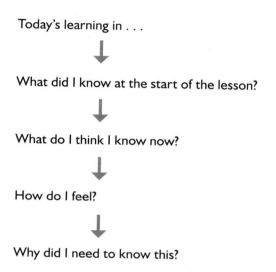

Today's learning in . . .

↓

What did I know at the start of the lesson?

↓

What do I think I know now?

↓

How do I feel?

↓

Why did I need to know this?

Figure 5.2 Reflection flow chart

This process could be aided by displaying a 'learning wall' which charts the progress through a topic and is added to daily. If the format were a mind map then it could be interactive and the children could add their ideas for experiences that would secure the next stage of learning (Harris and Caviglioli, 2003). Special provision, for example the deployment of support staff or strategic pairing and grouping of children will need to be made for children who have language acquisition problems or are reluctant to speak.

The use of flow charts makes learning visible and provides both teacher and children with a picture of their thinking and also a self-assessment tool. Additionally this conceptual link will ensure that the learning is more likely to be embedded.

Reflective journals that have a focus on learning can also be useful but probably more time consuming and the physical act of writing in sentences may actually distract from the process of reflecting for young children. The ability to reflect on their learning will be of enormous benefit to children not only during their school years but it is a skill that once mastered will impact positively on their entire lives.

CASE STUDY CAMEOS

The teachers in the following case studies were encouraged to develop the quality of their reflective practice throughout their PGCE course. At the start of the course they were encouraged to keep a reflective journal of things that happened throughout the university phases and the school experiences. They were asked to identify and consider their preconceived views on educational theory and practice; these would have usually been formed as a result of their own educational experiences, and to monitor if and how these changed as they gained more insight into the models of learning that they were exposed to. In addition they were encouraged to enter into discussions and debates during the lectures and seminars at university, to question received wisdom and to critique educational initiatives and practice. This enabled them to access the multiple perspectives of their peers. Towards the end of the course they were expected to provide a portfolio of evidence of their reflective journey and to write an essay that critically analysed frameworks for reflection using a self-chosen theme as the vehicle for analysis, noting any surprises or pivotal moments.

James

James has always been passionate about mathematics. Whilst at school he was taught mathematics through the use of textbooks. He asserts that this method of teaching suited his personality as he is quite competitive and enjoys a challenge. He worked his way through the exercises, learning rules and routines always aiming to reach the most challenging questions. He achieved well in mathematics and therefore believed that this was the most effective way to teach it. His first school experience reinforced this viewpoint as they too worked almost exclusively from textbooks. As it was considered a high achieving school he didn't question the approach.

During the university phase of his teacher training he was introduced to a research brief (Nunes et al., 2009) that suggests that mathematical reasoning is more important for children's later achievement in mathematics than the ability to calculate. For the first time he felt confused about his belief of how mathematics should be taught. He wondered why the findings were ostensibly ignored by schools and why the focus was on knowledge and procedures rather than investigative problem solving skills. He recognised that because of his limited experience he had relied on his own experience and the practice of more experienced others to dictate his approach. In line with Pollard's framework he decided to consult and collaborate with his mentor and as a result he implemented investigative mathematics sessions where he supplied resources that helped children to construct their own knowledge. He observed a surge in enthusiasm and motivation in children who previously seemed to be disinterested in mathematics. Conversely he also noted that some children who appeared to excel at mechanical mathematics struggled with the investigations. His research into the theories of proponents of reflective practice, especially Pollard, enabled him to focus his confusion. This was a very powerful lesson for James and one which he took very seriously, stating 'not only did I need to focus on the personal and academic consequences of my teaching but I also needed to identify with the social consequences of my teaching'. He adopted the characteristic of open mindedness as proposed by Pollard and researched further. He became aware of the negative culture surrounding mathematics teaching and learning and became more focused on ways to increase engagement and motivation for children. This led to further confusion and he was uncomfortable about challenging the teaching methods employed in his practice school.

James has been able to question attitudes and teaching models subsequently through opportunities for discussion with tutors, mentors and peers as well as adopting a different approach in a different setting. The opportunity to research, discuss and observe was crucial to him in forming an objective view about what constitutes effective teaching. He developed the view that a textbook approach had merit but mathematics learning needed to be enhanced by mathematical investigations. He recognises that reflection is a personal activity but that it is important to collaborate and discuss with colleagues in order to maintain professional development.

Sam

Sam is in his second year of teaching. As a PGCE student he had been extremely reflective about his practice and this impacted significantly on the positive way he was perceived by his professional colleagues in school. It was interesting to contact him towards the end of his NQT year to determine how much time he had been able to dedicate to the reflective process and whether or not he had been able to employ the same depth to the process. His answers to a questionnaire which set out to determine this are below.

- *What did the term reflection mean to you by the end of your PGCE year?*
  Reflection meant thinking back to previously taught lessons, identifying areas which worked well and those which needed improving. It meant looking at why things worked well and how things could be done differently to change the outcome. As I reached the end of the PGCE I realised the importance of reflecting on the positives as well as the negatives. By reflecting on the positives you can think about why things went well, and can identify ways to extend that success in future practice.

- *How has your understanding of reflective practice developed or changed during your time as an NQT?*
  I find that I am reflecting a lot more on wider school issues, and that this reflection is not just isolated to teaching. For example, I reflect on the way I deal with parental conflicts, which has helped me solve issues in a much more positive manner, whilst preserving my own confidence in my abilities as a teacher. I am now reflecting with a broader view of the implications for future practice. For example, identifying what has gone well in a topic so that I can think about what I might like to change for future years. The children's reflective process has also been important in this.

- *Whilst you were a trainee teacher you were supported to develop reflection as it was considered a valuable characteristic. How is your present working environment conducive to the reflective process?*
  I feel that I left university with a good grounding in reflection and this has enabled me to continue to be reflective. I have a very strong mentor at work who has helped me as I reflect on my own abilities as a teacher. I feel that I am reflecting

in a much more collaborative manner now than perhaps I did in my PGCE year and this is just another development in my process. I don't think that I would be such a strong reflector if it had not been taught as well at university. As it was incorporated throughout the course, this has helped me to carry this on and develop it further.

- *How often do you apply reflection to your teaching?*
  Daily, weekly, monthly, termly? Please clarify.
  Daily: I find that I am reflecting in different ways throughout the day. I reflect a lot after lessons, and find marking straight after helps me in this process. I can then use this to alter my next lesson accordingly. There is also a good chance to reflect with others during lunchtimes and I find that as a school, the staff talk a lot about how days have gone which helps the reflective process. At the end of the day, if needed, my partner teacher (who is also my mentor) and I will casually discuss certain elements of the day and reflect this way as well.

- *Do you use a framework to structure your reflection?*
  Not consciously. I find that I usually take some time to personally reflect after lessons/after issues. Thinking of what was successful/unsuccessful, making notes and working out ways I can achieve better outcomes. Then I might talk to my mentor or other members of staff and this helps to reflect in a different way.

- *If the answer to the previous question is yes, is it*
  1. *a known theoretical framework, e.g. Pollard?*
  2. *a devised personal framework?*
  3. *a school policy framework?*
  I'm not aware of a school policy framework and it isn't really a thing which is discussed in staff meetings or at the start of the year. I think it is expected that reflection is done which is why I am very pleased that there was such a significant input during the university course as it has enabled me to take control of my own reflection and identify ways to improve this process.

- *Do you reflect*
  1. *alone?*
  2. *with professional colleagues?*
  3. *with friends/family?*
  I usually reflect on my own, then when needed with my colleagues. Usually my mentor, though it can be my TA as well depending on the reflection.

- *Is your reflection*
  1. *an internal process?*
  2. *a written process?*
  3. *a discursive process?*

It is mostly an internal process.

- *Do you experience negative emotions when you engage in the reflective process and if so how do you respond to them?*
  Quite often, especially when reflecting alone after school. I try to go back over the situation or lesson and try to balance out the negative with the positive aspects of the situation. I often also think of how situations may have developed differently, and often then find that I did take the right decision or a decision which was better than others I could have made. I also try to talk to my mentor as she will often put the situation into perspective, which is often the most important part that I can miss.

Reflecting on the case study cameos

- What is Sam's school doing to develop reflection?
- Are the teachers in the case study cameos reflecting in the same ways and to the same depth?
- Which aspects do you feel are most likely to be effective?
- What do you feel is missing?
- How does this compare to your own experience of reflection?
- Describe and discuss how refection could have wider societal impact.

 TRY THIS

The suggestions below provide opportunities to develop both teachers' and children's ability to reflect on their learning.

Try this 1: Managing learning

Activity 1

Periodically present a lesson where the learning objective is not explicitly defined. Tell the children that they are going to determine what they think they were supposed to learn from the lesson, what they think they learned and what evidence they have to support their thinking. This activity would benefit from group or paired discussion.

Teacher reflection:

Were the children more focused?

Were they able to support their statements?

Were there any surprises about the learning that took place?

Activity 2

Provide children with written or oral feedback and give them time to reflect on the feedback with responses, individually or with a peer.

This could provide on-going discussion about the specific learning that is taking place.

Is this manageable? If not, try focusing on six children in one week.

Do children become more interested in their learning and take more responsibility for the development?

Activity 3

Give children the responsibility of sharing their understanding and 'teaching' another child who finds a concept difficult to understand.

Does this create an undesirable hierarchy?

Does this approach make children more aware of different learning preferences?

Activity 4

Provide the space to allow older children to record their ideas of their learning in a learning log at the end of a lesson/day/week. Scaffold the approach by displaying an appropriate questioning approach on a 'learning wall'.

Encourage an oral analysis with younger children.

How does this affect the children's understanding of their own learning journey?

Do children become more focused and proactive about developing their learning or do they consider it an extra unwanted task?

Try this 2: Monitoring different stages of the lesson

Activity 1

Consider the appropriateness of the first stage of the lesson. Do you always use it for the same purpose – e.g. to set the nature of the lesson, to elicit understanding, to prepare for the main teaching, to rehearse skills? Try changing the focus frequently as appropriate to secure and develop understanding.

Are the children excited by the unpredictability or confused and insecure?

Activity 2

Try changing the usual grouping and seating positions for the main activity.

Use extra adult support in different roles.

Allow children to self-differentiate.

How do these changes impact on the motivation and attainment of individuals?

Try this 3: Gaining attention

Activity 1

Monitor the impact of your current behaviour for learning strategies on the flow and pace of the lesson as well as the effect on engagement. The ideal situation is for all children to be actively involved in the work because they are appropriately challenged within a classroom culture of mutual respect; however, in reality it sometimes takes a period of time to establish this culture and it is necessary to use strategies to ensure that children can focus on the teaching and learning.

If necessary try the following:

At the start of a lesson use silent body percussion to gain the attention of a noisy class then hand over the leadership to reward individuals.

Prepare large paper strips of green, amber and red. Place everyone's names on the green at the start of every day and move down through amber to red if the behaviour is inappropriate. This should be done without verbal reprimand which will disrupt the flow and pace of the lesson. At the end of the lesson there will be a consequence for the children on red. The children can also move up if they reflect and remediate their behaviour.

Activity 2

Ask children to consciously reflect on their seating positions and interactions during learning. What and who disables the learning?

How successful are these strategies?

Do you find it difficult not to explain why you are moving a child's name to a different colour?

Are the children mature enough to recognise that some children or some situation could 'block' another child's learning?

Try this 4: Professional development

Activity 1: Analysis of practice

Consider an element of your practice that you have employed consistently throughout you career to date. It may be about teacher approach, the use of worksheets or textbooks, assessment procedures or using the outdoor environment. Critically analyse that practice and research alternative approaches to try out.

Are you surprised by the emotions this engenders?

Are you surprised by some research findings?

Does the change impact positively or negatively on either you or the children?

SUMMARY

This chapter explores what it means to be a reflective practitioner and how it is important to plan and organise opportunities for reflection so that it becomes embedded in practice. The reader is introduced to frameworks, constructed by significant proponents of reflective practice, which might assist them in the proactive analysis of teaching and learning. It is important to develop the right mind-set and approach whereby this intellectual analysis is not undermined by the negative emotions that may arise as a result of reflection. The chapter also discusses the place of collaboration and consultation with colleagues as a necessary support element in furthering the reflective process.

Reflection is recognised as the vital ingredient for deep, sustained learning and a classroom environment that challenges and interests both teachers and children. The Try this section presents suggestions to help the teacher encourage reflection in children.

FURTHER READING

Frangenheim, E. (2005) *Reflections on Classroom Thinking Strategies*, 6th edn. London: Paul Chapman Publishing.
   A wealth of ideas; lots of practical suggestions on how to create a successful thinking classroom.
Hughes, M. (1999) *Closing the Learning Gap*. Stafford: Network Educational Press.
   Written in an accessible style, this book presents a range of strategies to develop effective learning which have been created as a result of consideration of research about the brain and learning.

Manchester, H. (ed.) (2012) *Creative Approaches To Improving Participation. Giving Learners A Say.* Abingdon: Routledge.
This book looks at imaginative and creative ways in which to involve young children in their education. It presents a number of interesting case studies and also practical suggestions for reflective practice and professional development.

Russell, M. and Munby, H. (1992) *Teachers and Teaching from Classroom to Reflection.* London: The Falmer Press.
This book develops important ideas about reflection in teacher education. It introduces case studies and action research in a bid to empower teachers to be proactive about their professional development.

Tileston, D. (2011) *10 Best Teaching Practices*, 3rd edn. Thousand Oaks, CA: Corwin Press.
This book focuses on differentiated teaching strategies, teaching for long-term memory retention, collaborative learning strategies, authentic assessment and higher order thinking skills and gives lots of practical suggestions.

REFERENCES

Boud, D. and Walker, D. (1998) Promoting Reflection in Professional Courses: The Challenge of Context. *Studies in Higher Education*, 23(2): 191–206.
Boud, D., Keogh, R. and Walker, D. (1985) *Reflection: Turning Experience into Learning.* London: Kogan Page.
Brookfield, S. D. (1995) *Becoming a Critically Reflective Teacher.* San Francisco: Jossey-Bass Inc.
Cole, A. L. and Knowles, J. G. (2000) *Researching Teaching: Exploring Teacher Development Through Reflexive Enquiry.* Boston, MA: Allyn & Bacon.
DfE (archived 2011) *Assessing Pupils Progress (APP)* http://webarchive.nationalarchives.gov.uk/20110202093118/http:/nationalstrategies.standards.dcsf.gov.uk/primary/assessment/assessingpupilsprogressapp
DfEE (2001) *Continuing Professional Development.* Nottingham: DfEE.
Freire, P. (1973) *Education for Critical Consciousness*, 3. New York: Seabury Press.
Ghaye, T. (2011) *Teaching and Learning through Reflective Practice: A Practical Guide for Positive Action*, 2nd edn. Abingdon: Routledge.
Harris, I. and Caviglioli, O. (2003) *Think it – Map it: How Schools use Mapping to Transform Teaching and Learning.* Stafford: Network Educational Press.
Hayes, D. (2006) *Inspiring Primary Teaching.* Exeter: Learning Matters.
Jensen, E. (2005) *Teaching with the Brain in Mind*, 2nd edn. Alexandria, VA: ASCD.
Larrivee, B. (2009) *Authentic Classroom Management. Creating a Learning Community and Building Reflective Practice*, 3rd edn. Upper Saddle River, NJ: Pearson Education.
Moon, J. (1999) *Reflection in Learning and Professional Development.* London: Kogan Page.
Nisbet, J. and Shucksmith, J. (1986) *Learning Strategies.* London: Routledge and Kegan Paul.
Nunes, T., Bryant, P., Sylva, K. and Barros, R. (2009) *Development of Maths Capabilities and Confidence in Primary School.* DCSF. Available at www.education.gov.uk/publications//eOrderingDownload/DCSF-RB118.pdf (accessed 28 May 2012).
Pollard, A. (ed.) *Readings for Reflective Teaching.* London: Continuum.
Pollard, A., with Collins, J., Simco, N., Swaffield, S., Warin, J. and Warwick, P. (2005) *Reflective Teaching*, 2nd edn. London: Continuum.

Pollard, A., Anderson, J., Swaffield, S., Warin, J. and Warwick, P. (2008) *Reflective Teaching*, 3rd edn. London: Continuum.

Race, P. (2002) *Evidencing Reflection: Putting the 'W' into Reflection*. Bristol: ESCalate.

Schön, D. (1983) *The Reflective Practitioner*. New York: Basic Books.

Scardamalia, M. and Bereiter, C. (1994) Computer support for knowledge-building communities. *Journal of the Learning Sciences*, 3(3): 265–83.

Warwick, P. (2007) *Reflective Practice: Some Notes on the Development of the Notion of Professional Reflection*. Bristol: The Higher Education Academy.

Zimmerman, L. (2009) Reflective teaching practice: Engaging in praxis. *Journal of Theory Construction and Testing*, 13(2): 46–50.

CHAPTER 6

LEARNING THROUGH ASSESSMENT

Anitra Vickery

Instruction begins when you, the teacher, learn from the learner;
put yourself in his place so that you may understand what
he learns and the way he understands it.

Søren Kierkegaard

Chapter overview

This chapter explores the role of assessment in developing children's learning.
Throughout the chapter we consider the active involvement of children in their
learning and make suggestions about how they can be proactive about their own
development. We examine the role of self and peer assessment and discuss how
we can move the children on from superficial assessment responses. Strategies
and approaches that develop metacognition are discussed as well as assessment
procedures that will make assessment judgements secure and the whole
process manageable and productive. A short case study describes the approach
one school is following to develop its use of assessment and records their
aspirations for a greater use of assessment throughout the school and across the
curriculum. The chapter concludes with activities to develop learning through
assessment and suggestions for further reading.

INTRODUCTION

The chapter begins with a brief discussion of assessment in education which
introduces the reader to historical and current perceptions on the role and different
modes of assessment. Approaches that take relationships and learning styles into
account will be explored in the context of current thinking. This chapter will focus

on assessment which results in action which has a direct effect on the learning of individuals. We will examine the essential role of planning in making assessment a powerful tool which supports as well as measures learning. Approaches which lead to improved teaching and learning including setting and sharing clear objectives and success criteria, planning probing questions and encouraging self and peer assessment will be explained and illustrated. The full 'checklist' of the strategies that contribute towards effective assessment could be overwhelming for the beginning teacher so we will encourage you to analyse the efficacy and fitness for purpose of the strategies for each type of lesson, and we will discuss whether or not it is always productive to set objectives.

The chapter reviews the difficulties associated with self and peer assessment and discuss ways in which these approaches can become meaningful and effective in developing independent critical thinkers. The chapter includes practical suggestions and advice about how to make assessment manageable for the classroom and references to further reading.

THE ROLE OF ASSESSMENT

There are two main purposes for assessment in education: to monitor and enable the development of the child and teacher and to report achievement. Assessment carried out in pursuance of the first purpose is normally referred to as formative, and that which is aimed at the second purpose is called summative assessment.

The terms formative and summative assessment and the practices associated with them have been debated over decades. Scriven (1967) was the first to use the terms formative and summative assessment and argued for summative assessment to be used formatively, which may seem a contradiction. He suggested that there is much more rigour attached to summative tests and examinations and that it was the interpretation of those tests that validated the particular benefit of summative assessment. In other words, if the children were tested systematically and the results of the tests were analysed properly with a view to addressing the development of learning for each individual, summative assessment could be used effectively for formative purposes. This approach, he believed, would be of immense benefit to each individual. He argued that formative assessment did not have the same rigour attached to it and therefore the analysis could not be as complete. There is a synergy between formative and summative assessment resulting from internal testing and both can be a valuable part of the learning process. This synergy does not, however, operate with exams set externally as there is no feedback process on the knowledge that has been presented in the exam. The marketisation of education since the 1980s has meant that the term summative assessment now has a very different meaning and use from Scriven's definition. National summative tests set out to provide information based on the aggregation of children's results that can be used to compare the performance of schools.

Historically, effective teachers have always applied assessment techniques to further the development of the children in their care even though the terms formative and summative assessment may not have been used. Effective teaching was based on knowledge of where each child was and analysis of how the attainment of each child could be improved.

For ten years from 1987, members of the Assessment Reform Group (ARG), a group of academics funded by the British Educational Research Association, commissioned Paul Black and Dylan Wiliam to research the impact of classroom assessment practice. The results of the research, printed in a pamphlet entitled *Inside the Black Box* (Black and Wiliam, 1998), claimed that when carried out effectively formative assessment which resulted in constructive feedback and action raised levels of attainment. This informal assessment was called 'Assessment for Learning'. Assessment for learning then became the term that encapsulated recommended practice and its profile was raised by policy makers who promoted it as a vital ingredient of teaching and learning.

In many schools assessment for learning came to replace the term formative assessment as assessment which leads to action. Regardless of the term used the purpose is to identify where a child is in their learning and identify the strategies that could be applied to further develop that learning. You may encounter further terms for assessment with the primary purpose of developing the learning of each child including assessment *as* learning and assessment *is for* learning, the term favoured by the Scottish Curriculum for Excellence. These terms reinforce the message that assessment should be inextricably linked to and enable the learning of each individual. The principles that underpin the approach to assessment described by these terms are the same and each places great emphasis on the active involvement of the learner in setting goals and assessing progress. One of the great strengths of these approaches to assessment is that it enables the teacher to diagnose misconceptions and potential barriers to learning for each individual.

Summative assessment is primarily an assessment *of* learning. It is a measure of a child's attainment at a particular time. Summative assessment information usually comes as the result of a test or examination. The test could be an external or internal measure and its value as regards the development of learning depends on whether or not it can be analysed and used as a starting point for further teaching and learning.

Externally produced summative assessment is linked to accountability and judges the effectiveness of teachers and schools.

USING ASSESSMENT

The term assessment has both negative and positive connotations. It is interpreted by many as being synonymous with the words: test, exam, evaluate, estimate ability, accountability. An online dictionary definition defines assessment as a judgement of the value, quality or importance of something. Linking assessment with the notion of 'judgement' can be off-putting. The word assessment originates from the Old French *assesser*, based on Latin *assidere*, meaning to 'sit by'. The etymological roots conjure a more congenial picture of children and teachers supporting each other in their learning journey.

The Assessment Reform Group state that the process of assessment for learning should encourage both children and teachers to find and interpret evidence to secure development and interest in order to encourage children to be active participants in their learning (ARG 2002).

Assessment can be a very powerful tool; however, the degree to which it can have a positive effect on learning is largely dependent on the following key factors:

- The purpose of the assessment – when is it targeted at the development of individual learners and when is it carried out to meet demands for accountability?

- Your philosophical position – the way that you engage with and value assessment.

- The process – the procedures that are undertaken to gain an assessment of learning and the action that results from an analysis of that assessment.

- The perspective of the learner – do the children recognise the benefits to their development?

It is important to recognise why you might want to assess pupils. This chapter focuses on formative assessment but it is important to acknowledge that using internal summative assessment to provide a snapshot of attainment or understanding at a point in time will form a valuable part of your assessment toolkit. All internal assessment should be an integral part of teaching and learning where an assessment of understanding and attainment in the children is undertaken with the objective of improving and developing the understanding and learning of each individual. The analysis of this assessment requires you to be reflective about both your practice and the children's learning. In this way you will be able to identify barriers to a child's development as well as any blocks that indicate that teaching approaches need to be adjusted. In other words you need to remain open to the possibility that a child's failure to progress could be as a result of the teaching style as well as ingrained misconceptions or a reluctance to engage in the learning on the part of the child. Assessment should help to provide a clear picture of a child's journey and the pitfalls she encounters as well as the impact of the teaching.

If a child is to be encouraged to take an active part in developing their learning through assessment then the support of the teacher and the design of the environment must impact positively and be enabling. The design of that assessment should take into account the ways in which individuals learn so that children are able to demonstrate what they have learnt and what they can do. Think about how children might prefer to record their understanding. Would they be more confident speaking or recording with a partner or group? Would they prefer to record pictorially or orally sometimes?

You should try to embed assessment for learning throughout the day so that the children recognise that the classroom is a learning environment where they are encouraged to be proactive about and celebrate the learning that takes place. (See case study on p. 105, and Try this on p. 107) All interactions and observations should feed into the profile of learning that you are building of each child. You should gather evidence of a child's learning from across the curriculum so that it will feed into your understanding of that individual and give you a clearer picture of the learning needs and preferences of that child. You should also guard against only using assessment in core subjects as the child will then develop a picture of what she thinks you value. The children who excel in creative subjects will not recognise their achievement because they will assume that learning in those areas doesn't matter. You will need to bear all these factors in mind when you assess so that both you and the children benefit from the process. You should aim to ensure that you include opportunities for assessment on your plans as well as taking every opportunity to respond to assessment situations that present themselves throughout the day.

In order to fully engage the children in the assessment process they should be consulted about what they think the next stage of learning is and how it can be achieved. This will give them choices and empower them to be proactive about their development. They will be more likely to do this if they are confident about the process and familiar with the support structures that accompany assessment. Obviously the extent to which this is possible will depend on the age of the child but including the child in this process from the beginning will secure engagement and motivation.

Shirley Clarke states that the principle of active learning is at the heart of formative assessment (Clarke, 2008: 2). It requires:

- collaboration between teacher and child;
- assessing with and for the development of the individual's learning;
- pupil talk.

Any assessment in order to be motivating and productive needs feedback which informs the child. Encouraging the child to be part of the analysis and decision making will empower the child by motivating them to take an active part in their development. Summative assessment will also be less threatening and less stressful if the child recognises that any measure of learning can be used productively to enhance and develop understanding.

AN ENVIRONMENT THAT SUPPORTS ASSESSMENT

If children are to be encouraged to take a major part in the assessment of their learning they need to feel safe and be able to take risks (Dix, 2010). Modelling the learning process yourself by choosing to engage in a new skill and exposing your problems and insecurities is a powerful example. Claxton (2000) cites the example of a headteacher sharing his learning of a new musical instrument with all the frustrations that accompanied it. This presented the children in his school with a powerful message about learning, persistence, setbacks, collaboration and resolution.

The Qualifications and Curriculum Agency list ten principles of assessment for learning (ARG 2006). Assessment for learning:

1. is part of effective planning;
2. focuses on how children learn;
3. is central to classroom practice;
4. is a key professional skill;

5.   has an emotional impact;
6.   affects learner motivation;
7.   promotes commitment to learning goals and assessment criteria;
8.   helps learners know how to improve;
9.   encourages self-assessment;
10. recognises all achievements.

Two of these clearly state the need to support learners emotionally in the assessment process: 'Assessment for learning should be sensitive and constructive because any assessment has an emotional impact' and 'Learners should receive constructive guidance about how to improve' (Dix, 2010: 102).

FEEDBACK

Receiving feedback about one's work can be quite stressful and demotivating unless a positive atmosphere is created. Feedback for those who have been unsuccessful must be sensitive but specific and enabling. How can they overcome misconceptions? What further practice do they need? The use of a positive approach can develop self-efficacy (Bandura, 1994). You will need to develop this positive approach by recognising achievement and addressing difficulties positively. The child should be given credible feedback and effective strategies to move forward. Any feedback needs to focus on what has been achieved so far and how that can be developed. If a child is convinced in her ability to achieve then that achievement is almost guaranteed. 'Feedback is one of the most powerful influences on learning and achievement, but this impact can be either positive or negative' (Hattie and Timperley, 2007: 81).

The process of improvement needs to be exemplified clearly. Your feedback should enable the children to think more clearly and carefully about the development of their learning. One way in which you can do this is to provide opportunities for the child to respond to both your feedback and that of their peers.

A demonstration of external interest, by teacher or peer, and self-belief are powerful motivators. Studies carried out by Rosenthal and Jacobson (1992) concluded that if you demonstrate that you believe that children can do something then they invariably can. This is often referred to as the 'Pygmalion effect', or 'Rosenthal effect'. Your feedback should focus on the development of each child's knowledge and understanding. In this way it will avoid comparison and competition with her peers. The routine application of this form of feedback develops a dialogue between the child and you where the child recognises that the aim is to help her to succeed rather than it being a judgement of her achievement (Swaffield, 2008). However, this process of individual feedback involving conversations between children or between you and the child can be time-consuming and could become unmanageable unless you employ some enabling strategies (Butt, 2010). It is therefore important to empower children to take more responsibility for seeking, receiving and acting on feedback. If you give written feedback then it should be directly related to the expectations for learning. It should express what has been achieved and, if desirable, at that point in the learning, should contain suggestions for activities to secure learning or address misconceptions. Marking alongside the child is a very powerful and worthwhile experience for both you and the child. Children need to be given time to respond to this marking and could engage in a written dialogue with you after peer discussion. It is a good idea to make sure that there is time during the day to do so. Indeed it is probably best to timetable sessions devoted to feedback dialogues, both written and oral, so that they become routine and are not just shelved for another time during particularly busy periods. It is sometimes helpful for children to discuss feedback comments with another person, for example teaching assistants (TAs) and teachers in turn, but also with a peer they relate to and trust. If a high level of trust is developed then this feedback can be extremely powerful, meaningful and motivating. Establishing talk partnerships; pairs of children who work together to facilitate discussion, is an effective strategy that develops security and encourages objectivity in the analysis of learning. You will need to monitor the functioning of the partnerships and consider changing partners at times to increase the positive atmosphere throughout the classroom. This process in turn builds up a more informed self-assessment because the children are fully aware of the expectations for the learning and become more involved in the analysis of their achievement at that point in time. During peer discussion about the learning you can take part by conferencing individual children about their learning and how to move forward. Try to provide a solution for their misunderstandings or failure to develop by engaging with 'how' rather than just by pointing out what is wrong. The process then becomes realistic and appropriately challenging. By timetabling feedback response sessions you will not only ensure that they actually happen but also create valuable time for uninterrupted interaction between you and individual learners.

SELF-ASSESSMENT

Initially it will be very difficult for children to self-assess; they must 'grow' into it. The key to its success is to be very clear about the learning intention so that children are able to appreciate whether or not they have attained it and to give them indicators, often referred to as 'success criteria', if appropriate, to aid their assessment. Children often find it easier to develop self-assessment skills if they have had experience with peer assessment. Indeed a peer can often help those who find it difficult to assess their own work by working alongside them or by engaging in genuine discussion, which is not dominated by the teacher, where children are encouraged to be reflective and analytical about their metacognition (Butt, 2010). Such interactions will promote thinking and enable the children to consider not just the learning that has taken place but themselves as learners.

One useful strategy is to explore, with the children, some work from an anonymous child. For effective learning to take place common misconceptions must be identified and explored as soon as possible (Askew and Wiliam, 1995). There is a strong connection between effective learning and children's articulation of their thinking therefore it is essential that discussions take place in a social environment (Askew et al., 1997). Research into learning conducted at Nottingham Shell Centre (Bell, 1993) suggests that learning is more effective if children identify misconceptions in their own work. If, however, children's misconceptions are exposed by the teacher they often experience feelings of anger and sometimes humiliation (Koshy, 2000). Therefore it is sometimes useful to remove the 'emotional backwash' that might exist by getting children to analyse and discuss pieces of work from anonymous children. In this way they will be able to discuss the content and suggestions for improvement objectively. It might be useful to scaffold this with a framework for analysis (Spooner, 2002).

Different forms of assessment address different styles of learning and impact differently on different learners. For example, assessment for learning ostensibly occurs throughout the school day. It can be applied through marking, as discussed previously, questioning, discussion or observation. The means by which children can engage in the assessment process throughout the day are many and varied. They can answer independently or with the support of a partner or group, depending on the level of emotional support needed. They can use a mini whiteboard or other individual feedback resource in group sessions or engage in a verbal or written dialogue with the teacher or more knowledgeable other. The ways children will be able to respond to your questioning and probing will vary too. See Chapters 3 and 4 for a discussion of creating a positive environment for responding to questions.

A strategy that is often used to demonstrate children's self-assessment is to encourage the children to indicate their confidence or success with the learning with a written mark, usually a smiley face, a coloured traffic light circle or by using a thumb up or down signal. This is fine as an introduction to engage the child in thinking about the process but unless this is developed it will continue to give a very superficial picture. To be fully engaged with the learning a child needs to be able to express why they think they have succeeded, or why they have had difficulties, or what it is they don't understand – only then can they be proactive about their development and engage in a consideration of future learning. It is a good idea to build in time for reflection at the end of lessons or units and allow children to discuss their perceptions. Children need to talk through their experiences in order to develop their thinking and learning (Alexander, 2006).

SUCCESS CRITERIA

Success criteria, whether generated solely by the teacher or in collaboration with the children, are a series of statements that guide assessment of the overall learning intention of the lesson. They are used to focus the children on the steps they need to take to achieve secure, successful learning and as such can be a scaffold for children's learning. Success criteria are usually generated at the start of the lesson but if the lesson doesn't have a stated lesson objective, which may sometimes be the case, the success criteria can be generated retrospectively. They provide a framework for a formative dialogue where the children become aware of what they have succeeded in accomplishing. However, this approach can have some drawbacks unless it is handled sensitively. Some children believe that they haven't succeeded if they haven't been able to 'tick off' all the statements and this can be very demotivating, especially if the success criteria were generated solely by you. Those steps were your measure of success and sometimes this restricts or ignores any other learning that has taken place and predetermines what the outcome should be. If, however, you recognise that other learning might occur and share that idea with the children then they will feel able to retrospectively record their individual learning which may be very personal to them. In this way they make the success their own and become more aware of their learning in the process.

Gipps et al. (2006) state that encouraging children to create their own success criteria to demonstrate their learning reaps dividends. The construction of success criteria can be done either at the start of the lesson or at the end during peer or self-assessment. For example, if children are told what the purpose of the lesson is and what they are expected to achieve during the lesson they can decide how they can demonstrate that they have been successful; however, deciding what they have achieved at the end of the lesson can help children to analyse what they perceive as learning and which skills or knowledge they have acquired during that time. By encouraging and listening to children as they create their own success criteria you are empowering them to be active about their education and recognise that learning is not linear. Children construct their own learning and being given responsibility on this scale will help to develop an intrinsic motivation to learn (Drummond, 2004).

LEARNING INTENTIONS

Many practitioners would argue that learning can only be measured by the observer and the participant if the desired learning outcome is shared with the children. Certainly sharing the objective informs the children what they are supposed to learn, and it also clarifies and determines the flow of the lesson for you.

All children need to know what they are supposed to be learning if they are to make a judgement on the success of that learning and it must be presented to them in a way that they can understand in order for them to do that (Leahy et al., 2005). However, sometimes that process of sharing the desired outcome can actually restrict the learning in that it doesn't take account of any other skills or knowledge that have been absorbed and may have a negative effect on children's desire to engage with self-assessment. If you expect children to achieve the learning challenge that you set then that expectation must be realistic and attainable. There is a danger therefore of restricting challenge by designing lessons that are perfunctory and limited in challenge. Adhami (2003) favours the term 'lesson agenda' in his discussion of lesson objectives and suggests that too rigid a use of learning objectives can limit or at the very least hide some important learning that has taken place, such as learning to collaborate and cooperate or engaging in meaningful discussion. He also believes that a cognitively-rich lesson cannot be limited to one lesson objective. This form of lesson will involve higher order questioning and thinking and usually involve extended, high quality discussions and interactions which might take the lesson into different directions which children will want to explore to gain new understanding. You should consider how to strike the right balance of introducing new learning that can easily be assimilated and creating challenge which provokes thinking and quality interactions.

KEEPING TRACK OF ASSESSMENT

Assessment for learning needs to be manageable. Initially it may seem overwhelming but with practice and routine it becomes a 'habit of mind'. The first step is to consciously plan for assessment. Record opportunities on your lesson plan. Devise key questions to elicit information at strategic points during the learning journey of the children and jot down any responses or surprises that add to the learning picture. These observations will enable you to redesign the activities to secure learning. It will also enable you to appreciate how individual children learn and what motivates that learning. Use a simple recording system such as post it notes to ensure that your minute-by-minute observations are not forgotten but feed into future planning and teaching. You might want to use something as straightforward as a diary page where you note observations of learning against a simple key or a class list. You can record perceptions of the learning that has taken place using something like traffic light colours and annotate as necessary.

Questioning can be a very useful strategy to gain information quickly; however, unless a teacher consciously uses a range of question stems she will tend to apply closed questioning (see Chapter 4). This form generally tests knowledge rather than understanding and gives an incomplete picture of the learning that has taken place. Learn to probe the understanding by using open and extended questions based on the question stems from Bloom's taxonomy (see Chapter 4). Some children find it difficult to take part in open questioning or discussions unless given time and support. You need to skilfully manage this by giving time and utilising and modelling extended questioning in a supportive manner. The essential thing to remember is that assessment for learning is a positive process. It should be a process whereby a child's learning is celebrated and steps to develop that learning further are explored and identified collaboratively.

Try to involve all interested parties in the assessment process, making sure that all the teachers the children come into contact with are informed of the learning development and style of each individual child. Make sure that you take feedback from the adult support working in the classroom. This can be difficult if they appear at the start of the lesson and disappear at the end. Try to devise a communication system between you using lessons plans or intentions, post it notes and feedback sheets to set up on-going conversations. If you are a Year 2 or Year 6 teacher the children will benefit enormously if you communicate with their teachers for the next stage of their education by sharing appropriate assessment results.

Parents can be very powerful motivators so try to be proactive about involving parents and carers by seeking conversations when they bring their children to and from school or enter into a written dialogue if desirable through homework tasks. In this way targets for development that have been highlighted through the assessment process can be negotiated through discussion with both the child and her parents (see case study).

In summary you need to consider what to do with the daily assessments you have made so that they feed into the development of learning for each child. You will need to share these with the child so that they are fully aware of where they are in their learning and what they need to do to improve. You should also use these analyses to inform your planning for the next stage of teaching and in the process share it with both colleagues and parents to ensure interest and consistency.

CASE STUDY

This case study looks at a school that was identified by OfSTED in 2010 as one that has a 'clear tracking system for pupils' progress which is used effectively to provide timely interventions' to secure and develop children's learning. They have also introduced a creative curriculum which provides many opportunities for active learning. This cross-curricular approach promotes the learning potential of the outdoor environment and has been designed to be relevant to individual needs and help the children to be creative and innovative. The assessment process within the school enables children to set personal goals by being aware of their learning and the way to develop that learning. The school vision statements include the desire to:

- create a vibrant learning environment;

- help children to value and enjoy life-long learning;

- equip children with the necessary skills for their personal, social and academic future.

The school is a large primary school of 13 classes with a small ethnic minority group of children. The number of school-identified school action plus children was slightly higher than the national average in 2011–12 but now is broadly in line; however, the percentage of school action plus and statemented children is lower than the national average.

   The school has developed assessment techniques greatly over the last few years for English and mathematics and is now focusing assessment in the foundation subjects. The school uses the WALT acronym ('We are learning to') to focus the learning in the lesson and also WINS ('What I need to succeed') to create the success criteria which can be either generated solely by the teacher or developed as a result of collaboration with or by the children. At the end of a lesson the children were sometimes asked to record their success or confidence about the lesson using a smiley, sad or in-between face. The assessment coordinator came to recognise that this was often an inaccurate judgement on performance as it was hard for some children to record anything other than a smiley face if they had enjoyed the lesson, even though their learning might not have developed at all during that time. She gradually introduced the notion of asking the children to write a comment relating to the WALT which gave her a better understanding of the achievement and need.

   Currently this practice is becoming more consistent in Key Stage 2 classes. In Key Stage 1 peer and self-assessment are carried out regularly in conversations with children. A system of smiley faces assesses how confident children feel about their learning, allowing teachers to revisit concepts and make formative changes to their planning. Children often identify aspects linking to the WALT by underlining it in their learning as part of the review or by drawing a star next to an aspect they feel fulfils the learning objective.

The school has developed genre ladders for literacy, used in Key Stage 2. These are based on the VCOP approach: vocabulary, connectives, openings and punctuation. The children focus on the statements on the rungs of the ladder and edit their work by placing a star if they have included the feature from the ladder that they are working on and then identify the wish, a picture of a magic wand, to indicate which feature they want to develop.

In Key Stage One, targets are directly linked to assessment. After assessing the children using work sampling, reading/writing and maths APP and other assessment materials, a gaps analysis is conducted. In so doing, areas of weakness for each child are identified which forms the basis of their future personalised learning opportunities and interventions. These targets also directly link to IEPs for children with Special Educational Needs and target books with individual targets are used for vulnerable pupils. Literacy targets are displayed on a bee hive with bees travelling to the Queen; numeracy targets are shown as spiders travelling to a fly in the middle of a web. Targets are based around the same focus but are differentiated for individual children. If children achieve their targets they are given a new target or challenge. This system has proved popular with children as it is both visual and child friendly.

This approach, which places the children at the centre of their learning, is also reinforced by including parents in their target or wish. Children are encouraged to take a target sheet home so that the parents can be involved in the development of learning. The sheet contains the sections Target, Example and How to help. The statements are linked to the Assessing Pupil Progress (APP) grid in both literacy and mathematics. In Key Stage 1, targets are shared with parents at Parents' Evenings where IEPs and target books are also reviewed.

In mathematics the children are encouraged to consider and achieve statements of increasing complexity for calculation. There is a reward structure in place in the form of bronze, silver and gold which not only makes the learning visible but allows the children to monitor their own development. In some cases this can be motivating, but at times the children are concerned about comparison and some parents are as well. The school would like to develop an ethos where learning is valued intrinsically and are considering ways in which this can be achieved.

In some classes the children are used to both peer and self-assessment and have benefited from the modelling of open questions. They have been encouraged to develop their own use of open questions through 'hot seating' and the Mantle of the Expert, a programme to develop engagement with real life scenarios. This approach has enabled many children to employ quite a sophisticated level of questioning and thinking about their own learning. The school hopes to make this consistent throughout the two Key Stages.

APP statements are reviewed three times a year for reading, writing and mathematics and are analysed so that vulnerable learners can be quickly identified so that effective intervention strategies can be put in place.

The coordinator has plans to develop assessment further in the near future. She has purchased some ICT software which will enable children to gain 'digital excellence' badges in ICT through the completion of tasks and then assessing their own learning. The program can be developed to include targets for other curriculum areas. During these activities children can work alongside others to develop and monitor their own learning through collaboration. The coordinator would like to give each child in the school a pennant on which they can display their achievement badges so that it becomes a visible celebration of each child's development in learning across the curriculum.

The coordinator is conscious of the fact that there is some tension and conflict about the preparation for SATs, in Key Stage 2, and the assessment of the process. She would like to introduce a more formative approach to SATs preparation where staff and children analyse all work with the aim of implementing actions for improvement. This process is already in place in Key Stage 1. There is also an intention to extend Early Years assessment practice into Key Stage 2 so that the good practice of observation and the collaboration of TAs 'post its' monitoring permeates the school.

In this school assessment is viewed very much as an enabling strategy. The approach is constantly being considered and reviewed because of the philosophy that the education they provide should enable the children to become responsible life-long learners.

Reflecting on the case study

- Are there any differences in the way that Key Stages 1 and 2 assess children's learning?

- Do you think that some assessment strategies are more suitable for Key Stage 1?

- Do you think it is difficult to develop a whole school approach?

- Which aspects do you feel are most likely to be effective?

- What do you feel is missing?

- How does this compare to your own experience of assessment?

 TRY THIS

Try this 1: Strategies for successful teacher assessment

Activity 1

During question time give the children mini whiteboards or individual resources so that their answers will be visible to you and you can make instant assessments which will feed into the next part of the lesson.

Is it possible to get a good general overview of the class's understanding or do you need to focus on a small group of children in turn?

Activity 2

Include opportunities for assessment on your plans and record a range of key questions to probe understanding.

Do you notice an increase in your use of open questions?

Are you able to extend the questioning to probe the children's understanding further?

Activity 3

Try to ensure that you give quality feedback. When you give written feedback concentrate on giving in-depth comments to a different group of children each time so that it becomes manageable. Allow children time to read and respond to the comments. Link all feedback comments, oral or written, to the learning and attitude to learning.

Are children keen to respond to written comments or do they regard it as just an extra task?

Does this give them time to reflect on their work before rushing on to the next piece?

Activity 4

Leave a diary easily accessible or carry post it notes so that you can note any significant learning daily throughout each lesson. Use a form of shorthand and reflect on it after the lesson so that you can plan subsequent actions that will feed into your teaching and planning.

Does your planning and teaching become more focused?

Do you notice a reduction in misconceptions as the topic progresses?

Try this 2: Strategies for assessing the starting point for new topics

Activity 1

Give children the opportunity to create a mind map of their understanding and or knowledge about the topic. Encourage them to share this with another child or small group in order to discuss the learning journey they would like to make. Develop a class discussion in this way the children feel empowered to take ownership for their learning.

Does this focus the learning?

Are you able to judge where to start the learning and create a visible learning journey at the start of each topic by sharing the 'big picture'?

Activity 2

Use post it notes and encourage any adult helper to do the same as you observe the interaction of the children and their security with the topic that is being proposed.

Does this help you to differentiate your questions and focus on the needs of individual children?

Activity 3

Encourage the children to create a large display of the proposed learning journey independently or with adult support starting with the known facts and indicating the stages of learning along the 'path'.

Duplicate this and allow each child to record her development on her personal copy.

Are the children confident in their approach?

Has there been enough discussion and generation of ideas to enable them to do this?

Are the children more focused on their own development?

Is the process too time consuming or is it justified by creating opportunities for individual's involvement?

Activity 4

Model the assessment of an 'anonymous' piece of work using and justifying the two stars and a wish approach (i.e. two positive comments and a target for improvement). Encourage the children to comment and discuss the analysis. When you feel that the children are confident with this process build time into a lesson for children to tour the class to look at the work of the class. Encourage them to record their assessment using two stars and a wish to indicate success and areas for improvement on post it notes placed on the work.

Give children time to read and absorb the comments and follow this with time for the children to report back.

Do children become more focused and objective in their assessment?

Do children concentrate more on the achievements they have made or do they find it competitive and threatening?

Activity 5

If children assess their work or confidence using visual indicators such as a thumbs up or down approach ask them to justify their choice either to a talk partner or you.

Are children increasingly able to analyse accurately?

Do they become more independent and objective in their analysis?

Try this 3: Strategies to develop engagement in the assessment process

Activity 1

Celebrate steps in children's learning through displays that recognise their development. Create pictures of both class and individual learning journeys that allow children to be proactive about recording their successes.

Do children become more involved and focused on personal achievement or does this approach encourage negative comparison?

Activity 2

Involve parents/carers in the assessment and target setting process by sharing the achievements and next steps in learning through regular written or oral dialogue. Illustrate how the parent/carer can help the child.

Do children benefit from the directed input of their parents?

What provision do you put in place for those children whose parents don't want to be involved? How might TA or peer help be utilised?

Activity 3

Involve the children in creating success criteria for the work and ask them to leave some space for them to add their own individual successes such as:

- I focused on my work throughout the lesson;
- I worked well with my partner/group.

Direct the children to work with a partner to check their work against the criteria and then evaluate their success adding their own perceptions of what they succeeded in as well.

Encourage them to discuss the next steps for each child and record it as a target.

Display it on their personal learning journey.

Are children able to analyse the work with the support of a friend and the success criteria?

Are they able to identify personal strengths that they have displayed in each lesson?

Does this added factor make them feel valued even if all the generated success criteria haven't been met?

SUMMARY

Learning through assessment is enabling. The child who is aware of their mis-understandings and misconceptions and is helped to reflect on ways to overcome these and recognise any barrier to their learning is being encouraged to take responsibility for that learning. In this way the child is being prepared for lifelong learning through the development of their reflection and analytical reasoning. These qualities are vital for engagement and development in learning. There are a range of strategies that the teacher can use to assess a child's learning but it is the action that follows that assessment that determines the success of the learners. It is important for children to develop an 'I can do' mentality as a result of the assessment of their learning but that will very much depend on the approach and reason for assessment. Those children who believe that they can influence their achievement will develop into adults who are analytical and reflective about the problems they encounter in life.

FURTHER READING

Blanchard, J. (2009) *Teaching Learning and Assessment.* Maidenhead: Open University Press.
 This book is written in a very accessible way. It suggests practical approaches to assessment for learning and includes case studies for reflection.

Gardner, J. (ed.) (2012) *Assessment and Learning*, 2nd edn. London: Sage.
 This second edition has been updated to contain the latest work on assessment and will be invaluable to teachers. It explores the inextricable link between assessment and learning and looks at the impact assessment has on a learner's motivation.

Rayment, T. (2006) *101 Essential Lists in Assessment.* London: Continuum International Publishing Group.
 This book contains a list of practical assessment ideas to implement in the classroom. It has useful ideas for analysing both children's and teachers' learning.

Torrance, H. and Pryor, J. (1998) *Investigating Formative Assessment: Teaching, Learning and Assessment in the Classroom.* Maidenhead: Open University Press.
This book explores the classroom assessment of young children but the ideas can easily be adopted for an older age group. The book is based on video and audio recordings of classroom interactions.

Johnson, S. (2012) *Assessing Learning in the Primary Classroom.* Abingdon: Routledge.
This accessible book links current theory with examples of assessment practice in the classroom. It identifies the principles that underpin effective assessment and considers the purpose and form it might take both within and beyond the classroom.

www.educationscotland.gov.uk/
This link takes you to the Scottish Curriculum for Excellence which has a very interesting section on learning, teaching and assessment.

REFERENCES

Adhami, M. (2003) From lesson objectives to lesson agenda: Flexibility in whole class lesson structure, in I. Thompson (ed.) *Enhancing Primary Mathematics Teaching and Learning.* Maidenhead: Open University Press.

Alexander, R. (2006) *Towards Dialogic Teaching: Rethinking Classroom Talk.* York: Dialogos.

Assessment Reform Group (ARG) (2002) *Assessment for Learning: 10 Principles: Research-based Principles to Guide Classroom Practice.* Cambridge: University of Cambridge School of Education.

Assessment Reform Group (ARG) (2006) *The Role of Teachers in the Assessment of Learning.* London: Institute of Education, University of London.

Askew, M. and Wiliam, D. (1995) *Recent Research in Mathematics Education 5–16.* London: The Stationery Office.

Askew, M., Brown, M., Rhodes, V., Wiliam, D. and Johnson, D. (1997) Effective teachers of numeracy in UK primary schools: Teachers' beliefs, practices and pupils' learning. *Proceedings of the 21st C conference of the International Group for the Psychology of Mathematics Education*, 2: 25–32.

Bandura, A. (1994) Self-efficacy, in *Encyclopaedia of Human Behaviour*, 4: 71–81. New York: Academic Press.

Bell, A. W. (1993) Some experiments in diagnostic teaching, *Educational Studies in Mathematics*, 24(1): 115–37.

Black, P. and Wiliam, D. (1998) *Inside the Black Box: Raising Standards through Classroom Assessment.* London: King's College School of Education.

Butt, G. (2010) *Making Assessment Matter.* London: Continuum.

Clarke, C. (2008) *Active Learning through Formative Assessment.* London: Hodder Education.

Claxton, G. (2000) *What's the Point of School?* Oxford: Oneworld Publications.

Dix, P. (2010) *The Essential Guide to Classroom Assessment.* Harlow: Pearson Education Limited.

Drummond, M. J. (2004) *Assessing Children's Learning (Primary Curriculum)*, 2nd edn. Abingdon: David Fulton.

Gipps, C., McCallum, B., Hargreaves, E. and Pickering, A. (2006) *Changing Teaching and Learning in the Primary School.* Maidenhead: Open University Press.

Hattie, J. and Timperley, H. (2007) The power of feedback, *Review of Educational Research*, 77: 81–112.

Koshy, V. (2000) Children's mistakes and misconceptions, in V. Koshy, P. Ernest and R. Casey (eds.) *Mathematics for Primary Teachers.* London: Routledge.

Leahy, S., Lyon, C., Thompson, M. and Wiliam, D. (2005) Classroom assessment: Minute-by-minute and day-by-day, *Educational Leadership*, 63(3): 18–24.

Rosenthal, R. and Jacobson, L. (1992) *Pygmalion in the Classroom* (Expanded edn). New York: Irvington.

Scriven, M. (1967) The methodology of evaluation, in R. E. Stake (ed.) *Perspectives of Curriculum Evaluation*, 1: 39–55. Chicago: Rand McNally.

Spooner, M. (2002) *Errors and Misconceptions in Maths at Key Stage 2*. London: David Fulton.

Swaffield, S. (2008) Continuing the exploration, in S. Swaffield (ed.) *Unlocking Assessment: Understanding for Reflection and Application*. Abingdon: Routledge.

CHAPTER 7

ACTIVE LEARNING WITH ICT

Keith Ansell

The great aim of education is not knowledge but action.
Herbert Spencer, English philosopher (1820–1903)

Chapter overview

To say that ICT in primary schools is in a process of change, is to state a truism. ICT is linked to the technology of the day. As tablets succeed netbooks, there will be evolution of technology in the classroom. What do we, as educators, do with the technology? How are we using technology for teaching and learning? Are we developing 'active learners'? There has been much recent debate about ICT in schools becoming a toxic brand, particularly in KS3. Instead of educating them, have we merely been training them, without enough emphasis on children using and applying ICT? A Royal Society report on computing in schools, 'Shut Down or Restart' (2012) said many pupils are not inspired by what they are taught and gain nothing beyond basic digital literacy skills such as how to use a word-processor or a database. The call from government and industry for a greater emphasis on computer science has been welcomed by Naace who point out there is much innovative, engaging work already taking place. ICT has become successfully embedded into the curriculum in many primary classrooms. Using case studies, I will reflect on good practice. It is an exciting time to be using ICT in primary schools. Although there aren't the streams of ICT funding and the software grants, to a large extent pupils and teachers have become familiar with the basic skills. Active learning with ICT is happening.

INTRODUCTION

The ICT toolbox

John Davitt's Learning Event Generator is a sublime idea. A fruit machine screen double tumbler selects a concept or area of learning, and challenges you to present it, as . . . an impressionistic painting; a haiku; a play in 3, 10-second acts . . . Davitt, a writer and digital toolmaker, is passionate about making the learning active. It is only when we reinterpret the idea/concept in a new form, that learning takes place, he says. Learning is made active. The Learning Event Generator will generate many ICT outcomes: . . . 'as an animation'; 'as a 20-second MP3 file'; 'as a word cloud in Wordle'.

As a judge in an animation competition, I came across one inspiring stop-frame animation produced by a class in the south-west. The Fruit and Veg team took on the Fast Food team in an Olympics-style 'Race for a Healthy Life', including Mr Banana's Top Tips for a Healthy Life. Their understanding of healthy eating was richly explained by the children through their animation. There are many opportunities for active learning that the ICT toolbox can support.

DIGITAL RECORDING IN THE CLASSROOM

McIntosh (2011) describes the idea of children filming their class at work and playing it back to them, as one of his best ideas. He goes on to observe just how cheap video cameras are now and how easy it is to quickly replay the clip back on the IWB, and points out how rarely he actually sees teachers doing it. Truly, the ability to play a short clip of a group collaborating together, played back in a mini-plenary session is a powerful device for getting learners to observe themselves working, enabling processes to be observed. Where children are learning to learn, exploring thinking skills, a small video camera is a perfect review tool. In a similar way, a visualiser enables teachers to place childrens' work under the viewer and get immediate feedback from them on grammar, spellings, punctuation and choice of vocabulary.

Let us pause and, using the language of film, zoom in here. Elsewhere in this book, we looked at how Papert (1993), the great thinker behind the computer language Logo, suggests that rather than teach children something about mathematics, we should be teaching them to behave as mathematicians. In all subjects, including ICT, children can be encouraged to think like a specialist. Photographers and film makers will have a range of shots: a panning shot, a zoom, a pull-back shot, to suit different purposes. Animators work together in a team – a camera person, a director, a props person. Each of these roles, and the collaboration, need thinking through to bring out quality outcomes. To extend the ICT toolbox metaphor, ICT and learning go hand in hand.

Our focus should be on the style of learning rather than the subject. Getting inside the subject by behaving as the specialist can work across the curriculum. A powerful ICT based resource such as www.artisancam.org.uk/ has an excellent series of videos where artists such as Andy Goldsworthy talk about what they are thinking and how they work as an artist. Hart et al. (2004) assert the importance of the children being engaged with the process of learning.

DIGITAL LITERACY

Technology is very much a part of the culture of society and should be used to support learning through integrating it into enquiry (Joyce et al., 2009). Searching for information needs be taught as an active process, as we aim to teach digitally literate citizens. The teacher will play a vital role in teaching the children to use this all-pervasive technology wisely. Children should be helped to recognise to comprehend the potential bias and moral implications presented through technology, so early KS2 children should be learning to recognise facts and opinions on websites. As a teacher we need to keep our own digital literacy updated. Try the November Learning Information Literacy Quiz (see further reading). Alan November is the acknowledged expert on digital literacy.

INTERVIEWING EXPERTS

We live in a media age where we can find video clips relating to any curriculum area. In school we consume ICT content using excellent online resources such as Espresso. If we want active learners we should also give the tools to the children. Using a Flip video camera or an Easi-Speak microphone can put the child into the role of the expert. It becomes 'here am I filming you/here am I recording what you are saying'. The video camera gives the eye to the child who is filming. Giving the microphone to the child to record, gives them the autonomy to capture what they think is important about the subject. In this way, they develop an interest in enquiry and consequently their questioning. Claxton (2008) notes that children's questioning skills can be moved to a higher level when a teacher asks learners to think of the questions a scientist/mathematician/writer would ask.

Bennett (2004) notes that audio allows learners to listen to, or watch the recording again. This facility to review the recording to extract information, gives opportunities for higher order thinking and supports talk into writing. He goes on to consider a progression of interview skills, and identifies planning and preparing questions at lower KS2 as learners, in group-based activity, discuss key issues which need to be addressed. At upper KS2, Bennett highlights skills of reviewing and extracting information as well as discussing and deciding how to present the information.

Later in this chapter we can see how it is now very easy to create a classroom blog to write about learning taking place in the classroom. The blog could also be used to share audio. Audioboo http://audioboo.fm/ allows you to create embedded play buttons so you can record, preview and publish your boo. Rylands (cited in Bober, 2010) suggests this could be a way of reminding children of a homework challenge, or perhaps learners could explain a science idea, or project, in 30 seconds. Echoes of the learning event generator, perhaps? Audioboo also allows upload of audio files, recorded on other devices. In this way, a pair or small group of children might publish their recount, or perhaps their song, to the blog to share with their parents and a much wider audience. Each audio posting has the potential to reach an audience of thousands and www.revolvermaps.com/ can show the children where their audience comes from. Publishing an audio clip online that parents and carers will hear later is a strong motivation towards a high quality finished product, so bullet pointing, scripting and rehearsing are all worthwhile preparation to make the most of the opportunity. Writing scripts and setting up interviews develops literacy skills, allowing children to develop and practise their speaking and listening skills. Purpose and audience are central to this type of learning activity.

There are many ways of creating and sharing audio, with different systems of varying complexity. Careful consideration should be given to the learning outcomes that teachers would like to achieve as well as the learning needs of their students before deciding which platform to adopt. Creating a podcast or a radio programme does require an amount of planning and classroom time. This can also be a very collaborative venture where they develop teamwork skills. Clear purpose can be sought right across the curriculum. A piece of persuasive writing presented as a radio show can link in to their own popular culture and knowledge of advertising and media. Rather than finding ready-made sound effect files there are curriculum opportunities with design and technology and music.

Adding of music and other sound to the soundtrack will make audio even more engaging. Presenting their audio as a radio broadcast or as part of a play, learners may well seek to add sound. Look Again (BFI, 2003) notes that from an early age, children come to 'recognise the sounds and music that signal danger, comedy, excitement and happy endings', suggesting that pupils should learn that moving image soundtracks have four elements: music, sound effects, voice and silence. All of these contribute to meaning. Sound can often do more to 'pin down' the meaning of a sequence than visual images can. Whitney (2010) noted a six year-old who responded to the way sound was used in a film soundtrack by drawing. His teacher later commented that it helped him make predictions in guided reading.

USING DIGITAL VIDEO

We can make learning active through digital filmmaking, which needn't be difficult. Photostory3 is a simple-to-use program which allows learners to combine a number of images with music or narration. When used by teachers or learners it has proved a very versatile tool in primary schools, particularly for working with narrative. A poem (text or spoken) could be enhanced with images and music. From a collection, learners assemble a series of still images to create a video. They can document their learning, perhaps supporting reflections on the process of a design and make task. Web 2.0 has made a range of video tools, such as Animoto for Education, available within a browser.

Data collected by Sigman (2012) suggests that by the age of seven years, a child born today will have spent one full year of 24-hour days watching screen media. Many ask whether children are too passive, sitting in front of screens. We are surrounded by digital media of all sorts, and children are immersed in this – very much part of our culture. But with many high-quality digital video clips available to us, could learners be making more active use of DV for learning in school? Chambers (2011) argues these visual, digital 'texts' can be used to develop comprehension skills in printed texts. We may have many in our DVD collection at home and many are available online. If we go to the Pixar website we can find many short, highly crafted videos that we know would be very engaging for the children in our classes. We know these clips will motivate learners, but how do we guide the discussion around a digital video clip?

There is evidence to suggest some children are failing to develop reading skills beyond basic skills of decoding texts literally, because they are not yet able to read between the lines and infer message not stated. Teachers also note that many pupils do not attempt to bring their own feelings or responses to texts read. We seem to be saying here that these children do not infer when they read, and yet, to infer is a natural state of mind. From a very young age, children are inferring, perpetually reading gestures, so they might infer anger or assertion if an adult bangs something down on a desk. Yet clearly many learners are not bringing this skill to their reading of text.

However, children who can read at only literal level with print text can, and do, infer at far more sophisticated level when presented with moving image clips. Waller (2008) suggests that at home there is often an environment rich in video and images, with narratives developed by television, film, games consoles, and increasingly on smart phones. Kress (2003) argues that we should more widely acknowledge these emergent digital literacies. It is necessary to start with those 'texts' that they are already reading actively so learning with moving image can have a key role to play in developing the higher order skills that children need to read and comprehend all texts. Moreover decoding the text is not a barrier.

In 1993 the writer Aidan Chambers published a book called *Tell Me* which had a powerful influence on teachers of children's literature. *Tell Me* was based on a questioning framework and outlined an approach for eliciting children's responses to the books they were reading. In the video, *Learning to be Literate* (1999), made by the Centre for Literacy in Primary Education (CLPE) emphasis is put on the need for teachers, and children, to learn and to practise how to ask, answer, and think about these questions. The effect is something more like a conversation than a lesson.

In 2003, the BFI approached the CLPE to join a collaborative research project investigating ways of working with film in Key Stage 2 classrooms. The CLPE introduced the Tell Me approach, and the BFI published their significant document, *Look Again*. The Tell Me framework consists of different types of questions under the headings 'Basic', 'General' and 'Special'. These subtle and open questions attempt to ensure that questions are generative. They create spaces for children to talk extensively and they do not threaten, or imply a right answer, anticipating a conversational dialogue. The outcome is cooperative talk in which a community of readers makes discoveries. There is also a desire for collaboration here that suggests that the teacher wants to know what the child thinks.

Returning to our initial question: Can we study these digital 'texts' to develop comprehension skills? The Tell Me approach means that a teacher can work from moving image texts, to printed text and back again. In this way they will foster their pupils' reading skills and responses in both media.

EXPLORING COMPUTER MODELS

As teachers we know that the learning environment is crucial to learning. Malaguzzi (Edwards et al., 1993) wrote about the three teachers of children:

adults, peers and the physical environment. He referred to environment as 'the third teacher'. By extension could we say that the environment of the digital simulation is also a child's third teacher? A computer-based model allows us to learn in a virtual environment. We can use the growing number of computer models, and simulations to try different possibilities and test them in a safe, virtual environment. As noted in previous chapters, subjects can be approached through active enquiry if the approach is valued, encouraged and facilitated by the teacher. It is important to recognise that the content can be the vehicle for the exploration (Hart et al., 2004).

A series of cross-curricular modelling activities based on regional themes which are aimed at KS1 (but very usable in lower KS2), Big Day Out provides mathematical and scientific challenges or investigations (see Try this 8, Activity 2 on p. 127). All modelling activities have multiple outcomes and are designed to encourage dialogue. For example, the user can set up the catapult at Warwick Castle. They can change the rope tension and distance to hit the rocks. In Torbay, learners can dispense as many ice creams as they wish that have different flavour combinations. Learners can reflect on their learning on a postcard which can be emailed to parents and carers.

The National Curriculum advised teachers to 'use simulations and explore models in order to answer "What if . . . ?" questions, and to investigate and evaluate the effect of changing values and to identify patterns and relationships'. The learning is not transmitted by the digital activity, it comes as children and adults discuss what is happening. As Alexander (2004) reminds us, at the heart of the matter, effective teaching is dialogic, rather than transmissive.

Learners can relate the experiences on the computer to investigate some of the ideas in the real world. The Torbay ice cream combinations activities could be extended with other flavour multilink cubes and an extension into a number investigation.

The phenomenon of the last 20 years has been the growth of electronic games, which have developed into fully immersive multimedia experiences. Children and adults fully engage in completely absorbing experiences. Players play for extended times and work hard to raise their skills and understanding of the virtual world they are in. They work together using collaborative skills to solve the problems which games present. As Bober (2010) notes, there has been increased interest in recent years in how games can be used to support teaching and learning in a more formal educational environment. When children are engaged in a game-related task, they are learning by doing. This is active learning. Csíkszentmihályi (2009) concludes that people are happiest when in a state of complete flow, or complete absorption in their task and the situation. Csíkszentmihályi refers to the issue of difficulty of task, observing that it is hard for a learner to achieve a state of flow if the task is too hard. Tim Rylands, on his website www.timrylands.com, quotes Papert who makes an important point about challenge:

> Every maker of video games knows something that the makers of curriculum don't seem to understand. You'll never see a video game being advertised as being easy. Kids who do not like school will tell you it's not because it's too hard. It's because it's – boring.
>
> (Papert, 1993)

Bober identifies challenge as one of the many motivational elements, that include action, adventure, strategy, suspense, coolness – characteristics present in electronic games that encourage learning. Bober turns to Tim Rylands who uses immersive landscape games to inspire children's writing. He has used games such as Myst, Riven, Wild Earth: Natural Safari and says he is always looking out for new Web 2.0 games. After asking children to describe what was present in a good computer game, Rylands came to the conclusion that challenge was the most important. He talks about the challenges within the game Myst:

> Myst itself has challenge elements hidden within it, in that to get to a new location you are set challenges to solve problems. In the Myst experiences they desperately want to find their way to a different landscape and they become passionate about solving the problem, however, I don't think the problem-solving is the challenge – the challenge is that the children start to bring their worlds alive through the power of words. It's giving them real reasons to want to polish up their writing, develop their descriptive skills, think about everything because we use it for everything; writing, music. It's not a specific challenge in the game, it's the challenge related to the games.
>
> (Rylands, cited in Bober, 2010)

Rylands (cited in Bober, 2010) asserts that the game need only be one part of the learning experience, and only one element of the technology. Myst may be the stimulus but there are a lot of other Web 2.0 technologies or analogue methods for the children to be able to record their experiences and their involvement with the process. He also thinks that the social aspects of the learning experience, such as collaboration, are crucial to engaging children. He has useful pointers: Using PrimaryPad, children can write at the same time as everybody else, interact, share ideas, build a document, literally writing at the same time as other people. A tool such as Scribblar could also give learners the opportunity to have a chat channel alongside, which means that they can draw interactively as well. Learners can be adding to the same text: correcting, chipping in, contributing. Rylands observes that it is 'games-based', in that the base is the game. What happens around it, is the important aspect.

Games-based learning has much to commend it. Learners can develop collaborative skills such as problem solving and team skills. The software can certainly engage children by building on children's existing skills and interests, and perhaps narrow that gap between children's home and school cultures. The power is in how we use them. Groff et al. (2010) assert that 'game-based learning approaches need to be well planned and classrooms carefully organised to engage all students in learning and produce appropriate outcomes'. After extensively examining Ryland's approach, Bober (2010) concludes that it is vitally important that 'games-based learning experiences are mediated by a teacher to facilitate learning and are supported by other digital tools and teaching methods'.

BLOGGING WITH YOUR CLASS

More and more teachers are considering setting up a class blog. Blogs, such as those supplied by Primary Blogger or Edublogs, are essentially websites with all the capability to share images, audio and video, but fluid and adaptable to the needs of the class and teacher (Fryer, 2012). School websites can suffer from lack of updating and lack of clarity about what they want to achieve, but with teacher and learners working together, a class blog can make a real impact.

Fryer (2012) summarised the positives, noting that with class blogging there is clearly a purpose and the children are writing for an audience. Furthermore a class blog gives the opportunity for video, audio and collaboration following a stimulus. Fryer cites the ability to produce wonderment and the freedom from worry about handwriting. Teachers and learners have autonomy or control of their own learning, enabling personalisation. He goes further, exploring the idea of blogging supporting self-efficacy, or the measure of one's own competence to complete tasks and reach goals. Blogging is indeed very straightforward to set up and can support teaching and learning in a number of exciting, motivating ways (see case study 2).

Learning how to create a blog might be called a routine skill that children have to acquire. However, maintaining and formatting a blog to include various types of visual media requires the child to demonstrate a combination of skills, understanding and knowledge. What is more, using a blog format to write a diary over a number of weeks would not only reveal much capability, but also constitutes a purposeful, cross-curricular application of technology in the context of a meaningful task and provides a powerful learning experience as a result.

(Barber and Cooper, 2012)

DISCUSSING ONLINE

Comments need to be moderated on a class blog. VLEs offer a walled garden where learners and teachers can participate in learning and teaching in an e-safe online environment. By using the online discussion function and putting peers directly in touch with each other, we have the opportunity, as Kress (2003) talks about, to 'get learners talking about their learning'.

Facebook and discussing online is a social phenomenon of our time and part of our culture. Waller (2008) writes about the importance of bringing home into school, observing that most children engage with a range of popular cultural forms outside of school. Cremin (2007), writing about creativity in writing, observed that boys become much more engaged when they can write freely, bringing in their own culture. Cremin links outcomes with boys very much to enjoyment and motivation. Barnes (2009) talks about the relationship between learners and teachers less in terms of language and more in terms of the kinds of access to the processes of learning that teachers make possible. Facebook is not an e-safe environment for children. Many schools subscribe to a virtual learning environment such as Kaleidos, It's Learning or SWGfL Merlin.

As part of e-safety responsibility, teachers need to address behaviour online. Thinking before they post is a crucial awareness for children, if emotional havoc is not to ensue. Children need to learn that a posting could convey unintended messages and emotions and is more open to incorrect interpretation as there are not the usual cues to assess the other person's reaction. Byron (2008) reminds us that equipping children with the skills to appropriately impart messages to others, is as important as helping them know how to interpret and cope with those they receive. The online discussion is a useful place to learn this awareness.

What makes an online discussion space a successful place for learning? In this context, interaction must be structured and systematic. Communication with the intent to influence thinking in a critical and reflective manner, is the intention. One successful example was – 'Space – what would you like to do in Space?' used with a Y5 class. Open-ended questioning is crucial, to get learners exploring different ideas. The scaffolding by the teacher should enable the children to 'take the major thinking role'.

Alexander (2004) emphasised that to provide the best chance for children to develop the diverse learning talk repertoire on which different kinds of thinking and understanding are predicated, dialogic teaching needs to meet five criteria. Dialogic teaching is collective, reciprocal, supportive, cumulative and purposeful. Guided by these five principles, online discussions become a powerful tool to enable learning to take place. Success rests on the extent to which discussions are dialogic. As teachers begin to use online learning for homework, the way that they structure the learning may well evolve, particularly using open-ended starting points. Fewer directives from teachers 'do this . . . ,' and more 'let's imagine': exploring lots of 'what ifs' suits this medium. The space discussion became a useful exploration of concepts such as gravity and its effects. There are many other science topics where learners could consider concepts and explore their misconceptions. In order for productive dialogue to flourish, as Scott and Ryan (2009) point out, insight is required of teachers as they act 'in the gap' between pupil understandings and scientific views. Dialogic teaching is a pedagogical tool that applies to all subject areas. Could online discussions therefore contribute to learning right across the curriculum?

> Children must think for themselves before they can really know something and teaching must provide the linguistic opportunities, the conditions for this to happen.
>
> (Alexander, 2004)

CASE STUDIES

Case study I: Dan Wilson

Dan Wilson, a Y6 teacher from St Andrew's Primary School in North Somerset has become well known for his creative use of ICT. His class won the best animated film in the North Somerset Oscar (Noscar) Awards. Viewing the outcomes you know the children have had total ownership of the project. They had applied a whole range of techniques, with the children completely engaging with the purpose, and taking delight in sharing their humour with the audience.

When I observed this lesson, Dan was using Scratch, a program that enables the user to program small games. I spoke to Dan about his sequence of lessons. He has a regular slot in the ICT suite and says weekly sessions give enough time between to incubate ideas. He generally uses open source (free) software that the children can download and use at home. Dan researches the software but feels no necessity to become an expert user, although he carefully maps out the learning possibilities using teacher forums. The high motivation factor ensures that a number of children carry on between teaching sessions and the format of the lessons allows space within to share their growing expertise.

In the first session, of possibly five sessions, children create in pairs. His intention is for the children to become familiar with the layout of Scratch and to move a sprite around the screen.

In the second session the children's task is to make a simple chase game with Scratch, using the key 'forever' function. They also create their own sprite, increasing sense of ownership. The children are highly energised and share the features that they have discovered, to tweak different elements. In a plenary, Dan asks what would they like to be able to do with Scratch in future? What sort of game do they think they could make? One child confides to me that she likes to, 'design and control my own things'. At this stage the aim really is ownership by the children, as he asks how they would like to develop their ideas using Scratch in their topic of Tudors.

In the third session Dan helps them prepare. His intention in this session is for them to be able to move the sprite continuously across screen, so introduces the feature 'if on edge, bounce'. He also asks them to experiment with pausing. The children are incubating ideas for their Tudor game.

The fourth and fifth sessions are about developing and refining their ideas towards an agreed time where they will present their Tudor game to others. The task now has both purpose and audience.

Dan says that he uses a similar approach with all of the ICT projects he undertakes. Whether it is an animation program to create a stop-frame animation, Google Sketchup to create 3D virtual models, Garageband to create space music, or Scratch to create a Tudor game, he uses the free tool in a series of sessions to produce an extended and refined piece of work. (We could add the tools Audacity or WeVideo, to the list with appropriate purpose and curriculum context.) ICT provides a whole toolbox of tools for active learning. Learners are motivated by collaborating and learning together to utilise the features and functions of the program in a purpose that is very much owned by them. In this approach the learners are fully activated.

Creative teachers show a considerable degree of ownership with regard to planning, teaching and assessment. They exert a strong sense of professional autonomy in the classroom and demonstrate flexibility and confidence, asserting their desire to create a co-constructed curriculum which builds on the learners' interests and their social/cultural capital, as well as curriculum requirements.

(Cremin, 2007)

Reflecting on the case study

- How would you sum up the characteristics of this approach to discrete ICT?

- What do you think are the strengths of this approach for
  a) the children?
  b) the teachers?

- Which aspects of the teacher role do you think are key to this being an effective approach?

- How does this approach compare to your experience in school?

Case study 2: Ian Rockey

Ian Rockey from Moorlands Schools Federation in Bath has created a blog, subtitled 'sharing our learning with the world', with his Year 2 class and speaks with great enthusiasm about how their blog has proved highly motivational, particularly for writing.

http://msfy2.primaryblogger.co.uk/ (2011–12) and http://msf2010.schoolblogs. org (2012–13) are full of examples of the children's writing published. The use of Picasa, Audioboo and PhotoPeach to add slideshow, audio and video clips has added a multimedia dimension. To show a knowledge harvest, an embedded Wallwisher displays what the children want to learn about the circus. A look at categories shows Ian has tried a range of purposes for posting with his class, including a five-sentence challenge and maths challenges for home. He says that, 'the blog takes the learning outside the classroom and engages the parents'.

Commenting is an important element to the blog dynamic, with children, parents, teacher and visitors leaving comments. Ian advises teachers to ensure they turn on the setting for moderation, to enable the teacher to read and approve comments before they are added.

Ian was careful to create some simple guidelines and suggestions with the children to 'help us to keep our blog safe and enjoyable for everyone to read'. Here are their useful Blogging Guidelines:

- Children should only use their first name when commenting.

- Parents who leave comments are asked to use their first name only so as not to identify their child, or post comments as 'Ian's Mum' or 'Amy's Auntie'.

- Do not post photos from or links to other websites without permission from Mr Rockey.

- All posts will be checked by Mr Rockey before they are published to the blog.

- All comments are checked by Mr Rockey before they appear on the blog.

- Be positive if you are going to comment. Say something that you like about a post and maybe even ask that person a question.

- Please write in full sentences and use proper punctuation. Make sure you double check your comments carefully before sending them.

The children have their own log-ins to the blog. With his Year 2s, Ian is moving from whole class to individual learner postings as the year progresses. A Year 5 blog at Moorlands has used Poll Daddy for surveys and the comments demonstrate more independent use.

Ian is keen to emphasise the role of the education blogging community. Following Deputy Mitchell on Twitter, led him to the idea of Quadblogging. Sustaining the enthusiasm for your class blog can difficult over the year, so classes join a quad of four classes around the world who comment on each other's blogs. Moorlands are currently in a quad with a class in New Zealand with whom they have built a good relationship, and continue a dialogue about their learning across the world.

A blog needs an audience to keep it alive for your learners. Too often blogs wither away leaving the learners frustrated and bored. Quadblogging gives your blog a truly authentic and global audience.

(Mitchell, 2012)

Reflecting on the case study

- What do you think are the strengths of using of a class blog for
  a) the children?
  b) the teachers?
  c) The parents?

- How could this approach support learning in your class?

- Compare class blogging with alternative ways of achieving the same goals.

- What are the barriers to setting up a blog, and how can these be overcome?

 TRY THIS

Try this 1: Introducing the ICT toolbox

Activity 1

John Davitt's Learning Event Generator www.newtools.org/showtxt. php?docid=737 Explain 'parts of speech as a radio advertisement', and other active learning permutations.

Try this 2: Digital images in the classroom

Activity 1

www.fromgoodtooutstanding.com/tag/flip-cam

Explore use of a Flip video camera to support teaching and learning.

Try this 3: Image resource sites

Activity 1

www.nationalarchives.gov.uk/education/default.htm

Activity 2

http://gallery.nen.gov.uk/gallery-swgfl.html

A search can return many images of objects, documents and paintings.

Try this 4: Research tools

Activity 1

www.taggalaxy.de/ Uses a 3D galaxy to navigate and select images to view. A visually stunning way of browsing Flickr content.

Activity 2

www.instagrok.com for a research tool based around an interactive concept map that incorporates a glossary, key facts, quizzes. It enables the learner to select content and assemble ideas in a journal.

Try this 5: Investigating digital literacy

Activity 1

Visit the All About Explorers site www.allaboutexplorers.com

Activity 2

Find out about the Pacific Northwest Tree Octopus found at http://zapatopi.net/treeoctopus.html

How might you use websites like these?

Try this 6: Interviewing experts audio tool

Activity 1

Croak.it http://croak.it/ Recommended by Tim Rylands, learners can record a thirty-second message. Your 'croak' is saved and you get a unique url address that you can share.

Try this 7: Video teaching resource using digital video

Activity 1:

For more on using digital video clips see www.literacyshed.com for a wealth of visual resources with ideas for teaching. These are high quality resources that can be used in stand alone or sequences of Literacy lessons. Have your Tell Me questions ready for a fascinating dialogue with your learners.

Activity 2

Inanimate Alice is a website www.inanimatealice.com/ with a series of high quality, award winning, multimodal stories that combine text, image, video, sound, sound effects and games. The story of Alice begins when she is eight and explores what it means to conduct your life online. Like another Alice, this international project has grown and now has an education pack including a tool called Snappy that allows the readers to become writers and compose their own multimedia story using digital assets from the stories. Suitable for upper KS2, Inanimate Alice is a great tool to motivate reading for pleasure. Interestingly all stories written in the first person and Alice the character is never shown.

Try this 8: Exploring Computer Models modelling activities

Activity 1

Explore BBC Science Clips www.bbc.co.uk/bitesize/ks2/science/

Activity 2

Visit Big Day Out www.bigdayout.swgfl.org.uk/flash/index.htm

SUMMARY

Ewan McIntosh says that children should be 'problem finders' and not 'problem solvers', noting that this is a subtle change but with hugely beneficial consequences. Children can only become 'problem finders' when we release the reins and allow them to lead their own learning.

This chapter explores the idea that, with open-ended questioning, and with learners taking the major thinking role, ICT has the capacity to change the way in which learning and teaching happen. With reference to Robin Alexander, we must enable children to actively think for themselves before they can really know something, and teaching and learning using ICT must provide the linguistic opportunities, the conditions for this to happen. With questioning style crucial, we examined how a particular questioning approach when learning with digital video can support reading development, and found that dialogic teaching is possible in an online discussion. We suggested that working online could extend active learning to home, as learners interact through their class blog or online discussion.

We investigated simple audio and video tools and approaches that support active learning across the primary curriculum, and saw the considerable value of challenge and motivation that games-based learning and computer models bring. It is not just about the computer science, the digital literacy or the ICT, essentially it is about the engagement that active learning with ICT can bring.

New technology gives us exciting new opportunities to all learn in an active way. Our two case studies showed two teachers who became aware of new opportunities in the form of Scratch and a class blog. By, to an extent, standing aside and ensuring learners are challenged, motivated and have full ownership of their Scratch game or class blog, they show how active use of ICT can produce high quality learning.

FURTHER READING

Chambers, A. (2011) *The 'Tell Me' Approach: Children, Reading and Talk and the Reading Environment*. Stroud: Thimble Press.
An excellent book to read in order to immerse yourself in the language of questioning.

British Film Institute Primary Education Working Group (2003) *Look Again! A Teaching Guide to Using Film and Television with Three- to Eleven-year-olds*. London: BFI Education.
This provides a wealth of practical ideas for engaging children in analysis of moving image media. It presents powerful arguments for the value of such work in children's learning and outlines the close connections between teaching literacy and cine-literacy, giving details of how to engage primary age children in discussing different aspects of moving image media. A practical guide, it details how to integrate these activities across the curriculum in primary schools.

Explore www.timrylands.com and follow @timrylands on Twitter.
Bober, M. (2010) *Games-based Experiences for Learning: Final Report*. Manchester Metropolitan University. Explore the research and read more about Tim's thoughts.

Follow Ian Addison @ianaddison and David Mitchell @DeputyMitchell to find many reasons to start class blogging, and ask questions.
Go to www.primaryblogger.co.uk to create a class blog in ten minutes. Ian advises setting to Easi-mode.
Consider Quadblogging: http://quadblogging.net/ Link up with other classes around the world.

Try the 'November Learning Information Literacy Quiz' at www.novemberlearning.com/resources/information-literacy-resources/1-information-literacy-quiz/
Consider what you know about information literacy, and what your class need to know.

REFERENCES

Alexander, R. (2004) *Towards Dialogic Teaching: Rethinking Classroom Talk*. York: Dialogos.

Alexander, R. (2005) *Culture, Dialogue and Learning: Notes on an Emerging Pedagogy.* IACEP 10th International Conference, available at: www.robinalexander.org.uk/docs/IACEP_paper_050612.pdf (accessed November 2012).

Allen, J., Potter, J., Sharp, J. and Turvey, K. (2011) *Primary ICT: Knowledge, Understanding and Practice*, 4th edn. Exeter: Learning Matters.

Barber, D. and Cooper, L. (2012) *Using New Web Tools in the Primary Classroom – A Practical Guide for Enhancing Teaching and Learning*. London: Routledge.

Barnes, D. (2009) *Exploratory Talk for Learning*, in N. Mercer and S. Hodgkinson (eds) *Exploring Talk in School*. London: Sage.

Bennett, R. (2004) *Using ICT in Primary English Teaching*. Exeter: Learning Matters.

Bober, M. (2010) *Games-based Experiences for Learning: Final Report*. Manchester: Manchester Metropolitan University.

British Film Institute Primary Education Working Group (2003) *Look Again! A Teaching Guide to Using Film and Television with Three- to Eleven-year-olds*. London: BFI Education.

Byron, T. (2008) Safer Children in a Digital World. The Report of the Byron Review. Available at: www.education.gov.uk/ukccis/about/a0076277/the-byron-reviews (accessed November 2012).

Claxton, G. (2008) *What's the Point of School?* Oxford: Oneworld Publications.

Chambers, A. (2011) *The 'Tell me' Approach: Children, Reading and Talk and The Reading Environment*. Stroud: Thimble Press.

Cremin, T. (2007) Creative teachers and creative teaching, in A. Wilson (ed.) *Creativity in Primary Education*. Exeter: Learning Matters.

Csikszentmihalyi, M. (1990) *Flow: The Psychology of Optimal Experience*. New York: Harper and Row.

Davies, J. and Merchant, G. (2009) *Web 2.0 for Schools: Learning and Social Participation*. New York: Peter Lang.

Edwards, C., Gandini, I. and Forman, G. (eds) (1993) *The Hundred Languages of Children*. London: Ablex Publishing.

Fryer, C. (2012) *Why Blog?*, a seminar by Chris Fryer at West of England Regional ICT Conference 2012.

Groff, J., Howells, C. and Cranmer, S. (2010) *The Impact of Games in the Classroom: Evidence from Schools in Scotland*. Bristol: Futurelab.

Hart, S., Dixon, A., Drummond, M. J. and McIntyre, D. (2004) *Learning without Limits*. Maidenhead: McGraw Hill.

Joyce, B., Calhoun, E. and Hopkins, D. (2009) *Models of Learning Tools for Teaching*, 3rd edn. Maidenhead: Open University Press.

Kress, G. (2003) *Literacy in the New Media Age*. London: Routledge.

Loveless, A. and Ellis, V. (2003) *ICT, Pedagogy and the Curriculum*. London and New York: Routledge Falmer.

McIntosh, E. (2011) A keynote speech at West of England Regional ICT Conference 2011.

Mitchell, D. (2012) http://quadblogging.net/ (accessed November 2012).

Naace (2012) *Response to the Royal Society's Call for Evidence on Computing in Schools*. Available at: www.naace.co.uk/1322 (accessed November 2012).

Ofsted (2012) ICT Subject Development Materials. Available at: http://www.ofsted.gov.uk/resources/subject-professional-development-materials-ict (accessed November 2012).

Papert, S. (1993) *Mindstorms: Children, Computers and Powerful Ideas*, 2nd edn. New York: Basic Books.

The Royal Society (2012) *'Shut Down or Restart': A Report on Computing in Schools by The Royal Society*. Available at: http://royalsociety.org/education/policy/computing-in-schools/ (accessed November 2012).

Scott, A. and Ryan, J. (2009) *Digital Literacy and Using Online Discussions: Reflections from Teaching Large Cohorts in Teacher Education*. Sydney: Merga.

Sigman, A. (2012) 'Time for a view on screen time', Archives on Diseases in Childhood. Available at: http://adc.bmj.com/content/early/2012/09/04/archdischild-2012-302196.short?rss=1 (accessed November 2012).

Waller, T. (2008) ICT and literacy, in J. Marsh and E. Hallett (eds) *Desirable Literacies*. London: Sage.

Whitney, C. (2010) A learning journey, in C. Bazalgette (ed.) Teaching Media in Primary Schools. London: Sage.

CHAPTER 8

THINKING SKILLS THROUGH MATHEMATICS

Anitra Vickery

One can always reason with reason.

Voltaire

Chapter overview

If we accept that a reason for studying mathematics is to prepare people to meet the mathematical demands of everyday life we must also accept that this cannot be achieved without emphasising the development of the transferable skills of reasoning and the ability to solve problems. This chapter discusses evidence that the study of mathematics is feared by many adults and children and sets out to explore how teachers can challenge this by helping children to develop problem-solving skills and strategies and foster a 'feel for number'. The chapter emphasises the importance of making mathematics fun and meaningful by articulating ideas in a supportive social context and linking it to the real world.

INTRODUCTION

This chapter begins with an exploration of issues that provide a context for anyone who is seeking to develop problem solving or thinking skills through the teaching and learning of mathematics. We look at the evidence of widespread negative attitudes that people hold towards mathematics and the prevalence of 'maths anxiety'. Statistically, many teachers will themselves be victims of a dysfunctional mathematics education and will work with children whose parents have been similarly afflicted.

The chapter goes on to introduce the debates about whether problem solving skills can be taught as opposed to acquired through experience and whether skills that are developed in the context of mathematics can be transferred to other subjects and to life outside the classroom. It will also look at shortcomings in the design of mathematical problems commonly presented to children.

The second section of the chapter looks at creating the classroom conditions in which an active engagement in problem solving can thrive. We introduce a short discussion about the need to get a balance between the relative importance of skills, concepts and knowledge in learning objectives for mathematics. We also consider ways to create the conditions for effective collaborative work, the importance of care in developing mathematical language and setting up a physical environment that facilitates active engagement in mathematical thinking.

A case study which explores one school's approach to the development of a mathematically rich language and logical thought is accompanied by prompts to aid discussion and reflection. The chapter concludes with a selection of activities which have been chosen to involve parents and give children opportunities to develop an investigative approach. Suggestions for further reading will enable you to find further examples for classroom investigations and explore the issues raised in greater depth.

ATTITUDES TOWARDS MATHEMATICS AND MATHS ANXIETY

As teachers we all need an awareness of how our experiences as learners affect our approaches to teaching. It can be argued that the need for this awareness is at its most acute when we teach mathematics. Research suggests that negative attitudes to mathematics are widespread in the UK. The Cockroft Commission of Inquiry into the teaching of mathematics (1982) commissioned a small study (Sewell, 1981) of the use of mathematics by adults in daily life. The study reported how the need to undertake simple mathematical tasks induced feelings of anxiety, helplessness, fear and even guilt in some of the subjects of the study. A further indication of the extent of the problem came from the fact that over half of those who had initially agreed to take part in the survey declined further participation when they discovered that it focused on the use of mathematics. The findings suggested that 'maths anxiety' impacted on all social groups and educational classes. A recent newspaper article (Brian, 2012) provided an estimate that as many as 2 million children in England are affected by maths anxiety and as much as 25 per cent of the population as a whole. If we accept the claims made in this article there has been little improvement in attitudes towards mathematics in the last 30 years. Ashcraft (2002) defines math (sic) anxiety as 'a feeling of tension, apprehension, or fear that interferes with math performance' (Ashcraft, 2002: 181). Boaler (2009) predicts that although there will be twenty million more jobs in the future for people with an aptitude for mathematical problem solving only a small proportion of the population, around twenty per cent, will possess the necessary skills.

Swain et al. (2005) believe that the role of the teacher, the attitude and enthusiasm is as crucial as the content of lessons. Burnett and Wichman (1997) recognise that primary teachers' own anxieties could be passed on to the children. If we are to enable children to become confident mathematicians it is essential to address any feelings of inadequacy that we hold as teachers.

Teachers' anxieties may result from poor subject knowledge which has a knock-on effect on their ability to plan and teach maths effectively (Goulding et al., 2002). It is very difficult, if not impossible, for teachers who are insecure about their knowledge to develop understanding or a sense of curiosity in children. Feelings of insecurity will also make it impossible to express enthusiasm for the subject and demonstrate mathematical curiosity. Enthusiasm generates enthusiasm (Day, 2004).

As teachers we often need to take on the role of learner. By embracing the need to prepare mathematics lessons by first researching the mathematical concepts, progression and potential misconceptions related to different themes, teachers can establish a confidence that equips them to provide a positive and enabling experience of the subject. There are a number of helpful books to aid this process cited in further reading at the end of the chapter.

Parental influence

The role of the parent is also of vital importance. Merttens (1999) believes that parents' attitudes shape a child's educational success. This suggests that parents who are anxious about mathematics transmit these fears to their children and are also more likely to accept failure in mathematics in their children. Gordon (1992) reported that it appeared to be socially acceptable for people to say that they weren't any good at or hated maths and that it didn't have the same stigma attached to it as people confessing to an inability to read or write. The benefits of working with parents cannot be over-emphasised. Schools and teachers who encourage their children to share their mathematics learning with their parents through well designed homework investigations, that need discussion and a collaborative approach, or where the child explains approaches in calculation, can achieve positive changes in attitudes. Schools can also actively change perceptions of teaching and learning in mathematics by inviting the parents into school to explain teaching methods and take part in mathematics investigations alongside their children (see case study on p. 139).

ACTIVE LEARNING THROUGH MATHEMATICAL PROBLEM SOLVING

The term mathematical problem solving in this chapter means any problem for which children need to select and apply mathematical skills and concepts to find a solution. Problems can include calculation, word problems and investigations or puzzles. The value of problem solving, however, is not defined by the nature of the challenge but by the extent to which children make autonomous decisions about the mathematics and the approaches they will employ.

Problem solving – the 'caught or taught' debate

Bandura and Damasio (cited in Wegerif, 2003) believe that patterns of behaviour are caught not taught and therefore it is essential that the teacher models appropriate approaches and attitudes. Many teachers believe that problem solving is a very difficult skill to teach, and indeed some categorically state that it can't be taught but that if children are given enough opportunities to be involved in problem-solving situations the appropriate mode of thinking might be acquired. This is in line with the constructivist perspective of learning in assuming that mathematics cannot be meaningfully taught as each learner constructs their own knowledge through interacting with the environment. In contrast, however, Wallace et al. (2004) suggest that children can be taught the processes of solving problems and supply a framework entitled Thinking Actively in a Social Context (TASC) outlining a staged process of thinking for the child engaged in problem solving. They cite the work of Robert Sternberg (e.g. 1985) and his definition of the nature of intelligence. Sternberg suggests that intelligence should be measured by one's ability to employ thinking and problem-solving skills in all aspects of life. He believes that it is possible to teach children to develop their approach to planning and carrying out tasks as well as recording and reflecting on their involvement. In this way children's intellectual function can be improved although differences in attainment will still exist because of the pre-school environment and genetics of the individuals.

Mason et al. (2010) also suggest a process for developing thinking skills loosely divided into three phases entitled Entry, Attack and Review. They focus on the types of questions that the individual should apply at each stage of the enquiry. It is suggested that mathematical thinking can be improved through the development of the pupils' engagement and attitude by questioning themselves about their level of conscientiousness, by reflecting on the situation, by linking emotions with actions and by studying the process of resolution.

Taking into account the competing views within this research it would seem sensible to embrace all theories by ensuring that problem-solving skills are modelled and are pursued through collaboration. The key is the articulation of thinking and this can be achieved through class, group or paired discussion.

The design of problems

Groves et al. (2000) believe that there are three areas that are critical in supporting the development of mathematical reasoning in children: the role of the teacher, the design of the problem and a classroom culture; all of which encourage and support children in explaining their thinking.

Selter and Spiegel (1997) report concerns about the irrational answers that children give when faced with questions that are impossible to solve. The following question is often used as an example: *A boat is leaving the harbour carrying 10 goats and 26 sheep. How old is the captain?'*, to which a disturbing number of children provide the answer 36. Problems that are designed to trigger calculation, as opposed to problems that are encountered in real life, rarely contain redundant information or indeed insufficient information to extract a solution. When faced with such questions children simply perform any operation on the numbers presented to them to obtain a solution (Vickery and Spooner, 2011). It is important to present the children with scenarios where some of the information is redundant, where they have to identify the question and where they have to recognise that sometimes there wouldn't be enough information to solve the problems. This situation would create a catalyst for meaningful discussion. All children, but particularly those who have concerns about mechanical mathematics, should be presented with some problems that require reasoning rather than calculation. They would then perceive problem solving in a new light. Orton and Frobisher (1996) reason that if a problem is perceived as an exploration of a situation it is of far more value than one that just involves the application of a method to a recognisable problem set in words. Wallace et al. (2004) believe that this form of hands-on enquiry will not only stimulate the brain because of active participation and engagement but will also increase motivation, confidence and self-esteem.

It is advantageous to teach the skills that will facilitate successful problem solving. If the children are encouraged to organise their information, for example, it will be easier for them to identify patterns and explain their thinking. If they learn to approach problems systematically it will enable them to persevere with confidence, knowing that they are not 'going round in circles'. You will need to decide whether to teach these skills explicitly or to intervene at appropriate times to direct children in their approach. If intervention occurs it should be handled sensitively and in a way that doesn't suggest that the children should do it your way. Problem solving should not just be presented in a way that prompts a mechanistic approach through looking for clues in the vocabulary used to present the problems, and then employing taught procedures. This approach, which is often associated with traditional word problems, has a place in encouraging the child to really understand the problem; however, if used exclusively, it becomes yet another taught procedure. In essence the approach, if overused, militates against the development of logic and intuition. 'Children answer word questions on the basis of superficial clues going from text to solution without passing through a thinking brain' (Verschaffel et al., 2000: 181). There is no doubt, however, that teaching children to approach a problem systematically and to collect and organise findings in a clear way will enable starting points in the process of problem solving. It could be argued then that teaching some strategies will help children to make logical deductions earlier.

It is important that mathematical problem solving is linked closely to real life. Some school events provide problems that need real solutions, e.g. the Christmas and summer fairs, sports day, classroom and playground design, concert seating and refreshments, etc. The fact that solutions to this type of problem will be implemented introduces a genuine need for accuracy and results in high motivation. At other times situations can be contrived in a way that excites and engages all learners (see case study on p. 139). Word problems that are written about children or situations that the children are familiar with also facilitate engagement. Verschaffel et al. (2000) suggest that if children are encouraged to visualise situations described in problems then these become more meaningful and they have a better chance of solving them.

The transferability of skills

Different authorities have different opinions about whether or not the skills acquired through problem solving are transferable to other subjects or situations. Muijs and Reynolds (2010) firmly believe that active learning enables the transfer of knowledge and skills. Wegerif (2003) also suggests that there is evidence to support the fact that if these thinking skills activities are developed in a culture of collaboration and cooperation then they are more effective, particularly if the group discusses, shares their reasoning and presents their ideas to others. If children frequently address problem solving in groups then the skills they learn through collaboration such as listening respectfully, speaking in turn and sharing ideas are social skills that will transfer to other situations easily. The process of analysing problems, suggesting and persevering with different approaches and reflecting on outcomes should equip the children with strategies that they can apply to all problems and then transfer to their own lives. Additionally, as the children present their thinking to others within the group or class they will develop their own metacognition. This would then enable children to be better at self-assessment, thus taking an active role in their development. Wallace et al. (2004) state that the development of thinking skills is a key factor in the development of children's self-esteem and confidence.

FACILITATING ACTIVE LEARNING IN THE MATHEMATICS CLASSROOM

To create a classroom environment that promotes and facilitates active learning through problem solving we need to consider:

- the role of collaboration and discourse;
- developing the language of mathematics;
- the development of mathematical concepts, skills and knowledge;
- the physical environment of the classroom.

Effective collaborative work

Problem solving should be pursued as a paired or group activity where the teacher is viewed as an active participant in the process. Collaborative work leads naturally to discussions, teaching and learning from others, practising by doing and demonstrating (Wallace et al., 2004). The skills developed through collaborative work combine four of the most effective ways of learning presented on the 'Learning Pyramid', reproduced in Koshy et al. (2000). The learning pyramid, developed by the National Training Laboratories (NTL) in the USA, is an image that maps a range of teaching methods and learning activities on to a triangle in proportion to their effectiveness in promoting student retention of the material taught. The factors that need to be taken into consideration in setting up a successful collaborative culture are discussed in more detail in Chapter 3.

The art of discussion and collaboration needs to be taught if it is to be effective in promoting creativity, as well as generating meaningful interaction and understanding for the learner (Scardamalia et al., 1994). Galton and Williamson (1992) report that initially children tend to collaborate more if they are working on problems that have a clear solution rather than those that are more open-ended. There is a tendency not to challenge their peers until they are more familiar and secure with the group work.

It needs to be recognised that the success of any collaborative work is determined

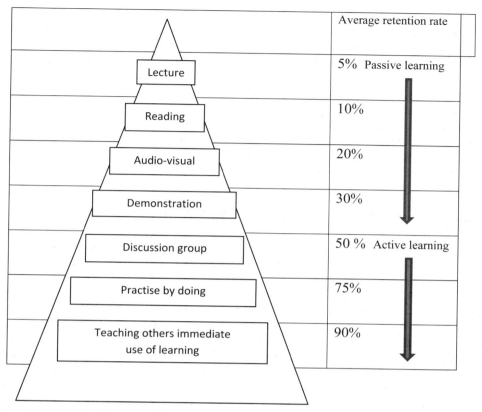

Figure 8.1 The learning pyramid

Source: NTL Institute for Applied Behavioral Science, 300 N. Lee Street, Suite 300, Alexandria, VA 22314. 1-800-777-5227

by the dynamic of the group and that every group needs to be monitored for effectiveness frequently. It is crucial to consider the composition of the pair or group carefully if collaborative work is to succeed. It should not simply mean that the groups are formed at the beginning of the year and exist for set periods of time. The organisation requires careful planning and the use of on-going assessment for learning. Group composition should be changed to suit personalities and tasks and there is no prescribed recommended size or composition or indeed period for which a group should exist.

Mathematical language

Mathematical language consists of words, symbols and graphical representations which are often interchangeable. When we study mathematics we learn new concepts by building on what we already know. The starting point for looking at mathematical language is to recognise that children learn their language by hearing and using the language in context to explain ideas and concepts. Language should be more than just learning the pronunciation and spelling of the words (Partnership for Reading 2006). When we talk about using mathematical language the focus needs to be on the mathematics, and not just the rote learning of words. It is important to define words clearly and point out incorrect uses as well as being aware of the differences in meaning between words used in everyday language and words used in mathematics, for example 'difference' and 'take away'. A further area of tension is created by the number of different terms that can be used to express a concept. For example, in calculation a child will encounter a variety of terms related to the concept of subtraction such as take away, difference, less than and more than.

Sometimes it is useful to make connections with classical roots such as tri in triangle; examining the construction of a word enhances understanding.

The development of mathematical concepts, skills and knowledge

Mathematics, in our culture, is perceived by many as a subject where answers are either right of wrong whereas, in Japan, the aim of mathematics lessons is to encourage new thinking and to see relationships between numbers and operations (Swan, 2006). Practising procedures is considered a necessary part of Japanese mathematics lessons but a greater percentage of time is spent on developing thinking and discussion. Nunes and Bryant (1996) believe that children's mathematical learning involves learning conventional mathematical systems, developing knowledge about logic and the wider use of mathematical relationships. If we place too much emphasis on correct mechanical mathematics then those children who find calculation difficult develop a lack of confidence about their ability to 'do' maths. Although many children learn to count and to perform operations with numbers, evidence exists that children learn procedures without any understanding of connections or relations and this is not sufficient to understand mathematics (Nunes et al., 2009). One of the key findings of the study carried out by Nunes et al. (2009) was that the ability to reason rather than success with arithmetic was a better indicator of children's later achievement in mathematics. If children become familiar and comfortable with numbers then this can facilitate and encourage not only computation but investigation. Children should be provided with opportunities to 'play' with numbers, generating a 'feel for number'. There is no doubt that it is necessary for children to be able to do mental calculation, to understand bonds and multiples, but accompanying this should be that deep understanding of number (see Try this) Memory serves a useful purpose in committing multiplication tables and mathematical fact to memory but it doesn't replace the thinking and reasoning processes that precede it. Working with number facts shouldn't just be a memory task but an investigation. Children should be encouraged to look for patterns and discuss and compare their findings. In this way learning to calculate can become very much a part of learning to think and reason. Developing thinking shouldn't be just an 'add on' but should permeate a child's education because we learn best when we understand why (Wallace, 2001).

The physical environment of the classroom

Specific areas of the classroom can be dedicated to mathematics by creating interactive displays for problem solving where the teacher or children present a problem and invite everyone else to solve or extend it so that the board becomes an area of on-going discussion and collaboration. Mathematical investigations can be provided through software and online sources which could be accessed in an area which promotes collaboration and enables the children to develop and present their thinking. Opening up the classroom to allow children to investigate mathematics at a level that challenges them might put a strain on the security of the teacher. This is where the essential feature of a participatory problem solving environment becomes particularly important. In such an environment the teacher is a participant and not the ultimate expert and every opportunity should be taken to allow children to demonstrate processes followed or solutions to an investigation. In this way the children who are operating as presenters develop and secure their own thinking and the audience gain insight into a higher level of mathematics.

CASE STUDY

This case study considers the practice of mathematical problem solving pursued in a small one form entry, rural school. The school is situated in an apparently affluent area but the children are drawn from a mixed social background. The school has been recognised by OfSTED for its caring approach which focuses heavily on the well-being of the children. The coordinator is passionate about the teaching of mathematics and supports and leads the rest of the staff. She promotes a problem-solving approach for all mathematics but insists that the foundation of bonds and table knowledge is secure and this often results in an emphasis on committing number facts to memory. Problem solving is embedded throughout the lessons. Problems can range from an exploration of multiplication and division facts by using supplementary questions (e.g. what is the answer to 6 ×7? If you know that what else can you tell me? Explain how you know the answer couldn't be 43?), to more complex investigations that would benefit from discussion and collaboration as well as extended time.

The parents are very supportive and the homework policy, of sending home activities that promote discussion as opposed to tasks that focus on mechanical calculation with increasing complexity, has been explained and respected.

The school has bought in support from the education authority which has resulted in a number of INSET days devoted to the development of problem solving. Staff meetings have focused on the use of questioning to open up the Assessing Pupil Progress (APP) statements and the strategic use of precise mathematical vocabulary. The school also believes that children, particularly those in Foundation Stage and Key Stage 1, should be immersed in the use of concrete resources to support the development of a good understanding of number and the associated concepts. Since this policy has been adopted they have noticed a smoother and swifter transition from concrete to abstract mathematics in Key Stage 2.

The coordinator often models approaches to her colleagues and suggests resources including online materials to facilitate problem solving. Children are provided with 'jotters' where they can record trial and improvement techniques which might be facilitated by a diagrammatic or pictorial approach. This approach to an investigation encourages the children to take risks and understand that they cannot always be right and that there is much to be learned from 'failing' to find a solution. The staff use a mixture of discrete teaching and collaborative discussion in problem solving and tend to introduce the strategies of planning, organisation and prediction through easily accessible problems.

The coordinator's philosophy about the use of problem solving can be summarised by the following statements:

- It helps children to understand real life and gives mathematics a purpose and just as importantly it can be great fun.

- It encourages children to:
  - persevere;
  - take risks;
  - embrace challenge.

- It develops the skills of:
  - communication – explaining and justifying, listening;
  - reasoning;
  - discussion;
  - logical and systematic thought;
  - decision making;
  - identification and analysis of patterns;
  - independence;
  - negotiation;
  - cooperation.

She recognises that a problem-solving approach to mathematics presents the staff with challenges; the main one being the need to balance the time it takes to cover the required content of the curriculum with the time needed to allow children to develop skills through a trial and improvement approach to investigations. The staff as a whole need to be convinced that this is time well spent and that it impacts more positively on SATs than constant coaching. They also need to believe in the merit of using a mixture of mathematical problems not just word problems and that the process is more important than the answer. The staff work well as a team and have collaborated effectively to enable this approach. They recently invited eight trainee teachers into their classroom to spend one day a week for four weeks to engage in problem solving with all the classes.

The children are enthusiastic and talk excitedly about their work. Recently a Year 3 class went on an overnight stay and during the day they engaged in mathematical problem solving. Their teacher presented them with a problem that had been posed by a fictitious IT company. The children were told that the company planned to strengthen the keyboards they manufactured but because of cost implications intended to strengthen only the most commonly used keys. The task for the children was to identify which keys should be strengthened. The children discussed it as a class first before splitting off into smaller groups which were chosen by the teacher. During this time the children independently made suggestions such as:

- 'They must be the vowels because I've never seen a word without a vowel.'

- 'Let's test it then, let's look at some writing from a book.'

- 'Shall we look at different genres? We'll do a recipe.'

The children then worked together in small groups to discuss approaches. They used tally charts to count the number of times different letters appeared. Some children presented a rationale for including different punctuation keys and the space bar. A discussion about capital and lower case letters resulted in some children creating Carroll diagrams. These results were then transferred to block graphs and spike charts and analysed for patterns. The children stated that during this time their teacher had no involvement other than to show some children how to use some software to draw graphs. They were clearly enthused and motivated. They spent one and a half days pursuing this without any dissent.

This enterprise gave children the impetus to work collaboratively and to persevere to present a credible solution. It appeared to challenge and engage all children and as a result they developed increased confidence.

The children are now coming to the end of their year in this class and the teacher remembers the initial difficulties of dealing with children's emotions when they 'failed' to reach solutions for investigations. She believes it is important to develop the qualities of resilience and perseverance for life and problem solving is a good medium in which to do that. The children have become more confident about tackling problems but have definitely been helped by her rationale for using the question 'why'. The school make a point of paying careful attention to the position of the word 'why' in a question. 'Why did you do that?' might not get a confident answer whereas placing why further along in the sentence, 'Explain to me why you did that,' the first word the child hears, 'explain', suggests quite a different exchange.

The school is pleased with the move to increasing the profile of problem solving and believe that this approach provides opportunities for all children to extend their understanding of and proficiency in mathematics.

Reflecting on the case study

- Which aspects of this approach do you think are most likely to be effective?

- How does this approach compare to your own experience as:
  (a) a child?
  (b) as a teacher?

- How important is parental approval?

- How realistic is it to include or duplicate real life situations in problem solving?

- Does embedding problem solving in the curriculum adequately prepare children for mandatory tests?

TRY THIS

The suggested activities are split into five sections which focus on the following:

1. Involving parents and using events from the school calendar to engage children in 'real' problem solving.
2. A selection of activities that will help children to develop a feel for number.
3. Encouraging children to extend their investigations.
4. Mathematics and art.
5. Developing logic.

The benefits of working with parents cannot be over emphasised.

Try this 1: Involving parents and using events from the school calendar to engage children in 'real' problem solving

Activity 1

Create a lending library of board games, playing cards, dominoes and dice with instructions for games that allow children to practise calculation skills and logic. There are plenty of suggestions online as well as in books (see further reading).

Do computation skills increase?

How do parents react?

What strategies could be employed to support children for whom support is not available at home?

Activity 2

Design homework investigations that need discussion and a collaborative approach.

For example:

- What mathematics can we find in a kitchen cupboard?
- Record the numbers you see around you and compare them in whichever way you want to.
- What information would I need to find out to completely redecorate my bedroom?
- Which room has the most free floor space and how could I measure it?

What support would parents need to be able to engage in this type of task?

Activity 3

Ask the children to 'teach' their parents some of the mathematics the children have covered during the week. It is particularly important to inform the parents of the different procedures used in calculation.

Would parents be more or less receptive if they were invited into school with their children for this?

Activity 4

Allow children to take responsibility for aspects of the organisation of school fairs and social events and encourage them to take a leading part in organising out-of-school visits and the use of the outdoor environment by creating maths trails.

Is this too time consuming and difficult to negotiate?

Do the benefits include an increased motivation for problem solving?

Try this 2: Developing a 'feel for number'

Activity 1

An exploration of numbers, e.g. what is 8?

This shouldn't elicit just the usual response of:

- $8 + 0 = 8$
- $7 + 1 = 8$ etc.

Instead, it should encourage a broader and deeper analysis, e.g. looking at even numbers, multiples, and situations that require different forms of partitioning:

- I could partition 8 into 6 and 2 to help with the calculation $58 + 8$;
- or I could partition 8 into 7 and 1 to help with the calculation $8 + 7$ (double 7);
- or I could partition 8 into 4 and 4 to help with the calculation $56 + 8$, etc.;
- if I know that $56 + 8$ is 64 what do I know about $560 + 80$ or $5600 + 800$, etc.;
- how does this help me with subtraction?

Activity 2

How do I know that the following calculation is wrong without working it out?

- $53? \times 68 = 36525$

Consider any multiple of 8; it is always an even number.

Activity 3

If a child finds it difficult to 'learn their tables' supply them with strategies to reason the answer e.g. an ability to count in 2s is the starting point for securing any group of even multiple. A visual aid to make it more accessible could be:

Counting Stick showing multiples of 2

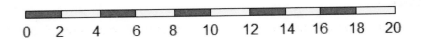

What process enables us to calculate the multiples of 4?

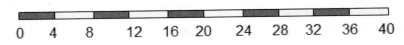

And the multiples of 8?

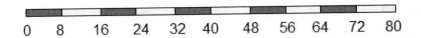

Leave some out

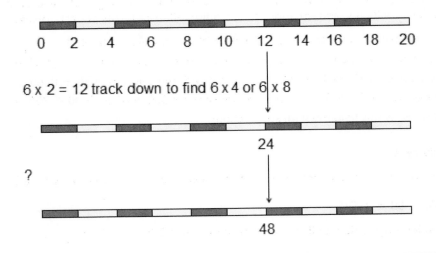

6 x 2 = 12 track down to find 6 x 4 or 6 x 8

24

?

48

Children could design their own resource which would just be a series of horizontal lines.

Multiples of 3, 6 and 9 could be calculated in the same way. Multiples of 7 would involve an understanding of the commutative aspect for example 3 lots of 7 are the same as 7 lots of 3. Ultimately they need to know the tables, and there are many ways rote learning can be fun especially if set to music or raps.

Try this 3: Encouraging children to extend their investigations

Activity 1

Cross totals:

Note that these investigations can start with very simple numbers so that children are focusing on the process of engaging with a problem, organising their approach, reviewing it and extending it.

Can you put the numbers 1, 2, 3 and 4 in a cross so that the totals of both arms of the cross are equal?

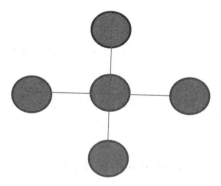

You may want to use counters with the numbers written on them so that they can be moved around easily.

Extending the problem

Below are a number of questions that will enable children to extend the problem. As children grow in confidence they should be encouraged to devise these questions for themselves by following a 'what if approach' and recognising it doesn't matter if it doesn't always lead to a solution it is the process undertaken that is the important element of the exercise.

Try these:

• Is there more than one way of arranging the numbers?

- Can you use other consecutive numbers, e.g. 3, 4, 5, 6?
- Do your solutions all have a pattern? Can you describe it?
- What about other sequences of numbers e.g. 2, 4, 6, 8, 10?
- The multiplication tables?

Can you think of any other ways to investigate numbers with this pattern?

What happens if you don't have a circle in the centre?

Can you extend the number of circles?

Do you need to have the same number of circles opposite each other?

What happens if you don't – is there a pattern?

What happens then?

Activity 2

A 100 square is a wonderful resource with which to explore number and extend investigations.

A.

Highlight the multiplication tables and look for shape and number patterns.

B.

Highlight different-sized squares contained within the hundred square, e.g. 2 × 2, 3 × 3, etc. and investigate patterns. Look at totals of diagonals, columns etc.

Using a 100 square

1	2	3	4	5	6	7	8	9	10
11	12	13	14	15	16	17	18	19	20
21	22	23	24	25	26	27	28	29	30
31	32	33	34	35	36	37	38	39	40
41	42	43	44	45	46	47	48	49	50
51	52	53	54	55	56	57	58	59	60
61	62	63	64	65	66	67	68	69	70
71	72	73	74	75	76	77	78	79	80
81	82	83	84	85	86	87	88	89	90
91	92	93	94	95	96	97	98	99	100

C.

The following investigation is suitable for Upper Key Stage 2 or more able mathematicians.

To develop an algebraic approach to calculation create T shapes and calculate the total of the numbers in the square. Look for a quick method. Hint: look at the number below the top bar. If n = 12, then the other numbers in the T are n − 11, n − 10, n − 9, n + 10, n + 20.

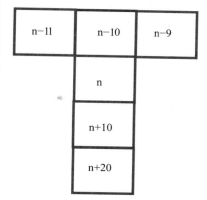

If you combine them all then the numbers cancel out and you are left with 6n so the total of the numbers in the T shape is 6n which in this case equals 72.

Can you find other ways of approaching this?

Using a 100 square

			4	5	6	7	8	9	10
11		13				17	18	19	20
21		23	24		26	27	28	29	30
31		33	34		36	37	38	39	40
41	42	43	44		46	47	48	49	50
51	52	53	54	55	56	57	58	59	60
61	62	63	64	65	66	67	68	69	70
71	72	73	74	75	76	77	78	79	80
81	82	83	84	85	86	87	88	89	90
91	92	93	94	95	96	97	98	99	100

What happens if both the horizontal bar and the vertical bar are 5 squares long?

Try this 4: Mathematics and art

Activity 1

Create the digital roots of numbers in the multiplication tables. To do this add the digits in the answer and continue to add until you reach a single digit.

e.g.

$9 \times 7 = 63$ $6 + 3 = 9$ so the digital root is 9

$8 \times 7 = 56$ $5 + 6 = 11$ $1 + 1 = 2$ so the digital root is 2

Write the digital roots in a 9 × 9 multiplication square as below. What patterns can you see?

Vedic square patterns from digital roots

1	2	3	4	5	6	7	8	9
2	4	6	8	1	3	5	7	9
3	6	9	3	6	9	3	6	9
4	8	3	7	2	6	1	5	9
5	1	6	2	7	3	8	4	9
6	3	9	6	3	9	6	3	9
7	5	3	1	8	6	4	2	9
8	7	6	4	4	3	2	1	9
9	9	9	9	9	9	9	9	9

Create a pattern by selecting a number (1 in this case) and joining that 1 to every other 1 by drawing a line from the centre of that square to the centre of each square that contains a 1. Then repeat with a second 1 as the starting point until each 1 in the square has been a starting point. See below.

Vedic square patterns from digital roots

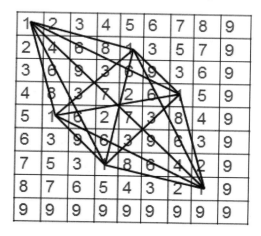

1	2	3	4	5	6	7	8	9
2	4	6	8	1	3	5	7	9
3	6	9	3	6	9	3	6	9
4	8	3	7	2	6	1	5	9
5	1	6	2	7	3	8	4	9
6	3	9	6	3	9	6	3	9
7	5	3	1	8	6	4	2	9
8	7	6	5	4	3	2	1	9
9	9	9	9	9	9	9	9	9

Activity 2
Working with squares

A.

How many ways can you split a square into 2 equal parts?

B.

Create a 12 × 12 square on squared paper. How many ways can you split it into 12 equal parts? Hint: Don't always use vertical, horizontal or diagonal lines.

Try this 5: Developing logic

Activity 1

Simple colour Sudoku using coloured counters.

The aim is to place one of each colour in the rows and columns.

The choice of using counters will allow easy access for all.

The size of the square can be extended to provide greater challenge for those who need it. You will need to use patterns and colours for larger squares.

Colour Sudoku

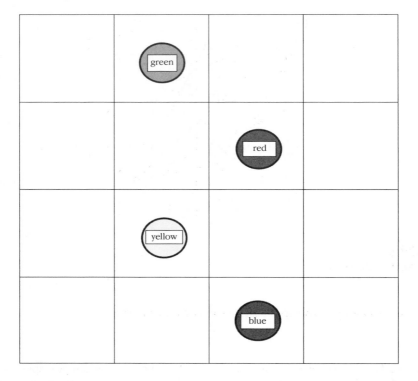

Activity 2

Take any 3 numbers and justify which could be the odd one out.

e.g. 25, 27, 29:

- 27 is the only multiple of 3
- 25 is the only square number
- 29 is the only prime number
- 25 is the date of Christmas
- . . .

Do the same with shapes.

Activity 3

Display a question such as, 'The answer is 27. What is the question?' daily and encourage the children to create their own.

Activity 4

Use sets of group problem-solving cards which contain the clues needed to solve a problem as well as some 'red herrings'. Some of these approach problem solving without mathematics as such but provide scenarios in the form of mysteries or puzzles that need to be solved.

These can be used with groups of 4 either in the classroom or at home (see further reading: Vickery and Spooner, 2004, 2011, *We Can Work It Out*).

Does raising the profile of problem solving impact positively on all children?

Are some children still reluctant to engage with the process?

SUMMARY

There is widespread acknowledgement of the negative attitude to mathematics that still exists for both adults and children. This chapter discusses the effect of 'maths anxiety' and explores what strategies can be put into place to ameliorate this. It champions the use of a problem-solving approach to all mathematics learning and suggests ways in which this can be made meaningful and accessible to all children. It recognises the role of the teacher in modelling enquiry and organisation and advocates the use of collaboration so that problem solving is a social activity where the teacher is an active participant in the learning. Consideration is given to the central importance of designing problems so that they require more than an application of mechanical calculation. You are introduced to ideas that enable the involvement of parents and suggestions for developing and extending a problem-solving approach.

FURTHER READING

Burton, L. (1995) *Thinking Things Through: Problem Solving in Mathematics.* Oxford: Nash Pollock Publishing.
    A practical guide, with advice for teachers to promote problem solving and investigations in their classrooms.

Haylock, D. (2010) *Mathematics Explained for Primary Teachers*, 4th edn. London: Sage.
    This book equips teachers with the confidence to understand and relay mathematical concepts. There is also a workbook that provides students with the opportunity to review and reinforce their understanding of the mathematics covered in each chapter.

Hughes, A. M. (2009) *Problem Solving, Reasoning and Numeracy in the Early Years Foundation Stage.* London: Routledge.
    A selection of good ideas for activities across the whole of the EYFS. It is reader-friendly with sound pedagogy.

Rowland, T., Turner, F., Thwaites, A. and Huckstep, P. (2009) *Developing Primary Mathematics Teaching*. London: Sage.
A book to help teachers to become more confident with the teaching of mathematics. It includes descriptions and transcripts of actual lessons (also available on the book's website) which enable teachers to reflect on teaching and learning.

Sellars, E. and Lowndes, S. (2003) *Using and Applying Mathematics at Key Stage 2: A Guide to Teaching Problem Solving and Thinking Skills*. London: David Fulton.
A series of problems that have been chosen to help children develop different strategies to solving problems. Each one is clearly explained with ideas of how to introduce it. Solutions and resources are included.

Straker, A. (1993) *Talking Points in Mathematics*. Cambridge: Cambridge University Press.
Suggestions for encouraging children to think and talk about mathematics. The ideas consist of both practical and imaginative scenarios and the focus throughout is on developing discussion. It also contains helpful ideas for teaching mathematics to children whose first language is not English.

Vickery, A. and Spooner, M. (2004, 2011) *We Can Work it Out* and *We Can Work it Out 2*. Derby: Association of Teachers of Mathematics.
Photocopiable books which contain sets of group problem-solving cards. Each set of cards contains the clues needed to solve a problem as well as some 'red herrings'. It is intended they should be shared out between a small group of children who have to share their clues verbally and solve the problem together. This method of working allows a match with 'speaking and listening' and thus fulfils some of the requirements of literacy across the curriculum.

Williams, K. R. (2006) *Vedic Mathematics [Elementary Level] Teacher's Manual*. Motilal: Barnasidass.
Written for teachers this book introduces Vedic Mathematics and was reconstructed from ancient Vedic texts early last century by Sri Bharati Krsna Tirthaji (1884–1960). It is a system of mental mathematics by which complex problems can be solved quickly. Try these ideas for fun and gain insight into the interrelated nature of mathematics.

REFERENCES

Ashcraft, M. H. (2002) Math anxiety: Personal, educational, and cognitive consequences. *Directions in Psychological Science*, 11: 181–5.
Boaler, J. (2009) *The Elephant in the Classroom. Helping Children Learn and Love Maths*. London: Souvenir Press Ltd.
Brian, K. (2012) Maths anxiety: the numbers are mounting. *Guardian Education*, 30 April 2012. Available at: www.guardian.co.uk/education/2012/apr/30/maths-anxiety-school-support?INTCMP=SRCH (accessed 30 April 2012).
Burnett, S. J. and Wichman, A. M. (1997) *Mathematics and Literature: An Approach to Success*. Dissertation submitted to the School of Education, Saint Xavier University, Chicago.
Cockcroft, W. (1982) *Mathematics Counts: Report of the Committee of Inquiry into the Teaching of Mathematics in Schools*. London: HMSO.
Day, C. (2004) *A Passion for Teaching*. London: Routledge.
Galton, M. and Williamson, J. (1992) *Group Work in the Primary Classroom*. London: Routledge.
Gordon, N. (1992) Children with developmental dyscalculia. *Developmental Medicine and Child Neurology*, 34(5): 459–63.
Goulding, M., Rowland, T. and Barber, T. (2002) Does it matter?: Primary teacher trainees' subject knowledge in mathematics. *British Educational Research Journal*, 28: 689–704.

Groves, S., Doig, B. and Splitter, L. (2000) Mathematics classrooms functioning as communities of inquiry: Possibilities and constraints for changing practice, in T. Nakahara and M. Koyama (eds) *Proceedings of the Twenty-fourth Conference of the International Group for the Psychology of Mathematics Education*, III, 1–8. Hiroshima, Japan: Hiroshima University.

Koshy, V., Ernest, P. and Casey, R. (eds) (2000) *Mathematics for Primary Teachers*. London: Routledge.

Mason, J., Burton, L. and Stacey, K. (2010) *Thinking Mathematically*. Harlow: Pearson Education Limited.

Merttens, R. (1999) Family numeracy, in Thompson, I. (ed.) *Issues in Teaching Numeracy in Primary Schools*. Buckingham/Philadelphia: Open University Press.

Muijs, D. and Reynolds, D. (2010) *Effective Teaching: Evidence and Practice*, 3rd edn. London: Sage.

Nunes, T. and Bryant, P. (1996) *Children Doing Mathematics*. Oxford: Blackwell Publishers.

Nunes, T., Bryant, P., Sylva, K. and Barros, R. (2009) *Development of Maths Capabilities and Confidence in Primary School*. London: DCSF. Available at: www.education.gov.uk/publications//eOrderingDownload/DCSF-RB118.pdf (accessed 28 May 2012).

Orton, A. and Frobisher, L. (1996) *Insights into Teaching Mathematics*. London: Cassell.

Partnership for Reading (2006) *Put Reading First*. The National Institute for Literacy: US. Departments of Education, Labor, and Health and Human Services.

Scardamalia, M., Bereiter, C. and Lamon, M. (1994) The CSILE project: Trying to bring the classroom into World 3, in K. McGilley (eds) *Classroom Lessons: Integrating Cognitive Theory and Classroom Practice*. Cambridge, MA: MIT Press.

Selter, C. and Spiegel, H. (1997) *Wie Kinder rechnen* [How children calculate]. Leipzig etc.: Ernst Klett: Grundschulverlag.

Sewell, B (1981) *Use of Mathematics by Adults in Daily Life*. London: Advisory Council for Adult and Continuing Education (ACACE).

Sternberg, R. J. (1985) *Beyond IQ: A Triarchic Theory of Human Intelligence*. Cambridge: Cambridge University Press.

Swain, J., Baker, E., Holder, D., Newmarch, B. and Coben, D. (2005) '*Beyond the Daily Application': Making Numeracy Teaching Meaningful to Adult Learners*. London: National Research and Development Centre for Adult Literacy and Numeracy.

Swan, M. (2006) *Collaborative Learning in Mathematics: A Challenge to our Beliefs and Practices*. London: NRDC.

Verschaffel, L., Greer, B. and de Corte, E. (2000) *Making Sense of Word Problems*. Lisse: Swets and Zeitlinger.

Vickery, A. and Spooner, M. (2011) *We Can Work it Out 2*. Derby: Association of Teachers of Mathematics.

Wallace, B. (2001) *Teaching Thinking Skills across the Primary School*. London: David Fulton Publishers.

Wallace, B., Maker, J., Cave, D. and Chandler, S. (2004) *Thinking Skills and Problem-Solving: An Inclusive Approach*. London: David Fulton.

Wegerif, R. (2003) *Literature Review in Thinking Skills, Technology and Learning*. Bristol: Nesta Futurelab/Open University.

CHAPTER 9

DEVELOPING THINKING AND LEARNING SKILLS IN SCIENCE

Chris Collier and Rebecca Digby

No great discovery was ever made without a bold guess.
Isaac Newton

Chapter overview

The chapter introduces the thinking and learning skills which lie at the heart of science. Approaches which advocate a practical, hands-on and minds-on experience in the pursuit of the development of these skills are discussed with reference to current research and literature. There follow suggested activities for the reader to trial exemplifying learning and skill development in science and a case study drawing on two different year groups presents an analysis of some of the activities explored in the context of the classroom. The chapter concludes with a summary and reference to further reading and resources including web-based materials and research.

INTRODUCTION

This chapter begins by questioning the importance of thinking and learning skills in science, followed by some discussion on the nature of science and its links to an enquiry-based approach to teaching and learning. There is exploration of the relationship between enquiry skills, procedural knowledge and process skills, with distinction made between those procedural skills that are thinking skills and those that are motor skills. The work of researchers in science education who emphasise the inherently practical nature of the subject is introduced with the notion that, through practical work, learners' understanding of scientific concepts can be developed. Further, there is recognition that practical work by itself does not necessarily develop these concepts and thus a hands-on and minds-on approach to learning in science is needed. Later in the chapter, case studies illustrate approaches that can be taken to develop understanding of scientific concepts.

Research on the development of higher order thinking skills through science education and the importance of dialogue within science lessons is linked to a series of activities which promote the role of talk. These are drawn from a range of topics across the primary age curriculum. The introduction to research also considers cognitive acceleration and the Cognitive Acceleration through Science Education (CASE) approach to teaching science. Reference is made to the importance of metacognition and schemata or reasoning patterns, and a series of activities for developing these are suggested.

WHY ARE THINKING AND LEARNING SKILLS IMPORTANT IN SCIENCE?

The skills that underpin scientific activity get to the very heart of what science is. Those skills which are inherently scientific in nature enable the learner to gain insights into and understand further the world around them when viewed from a scientific perspective. These skills require the learner to engage in thought. The case is made elsewhere in this book of the importance of generic learning skills. For example, in Chapter 4 developing learner questioning skills is discussed. In this chapter their importance in a scientific context is explained. Specific intervention programmes for developing thinking skills are analysed in detail and more general examples are presented of how thought on the part of the learner influences their scientific development. Developing children's scientific enquiry skills is fundamental to the development of their understanding of science, therefore those skills are identified along with examples of how this can be achieved.

RESEARCH REVIEW

Nature of science

In answer to the question 'What is science?', Howe et al. (2009) state that an important aspect defining the nature of the subject is arriving at explanations which help us make sense of the world through the use of evidence and logic. To reach these explanations scientists engage in activities which draw on a combination of skills, concepts and attitudes. Significantly, the types of skills used are considered by science educators as key factors in defining an activity as scientific in nature.

When deciding which skills should be part of the programme of study for science in primary schools, a group of leading scientists and science educators came to a shared understanding that both process and thinking skills were essential (Osborne et al., 2003). They suggested that the school curriculum should feature the teaching of scientific methods and critical testing, the diversity of scientific thinking, the role of hypothesis and prediction, the relationship between science and questioning, and the analysis and interpretation of data. In a further study examining the nature of science, the views of a group of practising scientists revealed similar ideas with 'overwhelming agreement in the importance of empirical data in the development and justification of scientific knowledge' (Schwartz and Lederman, 2008: 747). Also emerging from this study was the need for science education to broaden the range of scientific enquiry experiences for the learner. Indeed, there was consensus that teaching children only one approach or method in science will not provide them with an authentic scientific experience.

These studies reflect general agreement amongst scientists and researchers that it is the procedures supporting the construction of scientific knowledge which need a prominent place within teaching and learning in science. Consequently, it is clear that the skills of enquiry play an important role in developing children's understanding of the nature of science.

Enquiry skills

So what are the enquiry skills that should be such a central feature in the teaching and learning of science in primary schools?

There is agreement between Howe et al. (2009) and Harlen and Qualter (2004) that scientific enquiry skills can be divided into those which are mental in nature and those which are physical, thus acknowledging that there is an element of 'doing' in science. So as well as developing the mental capacity to question, predict, plan, interpret and reflect, children will also observe, measure and physically explore their environment. In describing enquiry skills, Harlen (2006) identifies seven outcomes to science education in terms of learners' development of 'process skills'. She states that science education should be contributing to learners' ability to:

- raise questions that can be answered by investigation;
- develop hypotheses about how events and relationships can be explained;
- make predictions based on hypotheses;
- use observation to gather information;
- plan and use investigation to search for patterns and test ideas;
- interpret evidence and draw valid conclusions;
- communicate, report and reflect on procedures and conclusions.

(Harlen, 2006: 38)

Goldsworthy et al. (2000) develop a further link between enquiry, process skills and thinking skills. They conclude that scientific enquiry should be seen as a cognitive process with children needing to develop thinking strategies in order to make progress in their investigative work. This principle suggests that children's developing capacity for thought will guide their practical activities and enable them to make the most of the data they collect. The work of Goldsworthy and others as part of the AKSIS project (a research project run jointly by the Association for Science Education and King's College London) led to the creation of a series of discrete activities, designed to help children develop their enquiry skills (Goldsworthy et al., 2000).

The approach advocated by the research team was to teach skills by atomising investigations into separate distinct processes. Although this approach may prove useful in targeting learners' specific developmental needs and it can be helpful when considering the different processes that make up an enquiry, Howe et al. (2009) raised concern that teaching each process discretely may lead children to believe science is a set of standard procedures to follow. This can be at odds with actual experience. For example, an enquiry might begin with a question being raised in response to an observation. After producing a tentative plan and having carried out some preliminary explorations, the child may want to revisit and revise their original question. Evidently, in such circumstances, the scientific method cannot be seen as a neat sequence (Howe et al., 2009). Despite this objection to the atomisation of investigations, it is still an approach worthy of consideration, particularly for the development of skills that children find difficult. For example, AKSIS resources target the skill of data interpretation, one of the most difficult enquiry skills to develop (Watson et al., 1998).

Conceptual development by active learning

Harlen and Qualter (2004) make the point that practical activity is at the heart of primary science teaching because children learn best from first hand experiences. However, they also state that the value of practical experience is enhanced by discussing and sharing ideas with others. They suggest children need opportunities to think about what they are doing and why they are doing it, not just experience following instructions. Further, children's questions need to be valued and they need to be encouraged to see the world through a different lens. For instance, children should be supported in developing their awareness of the validity of the experiences of others. In addition, Millar (2010) explains that practical science should be 'hands on' and 'minds on' if it is to be effective in developing children's understanding of scientific concepts. In order to realise this, children need to be challenged by questioning and provided with opportunities to engage in discussion so that a bridge can be built between the 'domain of observables' and 'domain of ideas' (Harlen and Qualter, 2004; Millar, 2010). This is significant in light of Ward and Roden's (2005) finding that primary children can have difficulties in interpreting data because insufficient time is devoted to this aspect of learning in science.

These findings suggest that children need time to discover the connections between their experiences in practical work and conceptual development. The case studies accompanying this chapter highlight the important role plenary sessions play in developing children's thinking and learning. Interventions throughout the lesson (mini-plenaries) can also be a particularly effective way of consolidating and extending learning. Whatever choices are made by you, it is clear that opportunity should be provided for the learner to reflect on their own experiences with the support of others.

Structured thinking skills development

Some process skills, it has been noted, are thinking skills while others are motor-sensory skills. Turning attention to thinking skills development, the Bright Ideas Project, which ran at Oxford Brookes University, took Bloom's taxonomy of thinking skills and considered how children can be encouraged to develop higher order skills through science education and in particular children's use of talk in a scientific context (www.azteachscience.co.uk). The project researchers identified how science education can support the development of such higher order thinking skills as synthesis, evaluation and analysis. Collaborative, investigative work can provide children with opportunities to engage in higher-level thinking and discussion. Skills of synthesis such as hypothesising, which show originality by creating and inventing or composing, are important parts of the planning process. The skills of evaluation (judging, rating and giving opinions) and analytical skills (categorising and comparing, distinguishing between fact and opinion) can be important for interpreting evidence and drawing conclusions.

Stimulating high-level thinking is also one of the aims of the Cognitive Acceleration through Science Education (CASE) approach to teaching thinking skills in primary schools (Adey and Serrat 2010). CASE, underpinned by the work of Piaget and Vygotsky, is the basis of intervention programmes published by Nelson, titled *Let's Think!* (Adey et al., 2001) and *Let's Think Through Science!* (Adey et al., 2003). It has at its heart three main pillars of cognitive acceleration that the CASE research team have identified as central to the stimulation of thinking abilities. Firstly, 'cognitive conflict' is the stage when the learner is presented with a challenge to their current level of understanding. This part of the programme draws on the work of Piaget in particular. Pitching the challenge at the correct level for the learner is of great importance – it should be neither too easy nor beyond the learner's potential for development. During the next stage, influenced by the work of Vygotsky's 'Social Constructivism', the learner is actively encouraged to work together with others to solve a problem. Later, the child is asked to reflect on the approach they took to solve a particular problem, a stage which is known as 'metacognition' (Adey et al., 2003). The categories of thinking ability that are developed by CASE activities are grouped together by their underlying reasoning patterns (schemata), providing a clear set of types of thinking that can be applied in many different scientific contexts (Adey and Shayer, 2002; Adey et al., 2003).

The importance of metacognition in cognitive instruction is confirmed by McGuinness (1993), who reviewed the methods employed by teachers during thinking skills development activities and concluded that to a greater or lesser extent all methods relied on an element of reflective thinking. These findings are similar to those of Larkin (2002), who found a positive correlation between metacognition and cognition.

Finally, a process of reasoning, termed argumentation, which was developed by Stephen Toulmin in the 1950s has influenced science teaching in recent years as part of a desire to focus on developing children's thinking skills (Trend, 2009). It is a model for learning based around five key elements: data, claim, warrant, rebuttal and qualifier. A proposition (claim) is made with reference to information (data). An explanation (warrant) is given that links the claim and data – why does the claim arise from the data? Possibly a challenge, accompanied by fresh supporting evidence, will then be made to the claim (rebuttal). The rebuttal may ultimately lead to a qualifier being issued, with the original claim being refined and modified in response to the challenge made. This model for argumentation has been adapted and developed as a means of promoting effective transition from primary to secondary school (www. azteachscience.co.uk).

CASE STUDY

This case study looks at initiatives that were implemented in two Key Stage 2 classrooms by an Advanced Skills Teacher in her role as science subject leader, with the aim of developing children's higher order thinking and questioning skills in the context of science. The rationales for developing these skills and key episodes in two lessons are documented, together with the successes and a reflection on difficulties faced. There is a discussion of the impact on learning and the next steps for the year groups involved.

The inner-city primary school involved in the study is a thriving and culturally diverse community which places quality learning within stimulating environments alongside support, challenge and encouragement highly in its ethos. A broad definition of learning is espoused with emphasis on creative, spiritual and social interactions, and the development of responsible citizens who can contribute positively to the world in which they live. The school's priorities, which included raising standards through the teaching, learning and assessment of speaking and listening, and further developing children's group working skills, have resulted in a focus on Assessment for Learning (AfL) and Collaborative Group Work (CGW). Staff within the school have taken part in meetings introducing the principles and approaches to AfL including the use of questioning and engagement in reflective discussion. This resulted in an agreement amongst staff to trial and document AfL strategies in English, Mathematics and Science.

Further to this, having received training in Cognitive Acceleration through Science Education (CASE) and taken part in a series of workshops led by the Wellcome Trust exploring the relationship between science and creativity, the science subject leader was working alongside Key Stage 2 teachers to support children in developing higher order thinking and speaking and listening skills during investigative activities. In particular, she was examining the potential of the CASE approach for promoting evaluative and reflective dialogue alongside the Year 3 teacher. In her own Year 6 class she was exploring the use of 'science starters' to develop opportunities for discussion and debate.

Year 3

As 'Rocks and Soils' was the current area of learning in science in Year 3, it was used as the starting point for introducing the CASE approach to the class. Teaching materials provided by CASE, including lesson plans and practical resources, formed the basis of a series of team-teaching sessions. Team-teaching is regularly used as an opportunity for professional development within the school and was seen as a highly successful strategy. Within the context of trialling the CASE approach, team teaching was described as an invaluable tool for promoting reflective discussion on the development of children's higher order thinking skills. Additionally, as one teacher was able to document and observe learning whilst the other led the session, a range of perspectives could be gathered and reviewed thus creating a fuller picture of events (Project Zero, 2010).

During a lesson focused on classification, the class was divided into groups and the children were invited as part of the 'concrete preparation' phase of the lesson to use their senses to explore a chosen rock and think about how it might be described. Ideas were shared within each group and then mapped in a 'whole class' word bank. The process promoted rich dialogue and provided children with the opportunity to consider and rehearse their ideas before they were shared (Alexander, 2008). Further, displaying ideas publicly in this form has been described by McMahon (2012) as both valuing children's contributions and creating an opportunity to revisit and develop scientific vocabulary at later points. It was apparent that this initial stage of orientating children in the context for learning promoted a positive culture in which discussion was highly regarded from the outset of the lesson.

During the next phase of the lesson (cognitive conflict) the class were invited to decide on ways in which they could sort the rocks into categories. During this episode the teachers observed interactions and listened to discussion noting both positive dynamics and issues which arose within the various groups. Whilst reviewing children's choices for classification, the teachers directed pre-planned questions to groups about the processes they had engaged in to arrive at decisions. The questions, which required analysis and synthesis from children in their responses (Bloom et al., 1956), and the use of 'think time' before answering, prompted complex and considered answers. Later, when the class as a whole were given the opportunity to reflect on each group's questions about choices made in categorising the rocks, the earlier modelling by the teachers was drawn on by children who readily asked questions such as 'Why was the last way you grouped them the best?' and 'How did you decide to put them into groups of smooth and rough (*textures*)?' involving evaluation and analysis, and so demonstrating reasoned thinking.

The cognitive conflict phase of the lesson contained several features which promoted conditions for children to engage in higher order thinking and questioning including the challenge of solving a problem within a group, use of direct questioning, encouragement of children to ask each other questions and use of 'think time'.

During 'metacognition' episodes in the lesson, issues which had arisen within groups, such as any difficulty in arriving at shared decisions, were used to further challenge thinking and invite groups to question both themselves and each other by considering what was difficult and how it might be overcome. The opportunity to engage in metacognition was woven throughout the lesson in a similar way to mini-plenaries. After each challenge or cognitive conflict followed a time for metacognition which was often focused on reflection and discussion of thinking processes initiated by teacher questioning, such as 'Can you explain how you sorted rocks this time?', 'What gave you this idea?'. These metacognition sessions provided children with space to review their learning experiences by reflecting both *in* action and *on* action (Schön, 1987), so engaging in sophisticated thought.

The structure of the lesson, with short focused cognitive conflicts followed by episodes of metacognition, provided children with opportunities to regularly reflect on the processes and the thinking that they were engaged in during challenges.

Significantly, a sense of openness and respect emerged as discussion and responses to questions increasingly involved self-reflection and honesty.

In their evaluation of using the CASE approach, teachers recognised it had made a positive impact on the development of children's higher order questioning and thinking skills. Factors which had a negative effect were related to time, resourcing and organisation. For instance, team-teaching was recognised as a unique opportunity by the teachers and it was noted that without two adults present in the class, the management of groups and collection of robust observations would become challenging. Further, as some groups had difficulty in working with each other, it was felt that they would need regular opportunities to practise this in order to overcome potential problems and get the most benefit from CASE sessions.

The science subject leader and Year 3 teacher agreed that the next steps would include:

- continuing to implement the CASE approach during science sessions;

- monitoring the impact on children's higher order thinking and questioning skills through observation and reflective discussion between the Year 3 teacher and science subject leader;

- observing the impact of the CASE approach in other subject areas, e.g. reflective discussion during thinking skills at registration time;

- utilising opportunities to engage children in metacognition during mini-plenaries in other curriculum areas.

Year 6

The science subject leader was keen to trial activities she had encountered during training workshops exploring science and creativity with her class. In particular, suggestions from the Bright Ideas Project (Wilson and Mant, 2004) such as 'Positives, Minuses and Interesting' (PMI), 'What if . . .' questions, and 'Odd One Out' were chosen to use as 'science starters' at the beginning of lessons. Concerned with challenging and extending high attainers during science lessons, the subject leader aimed to relate the starters to the topic being studied in order to encourage the development of questioning and thinking skills through whole class discussion and debate. Whole class discussion was considered by the subject leader as an opportunity for high attainers to both apply and share their understanding of scientific concepts.

To initiate these ideas, 'Interdependence and Adaptation' was chosen as the area for learning and the question, 'How could we adapt to live under the sea as well as on the land?' was posed to the class to stimulate discussion before the start of an elicitation activity exploring organisms, habitats and environments through concept mapping. Such a question has the potential to provoke not only scientific and creative thinking, but, importantly, the comprehension of possibilities. Craft (2001) describes this as 'possibility thinking', an essential skill which should be nurtured in both children and adults. Further, discussion around this question requires explanation, elaboration and justification of initial ideas, all key factors in supporting higher order thinking skills development (Bloom et al., 1956). However, most significant in the context of science, is the possibility for this type of question to provide a model for questions that children could ask themselves.

Children were invited to discuss the question with their science partners (partnerships close in attainment pre-selected by the teacher for talk during lessons). This practice provided children with the opportunity to exchange and develop ideas before sharing them publicly, an approach advocated by Black and Wiliam (1998) to ensure all learners are encouraged to think and express themselves. During this discussion and answer session, responses ranged from simple to sophisticated in thought. Suggestions such as 'the development of underwater food farms to provide energy' and 'growing gills or webbed feet to escape predators' demonstrated a progression from the understanding of established scientific concepts to an ability to make logical answers to the question. Evidently, as the question invited application of knowledge, it demanded further levels of higher order thinking.

Opportunities to use the skills of evaluation and justification were built into the session, particularly where children were asked to agree or disagree with each other's suggestions and then develop ideas further. For instance, an initial response from one group to the question 'How could seeing underwater be beneficial?' was 'it will help us to find our way easily'. This was challenged by the teacher who invited others to extend the answer and, after discussion, it was agreed that 'having a composite eye like an insect would increase chances of survival'. This process required children to critically and constructively debate ideas and resulted in the class arriving at collective agreements and shared ownership of ideas. Wegerif and Mercer (1997) describe this process as exploratory talk, important in developing reasoning in discussion in the classroom.

The science starter was revisited during the plenary session. During this episode, the follow-up question 'What if the underwater adaptations like gills caused problems once back on the land?' encouraged reflective thinking and refining of original ideas in the light of progression in learning that had occurred during the main body of the lesson. However, whilst evaluating the impact of the activity, potential issues with the use of thinking skills, questions in starters and plenaries arose. In particular, it became apparent that compartmentalising the opportunity to use these skills from the main elicitation phase of the lesson, when concept maps were completed and the tone of the session changed from active discussion to focused recording, could lead to a belief amongst children that certain parts of science lessons are dull and uninspiring.

In the light of these evaluations, the science subject leader outlined the next steps as involving:

- exploration of other opportunities for using Bright Ideas activities during science sessions;

- implementation of short, focused discussion activities during mini-plenaries;

- monitoring of the impact of Bright Ideas activities on higher order thinking of high attainers through observation and evidence of synthesis, analysis and evaluation in science investigations;

- dissemination of Bright Ideas activities to Key Stage 2 year groups.

Reflecting on the case study

- What do you think are the strengths and limitations of using the structured CASE approach for
  a) the children?
  b) the teachers?

- How could the use of Bright Ideas thinking skills starters be developed across the curriculum?

- Which aspects of the trialled initiatives do you feel are most likely to be effective? Why?

- How does this approach compare to your own experience of supporting the development of children's higher order thinking skills?

 TRY THIS

Try this 1: Holistic nature of skills development

It is possible for children to model the size and shape of meteorite craters by dropping different-sized balls into sand trays. Planning such an investigation requires the child to think about the practicalities of what can be done. By completing the enquiry from beginning to end, the child learns that their plans may be limited by what is procedurally practical. During planning the learner may identify a range of variables that can be tested: height of drop, weight of ball, diameter of ball and dampness of sand on to which the ball is dropped. Perhaps a decision may be made to test the height of the drop. This is a relatively easy variable to test because it is quite straightforward to control other variables such as the weight and diameter of the ball (the same ball can be used for each successively higher drop). However, investigating the effect of the weight of the ball on the size of crater will prove more problematic because now the diameter of the ball is harder to control – each heavier ball that is tested needs to be of the same diameter if the test is to be fair. The child may not appreciate that this is the case until the test is carried out. At this point plans will need to be revised or the limitations of the investigation reflected upon. Indeed the child may realise that scientific enquiry does not always proceed in a linear way from question to method, results and conclusion, but that original ideas may need to be revisited and altered in the light of subsequent actions.

What variables did you discover children found most difficult to test in a fair way?

Try this 2: Objective observation?

Optical illusions are a great way to get children to consider the role the brain plays in interpreting sensory information. The reliability of the measurements and observations they make may be questioned as they come to realise that the information transmitted by sense organs is processed by the brain. A way of demonstrating this is to look into mirrors. Our brains 'believe' that light travels in a straight line in all cases. An image received as a reflection from a mirror is interpreted in just the same way as if the image was received directly, therefore, the image appears to be behind the mirror. Obviously the object isn't actually there, it's just the brain coping with the information it receives as best it can!

What explanations do children come up with to explain optical illusions?

Try this 3: Precise predictions

One approach to developing children's skills of prediction is to ask them to say precisely what they think the results of an enquiry will be, even to the point of producing a graph or results table before the enquiry is carried out. For example, prior to a survey of grass height to the north and south of a wall, a prediction might be made that the grass north of the wall will be taller than the grass to the south. A causal relationship is established if the prediction is backed up with a reason (e.g. because the grass in shadow north of the wall will grow taller as it searches for light). However, by drafting a graph of the anticipated results (grass height versus distance from wall), further factors might be considered such as, will the grass that is protected by being close to the wall be taller than grass in the open? Is there a distance away from the shadow of the wall where we might expect the grass to be the same height both north and south of the wall? Making detailed predictions enables children to challenge their thinking prior to testing more explicitly.

Did you find that children's predictions improved as they were asked to consider in detail the potential results of an investigation?

Try this 4: Presenting and evaluating the results of different forms of enquiry

In these activities, how the type of enquiry influences the way the results are presented is discussed. We describe how different forms of scientific enquiry can produce very different types of results. For you the challenge is to identify in your planning the range of enquiries being taught and to consider the most appropriate way for children to present their results. We also explain how children might evaluate their work:

Classification/identification-type enquiry

Typically this type of enquiry might take the form of sorting a range of objects based on their properties or dividing living things into different categories. Enquiries such as these lend themselves well to children producing keys. This might be in the form of a branching database or another form of sorting diagram such as a Carroll diagram (see Figure 9.1). Once completed, the quality of the key or diagram can be peer-assessed (evaluated): How easy was it to use? Do two different groups using the key to sort the same objects replicate their findings? If there is a difference, was the reason for this that some parts of the key were unclear?

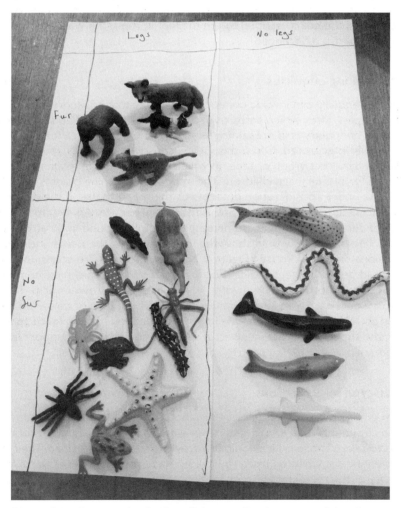

Figure 9.1 An example of a Carroll diagram. Eric has assumed the plastic toy animals are representations of the living animal and sorted them two ways: with/without fur, legs/no legs.

Design and develop enquiry

Often during these activities children draw on their scientific knowledge (as well as other skills) as they design and make artefacts to solve a particular problem. Take the example of children making a machine to sort magnetic and non-magnetic coins. Clearly the result of such an enquiry is the artefact produced by the children, and their understanding of magnets and magnetic materials will be reflected to a degree by the effectiveness of the machine to separate coins. In this context, when evaluating their work, children can ask themselves: Does the machine work? Is it fit for purpose? It may not be only their scientific understanding that they evaluate, they will also be assessing their design and make skills too so carefully chosen questions by you may help them focus on the science: Did all the coins respond to the magnet in the same way? Did the size of the magnet make a difference?

Pattern-seeking enquiries

This type of enquiry can involve conducting a survey that collects a record of lots of examples, after which patterns in the data are sought. The skill developed by this type of enquiry is in presenting large amounts of data in a form that can be readily interpreted. Often this means constructing tables and graphs. Choosing the correct graph or table in which to display these results can be a challenge for primary-age children. The important teaching point is that the type of data under consideration determines the graph to use. If the data set is categorical in nature, then a bar graph is most appropriate. An example of this is a survey of dandelion numbers, comparing the number found in three different localities. The bar graph would show the locations along the x-axis and numbers of dandelions on the y-axis (see Figure 9.2). If the variables are continuous, a line graph would be the correct choice. For example, children may have compared the distance a ball can be thrown with the length of the thrower's arm. The line graph would have arm length on the x-axis and distance of throw on the y-axis. In activities such as these, it is important that you make explicit to the children the thought process involved in selecting the graph, to support learner development.

Fair test-type investigations

One aim when teaching the skills of evaluation is to move away from non-scientific comments (e.g. 'the investigation was great fun') towards encouraging children to take a more critical look at the evidence as they evaluate their work more scientifically. Children need to have opportunities to assess the reliability and quality of their findings in order to discuss how they might refine their approach in the future.

In response to a fair test-type investigation, there are several areas children could focus on. Firstly they could consider how easy it was to control the

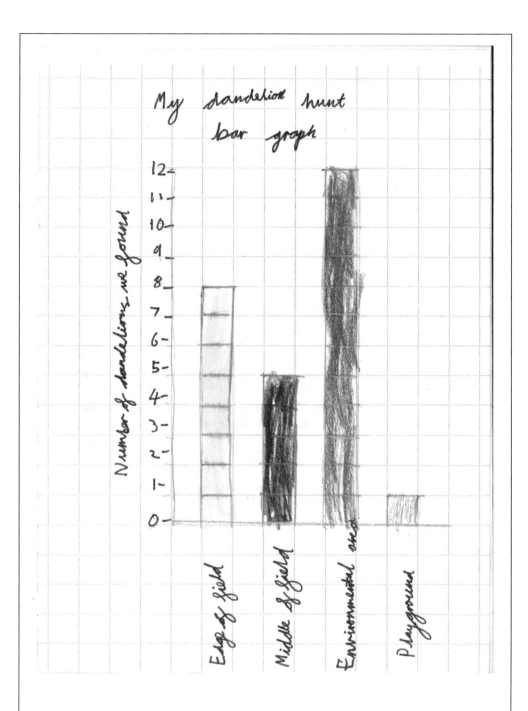

Figure 9.2 April has represented the findings of a dandelion survey on a bar graph in such a way that it is visually clear the school's environmental area has the greatest number of these plants.

different variables. Secondly, when considering the accuracy of their results, children could consider how difficult it was to use the equipment. Finally, they could assess the reliability of their results by considering if enough repeat measurements were made.

Introducing a metacognitive element to the process of evaluation no matter what the type of enquiry should be encouraged. This could involve children considering how their thoughts and ideas have developed over the course of an investigation by returning to the prediction they made at the start. As they do so, they should be prompted to consider how their understanding has developed and in particular which actions and experiences were influential in their development.

Consider the different approaches that might be taken to encourage children to reflect on their progress.

Try this 5: Interpreting findings

Taking the context of a parachute investigation, here are a range of conclusions ordered hierarchically in order of sophistication:

- 'One parachute took three seconds to fall.' (Child tells you one result.)
- 'The really slow parachute to reach the ground was the one that weighed only 20 grams.' (The extremes in results are described.)
- 'The higher that the parachute is dropped from, the longer it takes to fall.' (A pattern is described.)
- 'Large parachutes fall slowly because air resistance is greater.' (The response is related to conceptual understanding.)

By being aware of the types of responses that might be given, you can develop children's ability to interpret results by presenting them with statements connected to the investigation and asking them to rank them in order of sophistication.

Alternatively, play a 'Thumbs up/down' game, developed by Goldsworthy and Ponchard (2007). Children are given a table of results to study, after which the teacher reads out a series of statements. In groups children are challenged to decide if a statement is supported by the evidence or not, showing their understanding by thumbs up or thumbs down. A sideways thumb indicates the statement is partially supported by the evidence.

Consider the comments you might expect from primary children in response to an investigation with a different context (e.g. comparing bubbles formed by different-shaped bubble blowers). Can you place them in order of progression?

Try this 6: Identifying schemata

Primary science is characterised by children learning through hands-on activities. By understanding the different types of thinking that they use to make sense of these experiences you can design lessons for their development. The Cognitive Acceleration in Science Education (CASE) project has identified seven general ways of thinking (schemata). An example of each type is given below for you to try out. Alternatively use the list to review your science plans. Do they include provision for developing a range of schemata?

- Causality – Can children identify that the cause of the sound they are hearing is the triangle vibrating and that the effect of the vibration is the sound we hear?

- Classification – How can packaging be grouped depending on the property of the materials?

- Combinatorial thinking – Light and water are two factors that could be tested to see what difference each makes to seed germination. Even though each factor is tested separately, when considering all the results children could think of the four different possible scenarios: light and water, light and no water, dark and water, dark and no water.

- Concrete modelling – Can children develop concrete models for different types of rocks? Ball bearings held together by Blu-tak can model sand grains cemented together in sandstone. Different shapes of Lego bricks can model in a simplified way the interlocking nature of igneous rock grains.

- Conservation – Is the learner aware that the shape of one litre of water changes in different-sized containers but the amount stays the same?

- Relationship between variables – Is there a relationship between different factors in an enquiry? Does altering the tension of an elastic band alter its pitch when plucked?

- Seriation – Can objects or events be placed in order e.g. rocks in order of hardness, or the change in the appearance of the moon over the course of a lunar month?

Try this 7: Positive, minus and interesting

Creating your own Positive, Minus and Interesting scenarios is an opportunity to develop stimulating and creative sequences in science lessons. When used at the beginning of science lessons (or at any point during a session), they can add lively discussion and debate on scientific concepts and provide insight into children's existing thinking and ideas. Further, they have the potential to be a powerful opportunity for children to engage in higher order thinking and questioning as they consider abstract concepts in 'real-life' contexts. This activity comes from the Bright Ideas project referenced earlier. It involves considering the positives, minuses and interesting points of a scenario related to reversible and irreversible changes. The example given on the AstraZeneca website (see www.azteachscience.co.uk) is 'All door handles are made of chocolate'. Can you devise a scenario for some different topics such as micro-organisms or electricity?

Try this 8: Argumentation

Try using the context of floating and sinking to generate discussion and stimulate thinking:

Heavy objects sink (claim)

A lump of plasticine sinks (data)

Yes, the heavy object sank (warrant)

Plasticine shaped into a boat floats (rebuttal)

The amount of water an object displaces is important too (qualifier)

What other rebuttals did the children come up with?

SUMMARY

The development of children's thinking and learning skills in science is linked to a hands-on and minds-on approach to learning which includes a combination of procedural knowledge, process skills and enquiry. Ultimately, the development of these skills supports children in understanding the nature of science.

Through a research review, the chapter identifies the key factors which support the development of children's thinking and learning skills in science, namely:

- the process skills;
- practical activity;
- dialogue;
- collaborative cognitive and metacognitive activity.

Additionally, the chapter presents established pedagogical models and suggests practical activities which promote the above factors, including: holistic and atomised approaches to scientific enquiry; Bright Ideas; CASE; and Argumentation. The case study illustrates some of the suggested practical activities in classroom contexts and provides new topics for consideration such as the role talk plays in skills development. Both the range of activities for further investigation and the case study provide teachers with starting points for promoting children's thinking and learning skills and, in conjunction with the research review, offer approaches to facilitate children's development of a deeper understanding of the meaning of science.

FURTHER READING

Adey, P. and Shayer, M. (2002) Cognitive Acceleration Comes of Age, in M. Shayer and P. Adey (eds) *Learning Intelligence: Cognitive Acceleration Across the Curriculum from 5 to 15 years*. Buckingham: Open University Press.
Shayer and Adey's book will interest those wanting to know more about the Cognitive Acceleration through Science Education (CASE) approach to thinking skills development. The chapter referred to above includes an overview of the research and theory that underpin the authors' cognitive acceleration methods. Other chapters describe how these methods can be applied to thinking skills development across a range of age groups (both primary and secondary) and subjects.

Alexander, R. J. (2008) *Towards Dialogic Teaching: Rethinking Classroom Talk*, 4th edn. York: Dialogos.
This pamphlet is only 60 pages long but contains a great deal of useful advice about developing dialogic teaching in the classroom. It is not specifically about the role talk plays in scientific learning, but it was still found helpful as the authors of this chapter analysed observations made during science lessons (see case studies above).

Craft, A. (2001) Little 'c' Creativity, in A. Craft, B. Jeffrey and M. Leibling, *Creativity in Education*. London: Continuum.
Reference is made to Anna Craft's work on little 'c' creativity in this chapter (see case studies) although readers will not want to restrict themselves only to this part of the book. The authors argue the point that creativity is not just the preserve of the arts but applies to all domains of learning, including science.

Goldsworthy, A., Watson, R. and Wood-Robinson, V. (2000) *Investigations: Developing Understanding*. Hatfield: ASE.
This guidebook is focused on providing practical advice for teaching children about the skills and procedures of scientific enquiry. The point is made in the introduction that scientific enquiry is a thinking process and this is evident throughout the book. The activities described within it are designed to teach scientific skill development by developing the thought of the learner.

Harlen, W. (2006) *Teaching, Learning and Assessing Science 5–12*, 4th edn. London: Sage.
A very useful general text on primary science teaching and learning that places a strong emphasis on the role that enquiry skills play in developing scientific understanding.

REFERENCES

Adey, P. and Shayer, M. (2002) Cognitive acceleration comes of age, in M. Shayer and P. Adey (eds) *Learning Intelligence: Cognitive Acceleration Across the Curriculum from 5 to 15 years*. Buckingham: Open University Press.

Adey, P., Nagy, F., Robertson, A., Serret, N. and Wadsworth, P. (2003) *Let's Think Through Science!* London: NFER Nelson.

Adey, P., Robertson, A. and Venville, G. (2001) *Let's Think! A Programme for Developing Thinking in Five and Six Year Olds*. London: NFER Nelson.

Adey, P. and Serrat, N. (2010) Science teaching and cognitive acceleration, in J. Osborne and J. Dillon (eds) *Good Practice in Science Teaching: What Research has to Say*, 2nd edn. London: McGraw-Hill.

Alexander, R. J. (2008) *Towards Dialogic Teaching: Rethinking Classroom Talk*, 4th edn. York: Dialogos.

Black, P. J. and Wiliam, D. (1998) *Inside the Black Box: Raising Standards through Classroom Assessment*. London: King's College London School of Education.

Bloom, B. S., Engelhart, M. D., Furst, E. J., Hill, W. H. and Krathwohl, D. R. (1956) *Taxonomy of Educational Objectives: Handbook 1 Cognitive Domain*. New York: David McKay.

Craft, A. (2001) Little 'c' creativity, in A. Craft, B. Jeffrey and M. Leibling, *Creativity in Education*. London: Continuum.

Goldsworthy, A., Watson, R. and Wood-Robinson, V. (2000) *Investigations: Developing Understanding*. Hatfield: ASE.

Goldsworthy, A. and Ponchard, B. (2007) *Science Enquiry Games: Active Ways to Learn and Revise Science Enquiry Skills*. Sandbach: Millgate House.

Harlen, W. (2006) *Teaching, Learning and Assessing Science 5–12*, 4th edn. London: Sage.

Harlen, W. and Qualter, A. (2004) *The Teaching of Science in Primary Schools*, 4th edn. London: David Fulton.

Howe, A., Davies, D., McMahon, K., Towler, L., Collier, C. and Scott, T. (2009) *Science 5–11: A Guide for Teachers*, 2nd edn. London: David Fulton.

Larkin, S. (2002) Creating metacognitive experiences for 5- and 6-year-old children, in M. Shayer and P. Adey (eds) *Learning Intelligence: Cognitive Acceleration Across the Curriculum from 5 to 15 years*. Buckingham: Open University Press.

McMahon, K. (2012) Case studies of interactive whole-class teaching in primary science: communicative approach and pedagogic purposes. *International Journal of Science Education*, 34(11): 1–22.

McGuinness, C. (1993) Teaching Thinking: New Signs for Theories of Cognition. *Educational Psychology*, 13(3 and 4): 305–16.

Millar, R. (2010) Practical work, in J. Osborne and J. Dillon (eds) *Good Practice in Science Teaching: What Research has to Say*, 2nd edn. London: McGraw-Hill.

Osborne J., Collins, S., Ratcliffe, M., Millar, R., and Duschl, R. (2003) What 'Ideas-about-Science' should be taught in school science? A Delphi study of the expert community. *Journal of Research in Science Teaching*, 40(7): 692–720.

Schön, D. (1987) *Educating the Reflective Practitioner*. San Francisco, CA: Jossey Bass.

Schwartz, R. and Lederman, N. (2008) What scientists say: Scientists' Views of Nature of Science and Relation to Science Context. *International Journal of Science Education*, 30(6): 727–71.

Trend, R. (2009) Fostering students' argumentation skills in geoscience, *Journal of Geoscience Education*, 57(4): 224–32.

Ward, H. and Roden, J. (2005) The skills children need to learn science – process skills, in H. Ward, J. Roden, C. Hewlett and J. Foreman, J. *Teaching Science in the Primary Classroom: a practical guide*. London: Paul Chapman.

Watson, J. R., Goldsworthy, A. and Wood-Robinson, V. (1998) Getting AKSIS to Investigations. *Education in Science*, 177: 20–1.

Wegerif, R. and Mercer, N. (1997) A Dialogical Framework for Investigating Talk, in R. Wegerif and P. Scrimshaw (eds) *Computers and Talk in the Primary Classroom*. Clevedon: Multilingual Matters.

Wilson, H. and Mant, J. (2004) *Creativity and Excitement in Science*. Oxford: Oxford Brookes University.

WEBSITES

AstraZeneca Science Teaching Trust: www.azteachscience.co.uk (accessed 19 October 2012).
Project Zero (2010) www.pz.harvard.edu/ (accessed 1 September 2012).

CHAPTER 10

PHILOSOPHY FOR CHILDREN

Darren Garside

> *. . . the mind is not a vessel that needs filling,*
> *but wood that needs igniting.*
>
> *Plutarch*

Chapter overview

This chapter introduces the practice of philosophy for children. Although best practice requires undergoing professional development training, the chapter indicates how practitioners can develop techniques that are useful in the classroom. Some context is provided to understand the philosophy for children movement and from this it is emphasised that a practitioner's attitude is as important as their skill. Two case studies are provided from contrasting settings. One school in the east end of London begins philosophy for children from nursery age and sees it as vital in building a community and individual aspiration. The other school is in a rural, south of England setting and for them philosophy for children is at the heart of producing tomorrow's citizens. The chapter concludes with references and suggestions for further reading.

INTRODUCTION

During the course of her retirement year our sixth form Sociology teacher cleared out her stationery cupboard. One gift she gave me was an insubstantial book that she was turning out from her private collection. *Thinking to Some Purpose* by Susan L. Stebbing was a volume from the classic blue-covered Penguin range that covered archaeology, philosophy, politics, sociology, and the arts. The book was not particularly startling, it does not feature on any modern-day reading list, but its influence on me was profound and its influence is to be found throughout this chapter. Professor Stebbing was concerned with what would now be called 'critical thinking skills'. These skills are promoted as forensic tools of the mind, allowing the thinker to discern assumptions, arguments and rhetorical sleights of hand embedded in texts and discourse. Applying the scalpel of critical thinking allows the thinker to cut through the unnecessary, the illustrative and the downright deceptive to get to the heart of the matter; a heart that some still refer to as 'truth'.

Why should a modern reader concern themselves with a 50-year old book filled with outdated examples, and what relevance does that have to educational practitioners facing the complexities of modern classrooms? The answer to that question derives from the key word 'purpose' in the book's title. This chapter will argue that (educational) thinking is always for some (educational) purpose and that we must be clear about our purposes and our values before we can successfully promote good thinking in others; including children, colleagues, parents and the wider community. There is an implication to this argument and it is that thinking skills are not worthwhile educational aims in themselves. To make this argument I shall describe, analyse and evaluate the practice of philosophy for and with children. Philosophy for children describes both a pedagogical technique and a pedagogical movement that began in the USA in the late 1960s. However, there is not one thing called philosophy for children, rather there is a range of practices that share what the philosopher Ludwig Wittgenstein called a 'family resemblance' in contrast to a tightly-agreed definition. By describing the historical and geographical growth of the movement this chapter will illustrate how philosophy for children can help practitioners develop their techniques for promoting good thinking and derive standards by which their practice may be evaluated.

Most, if not all, philosophers engaged with the various philosophy for children movements argue that it is impossible to develop your practice without significant investment in your professional development, specifically through philosophising with your peers in a structured programme. There are many such courses that facilitate and recognise your developing philosophy for children practice and these are signposted at the end of the chapter. This chapter is merely an invitation to dip your toes into the waters, and in doing so you will join a worldwide community of practice dedicated to helping children.

RESEARCH REVIEW: THE PURPOSE OF THINKING IN CLASSROOMS

How does philosophy for children help children become more active partners in the classroom? To answer that we must consider why we want children to think well and then we might think about how we can help children to think well. We can think of two categories of reasoning, that can help us make judgements. The first type of reasoning is intrinsic; by intrinsic I mean reasoning that is worthwhile for its own sake, because it is a good thing for a child or person to do, it is something that ideally we would wish everyone to do. The second type of reasoning is extrinsic; by extrinsic I mean that the value placed upon the thinking is judged by some standard outside of the thinker or the context of the thinking. An example of this is where thinking is judged as worthwhile since it helps exam scores. Whilst acknowledging that teachers work in complicated, demanding and pragmatic circumstances, I agree with the philosopher Dewey that asking children to think better without good reasons for doing so is pointless. The ideal situation would be to engage in activity that has both benefits in the widest educational sense, and that is also a worthwhile activity in its own right. In this next section I describe how philosophy for children is one such activity. Before I go on to do this I will briefly justify why a purely instrumental attitude is not only wrong but harmful to children.

When instrumental thinking is wrong

In 1976 the then Prime Minister, James Callaghan, made his famous Ruskin College speech, where he challenged the teaching profession to give up its secret garden, a metaphor for the curriculum, and become more accountable to social and economic demands. Callaghan's demands were part of a wider movement known as neoliberalism. Neoliberalism is a movement that places its faith in the power of markets to determine good outcomes for individuals and consequently society. The rise of neoliberalism can be linked to a crisis of legitimacy in expertise and authority. In an era of increasing social liberty and cultural expression yet also of economic hardship and the breakdown of the post-war consensus, the appeal to the market offered certainty or at least solutions to otherwise seemingly intractable problems (Olssen, 2010).

The consequences of neoliberalism through education are both profound and long-lasting. The imposition of a national curriculum, the marketisation of school provision, and the involvement of the political class in not just the content of the curriculum but in the mechanisms of delivery have been well documented in education (Harris, 2007; Heilbronn, 2008; Green, 2010). Without going into the debate here, I would like to point out one effect of neoliberalism on the activity of children in the classroom. If the purposes of education are given to educators from outside of education there is a danger that all activity in the classroom becomes subordinated to ends the educators do not necessarily agree with. Colloquially this is known as teaching to the test and the effects of this teaching are felt not just in classrooms whose children are to be assessed in that year but in all classrooms throughout the school. There is a danger that thinking skills are seen merely as an end to improve performance; in other words in the production of children who can pass exams, thinking skills are a better type of machine. Yet focusing on outcomes, paradoxically can be counter-productive. There is a Zen koan which says 'the archer who aims at the prize will miss the target, whilst the archer who aims at the target will win the prize'. What this means for practice is that engaging in good educational activities will lead to good outcomes but focusing on good educational outcomes will not always lead to good educational activities.

This section has argued that thinking is not worthwhile for its own sake. What we should value are thinking persons; that is persons, and I explicitly include children in this category, with skills, dispositions and virtues who can think well to some clearly agreed purpose. Philosophy for Children (P4C) is a worthwhile practice when evaluated on the basis of the conventional educational goods it produces, such as reading scores, cognitive IQ tests, and interpersonal skills. Yet the next section provides an account that values P4C for other, intrinsic, reasons. Value is placed on reasonableness, the quality and re-balancing of relationships, the communal commitment to inquiry, and the care shown by members of the community both in the pursuit of truth and meaning and to one another in the course of that pursuit. It values a different conception of children – as active participants in learning with a range and potential that can both surprise us and also educate us. P4C is a pedagogy that encourages us to become learners *with* children rather than leaders *of* them.

What type of thinking is P4C?

This section explores the thinking and attitude of Socrates, the Greek philosopher and gadfly who lived in the fifth century BCE. Understanding Socrates is relevant now because it is in Socrates that we find the virtues of questioning, enquiry, and active participation in the world through his search for deep meaning. It is often remarked that young children are full of questions, wondering about the world, and that they display a thirst for enquiry that becomes lost through schooling – something which is regretted by all. Philosophy for children is both a pedagogical technique and a wider pedagogical movement. At its heart is a desire to reclaim education for children, to make space for their thinking and enquiry, and to facilitate them being active participants in their own learning.

P4C began with a philosopher called Matthew Lipman. Lipman was a trained academic philosopher specialising in art and aesthetics who was greatly informed by the twentieth century philosopher John Dewey. In Lipman's biography he described the growing recognition of the need of his students to think critically about the current issues of the day – in the late 1960s in the US, those were Vietnam and civil rights issues (Lipman, 2008). Despite his students' training in academic philosophy they were unable to think critically about the issues facing them and were therefore unable to think well about how to act. At the same time, in a burst of inspiration, the first chapter of a children's philosophical novel was written by Lipman as he realised that philosophy had to start earlier rather than later in a child's schooling. It is from Socrates that Lipman derived his values of enquiry; it is from Dewey that Lipman derived his value of the importance of the community of enquiry.

It is vitally important to understand the significance of the community of enquiry in P4C practice. Unlike most models of thinking skills that treat the brain as a central processing unit and treat thinking solely as the property of individuals, P4C practitioners understand thinking as taking place in a community. It is by thinking together, exposing our thoughts and beliefs to one another, and having those thoughts and beliefs explored and sometimes challenged that we learn to think better together. Thinking together this way is not always easy and certainly takes time to build a community. It is also challenging for the classroom practitioner since their role changes from being the 'sage on the stage' to the 'guide on the side'. In other words, teachers move from being leaders of learning, or didactic experts telling children what meaning they need to understand, to being facilitators and co-enquirers. The skill lies in helping the growth of the community by modelling the type of thinking and language that is indicative of good thinking, and most importantly modelling the openness to changing one's mind in the face of good reasons that is the mark of philosophy.

The structure of P4C sessions

The first thing you may notice on entering a classroom being used for a P4C session would be the unconventional layout. Philosophy for children values the community and places great store on the individual accounting their knowledge and understanding to the community. Everyone in that community is of equal standing, including the teacher/facilitator, and it is for those reasons that a P4C enquiry is conducted in a circle. You would also notice the importance of questioning in the session, and the giving and receiving of reasons; it would also become apparent that members of the community both cared for one another, directly by attending to the person and indirectly by attending to what is being said.

It is not appropriate here to go into a lengthy description of the different stages in P4C enquiry. There are plenty of books already published, that are very well established and respected, that can give the interested, beginning practitioner a deeper insight (e.g. Fisher, 2003; Haynes, 2008; Lipman, 2003; McCall, 2009; Saran and Neisser, 2004). What I shall do here is describe what purposes may lie behind the facilitator's decisions as she guides the community in its progress towards mutually negotiated goals. Whereas an experienced classroom teacher can explain the underlying reasons justifying their actions, a novice practitioner is less able to do so without structured support to aid their reflections. Therefore it is important to have a general understanding of what a P4C facilitator is trying to achieve.

The first stage is to bring the community together with some type of activity or game whose purpose is to encourage group ethos and togetherness and possibly activate certain types of thinking. From there the facilitator may well introduce a thought-provoking or emotionally stimulating resource, for example a picture book, film, or activity. Initial responses will be aired and shared either to the community as a whole or in small pairs or groups, eventually leading to the formulation of questions. These questions are invitations or candidates offered to the whole group so that the group can focus their attention through choosing one question to pursue further. Once the question has been chosen the community pursues the question, trying to get at the underlying meaning or truth. Before the session concludes a facilitator will often choose to finish with a final round where everyone has a chance to offer their closing thoughts and hopefully indicate how they think they may have changed their position over the course of the enquiry.

Although this is an outline of how an enquiry may precede, P4C methodology is not rigid prescription. Facilitators are wise practitioners in the sense that Aristotle means when he talks of practitioners' 'practical wisdom'. Someone with practical wisdom is not just a technician or rule follower but someone who is able to judge what type of situation this is and how one ought to act in this situation. Thus the practically wise teacher may respond differently from a novice practitioner owing to the depth and profundity of their understanding. It is the case that a huge amount of variation might be found in the facilitation of an inquiry. It is for these reasons that I urge and reiterate my earlier point that the only way to develop genuine expertise in philosophy for children is to take part in P4C professional development courses. The following section explores certain techniques and practices that are worthwhile in their own right and which might contribute to practitioners' emerging understanding of P4C.

CASE STUDIES

These case studies present an illustration of how P4C is implemented by two schools in the south of England. This is not educational research and the interrogation of the data is neither rigorous nor systematic but is, I believe, a fair representation of the voices of children and staff during short visits to the schools. Sceptics might claim that the perceived benefits actually derive from good schooling and teaching in general rather than from P4C in particular. That claim could be explored empirically through educational research. Here, I make no claim to truth that is generalisable or universal. What I do is illustrate how the ideas about purposeful activity and active engagement from earlier in the chapter are promoted in these schools' use of P4C.

Case study I: Fordingbridge School
School context

According to OFSTED, Fordingbridge Junior School 'is a junior school of average size. Almost all pupils are from a White British background, with few from minority ethnic backgrounds or who speak English as an additional language. The proportion of pupils eligible for free school meals is below average. While the proportion of pupils who have learning difficulties and/or disabilities is below average, the proportion who have a statement of educational needs is slightly above that seen nationally. There are currently more boys than girls in the school although this varies between year groups'.

Whilst OFSTED's description tells us very little of vital interest about Fordingbridge Junior, it is clear that P4C is integral to the purposes of the school. The school has a clear statement of its vision that derived from a communal consultation many years ago. The school's aspirations are supported by three strategies that act as effective means. The first strategy is a well-articulated set of key skills and values that allow children to understand their development as characters and citizens. The second strategy is the use of coaching across the school as a way of distributing authority and responsibility. The third strategy is the regular use of P4C in the classroom, during staff meetings, and its dissemination as a practice across the local school cluster. These three strategies are deeply integrated so that P4C sessions form the spine of strategic, medium-term and weekly planning.

Whilst being taken for a tour of the school I had the fortune to witness an episode that for me typifies the impact of P4C across the school. In a Year 6 class the children were completing a paired co-operative task as a numeracy warm-up. Matching equivalent measures such as 1.5 litres equalling 1500 millilitres, the children were reporting their results back to the class. The focus of the class teacher was not on the correctness of maths but on the underlying *reasons* and explanations for the match. The children displayed resilience as they were happy to accept challenges to their reasoning and emotionally lost no 'face' in such challenges. The focus was on gaining understanding in the sense of Dewey's 'warranted generalisation'. Furthermore, children displayed emotional resilience and maturity using phrases such as 'I struggled with . . .' yet showing a concern to understand rather than alleviate their anxiety. As the class teacher engaged with the misconception, about multiplying by one thousand and what happens to the digits and the decimal point, she made a highly philosophical move: using the phrase 'What are you actually *doing*?' she moved the discussion away from the means (erroneously moving the decimal) to a consideration of ends (multiplying by one thousand) and in this way the child could see how to go on. This is one example of how language structure developed in P4C enquiries is impacting across the school.

What the head says

The head's involvement with P4C stemmed from visiting a school in the same authority. Seeing an example of good practice he notes that he was 'blown away' by the maturity and articulacy of the host school, which they attributed in part to their use of philosophy for children. He resolved to bring P4C back to his school and saw it as central to his plans for school improvement.

Initially the adoption was piecemeal and fragmentary, spread more through demonstration and exemplification rather than systematic professional development and based upon the head's expertise that derived from his level 1 training with the Society for Advancing Philosophical Enquiry and Reflection in Education (SAPERE, 2010). P4C sessions were sporadic and not integrated into the school's customs and practices. From the perspective of the headteacher, the development of Fordingbridge Junior School reflects the growth of his own expertise. By moving through levels one, two and three of the SAPERE scheme, he systematically developed the capacity of others in the school. As things stand at the time of writing all members of staff are trained to level one, two members are trained at level two, with the head a fully qualified SAPERE trainer in his own right. (In a later section exploring teachers' reflections on their practice I elaborate upon what the different levels mean to teacher practitioners.) As the expertise of the staff has developed so also has the level of embeddedness of P4C in the school's implementation of the National Curriculum.

I have repeated often in this chapter that P4C and its techniques are not necessarily educational aims in themselves. For those who do not perceive themselves as philosophers there need to be clearly defined and perceivable benefits to practising P4C. Yet, paradoxically, without an initial commitment to P4C, as a practice sustained by regular time and implementation with children in the classroom, those benefits may never manifest themselves. Fordingbridge Junior's implementation of P4C in the classroom reflects the head's growing understanding of the necessary commitment. Initially P4C in the school was less systematic and embedded than current practices. The second stage of implementation committed to making P4C a regular part of the school timetable. On a fortnightly basis P4C was practised in every class across the entirety of Key Stage 2 and now P4C is central to each class's weekly timetable with an inquiry often split over two weeks in order to value each stage of the process. The first week is spent exploring a stimulus or provocation that is tightly integrated into the school's topic-based medium-term planning cycle. After initial thoughts have been aired and questions raised the question for the following week is then arrived at.

The influence of the head's commitment to P4C has been felt well beyond the confines of Fordingbridge Junior School. The head has worked with the National College of School Leadership (NCSL), and his local authority, where he is well-supported by his local authority advisor, and his local cluster of schools. It is clear that from his experience with working with keen but isolated practitioners and whole school staffs in other contexts that there are lessons for any manager wishing to develop P4C as a means to promoting children's active participation in their own learning.

- School development ideally starts with systematic mass participation.
- The more integrated P4C is to the curriculum, the more successful is its adoption and impact on school improvement.
- The ethos of P4C will only embed when it is congruent with the school's values and vision.
- The head needs to be fully committed and ideally trained in P4C.
- P4C provides high quality accredited whole school CPD.

What the children say

In the course of researching this case study I spoke to children across the age range (7–11) from all year groups and asked them to talk to me about their experiences of P4C. Their responses could be organised into two main categories: first, the interest in the methods and means of P4C and second, the impact on their life in school and beyond.

The children welcomed the affordances to participate that P4C provided. Throughout the key stage they saw P4C as something different, interesting and quite fun where they sat in a circle and discussed philosophical questions. They valued ('We really like . . .') hearing other peoples' thinking and that others' thinking helped them think. They noted that hearing other people's thinking, whilst not necessarily changing their own minds, made their own thinking clearer and made it easier to be clearer with others about what they themselves meant. It was generally agreed that P4C had a significant impact on language. Children commented that in sports it helped them to think more quickly and more strategically, and in maths and literacy it gave them better words and access to them more quickly. For literacy there were specific skills of empathy developed that were enormously helpful for comprehension and creating stories. Outside of the classroom it was noted that it helped with friendship problems by distinguishing between persons and their opinions and by helping children to 'calm down'. One respondent noted that as they got older P4C helped them to think about what is important and why. Going beyond the school walls, P4C was perceived to help with homework and being more respectful in general. The eldest children observed the following: that without the group or class they could not do P4C; they could not do P4C on their own, yet the benefits are accrued to each individual; and that it helped their own individuation or development as a person. For the younger children it was particularly important that the mechanisms of choosing the next speaker were just and openly fair and like the older children they noted how in P4C 'teachers speak less' and children do the ideas, which was regarded as an unqualified good outcome! Notably the younger children were as adamant as the eldest in emphasising the importance of reasons and using sentence scaffolds such as 'I agree/disagree . . . because . . .' and 'I think . . . because . . .'. The youngest children placed a little more value on how P4C fostered imagination and memory, especially in writing.

What the teachers say

The following composite account is derived from four teachers at Fordingbridge Junior School. Two of the teachers were at the school at the outset of the P4C project and are now level 2 trained according to the SAPERE scheme. One teacher arrived at the school as a newly qualified teacher (NQT) and was quickly inducted into the practice at level 1. The deputy has been at the school for a long time and is also a level 1 practitioner of P4C. When interviewing the teachers I asked them to reflect on how P4C related to their practice as professionals employed in state schooling.

In general the teachers noticed that attending level 1 made a difference by transforming isolated techniques into a rigorous practice that gained from its deeper coherence and accordingly had more impact. As formal training at level 1 provided rigour and coherence so level 2 training provided a genuine understanding of both philosophical ideas and the theory and practice of facilitation. One might see that formal training gives insight into the norms and methods of the practice and it is by understanding the wider purposes of the practice that individual techniques (outlined in the Try this section) become increasingly effective and have impact on children's learning.

As teachers became more secure in the practice of P4C they noticed and valued the following in both themselves and in the children:

- experience of deeper thinking – going beyond the surface;
- uncertainty – getting away from right/wrong;
- living their thinking;
- thinking for themselves;
- going beyond the orthodox or conventional;
- having time/space to deliberate and change;
- length of response time;
- greater reflection and pausing;
- confidence to work something out in other contexts;
- speaking and listening skills;
- children's reading and writing attainment;
- changed expectations;
- increased use of justifications, reasoning and resilience and accounting for themselves;
- 'the children are active participants in their own learning';

- the children often surprised themselves;

- increased confidence;

- greater sense of belonging;

- increased care – for each other, and for the words spoken to one another both inside and outside the P4C setup;

- a quality of thoughtfulness;

- greater engagement – more children feeling safe to engage;

- less dependence on others, i.e. more autonomous and less likely to follow the lead of opinion-formers.

Most notably it was reported that P4C had changed perceptions and that somehow they were a 'wiser teacher' and that P4C needed to be 'at the heart of what we do' and that it 'related to all parts of the curriculum'. I would suggest that the development of this self-concept of wiser teacher derives explicitly from the statement by one teacher that they now 'explore concepts at the heart of learning'. The idea of the wise teacher is an old one; Aristotle referred to the practically wise person as someone who could go beyond technique and method to genuine expert understanding. One teacher called this 'weaving technique into deeper understanding'. It was interesting to record that teachers were keenly aware of when and when not to make a judgement. Also one person initially felt challenged as the group started to run itself but soon welcomed the increased opportunities this afforded her to listen, observe and think. Another commented that when the (questioning) genie was let out of the bottle there was no putting it back; P4C is a way of empowering children that cuts across everything they and we do.

Reflecting on the case study

- What value is placed upon P4C by
  - children;
  - teachers;
  - management; and
  - other interested parties?

- To what extent is the experience of Fordingbridge transferable to other contexts?

- What techniques and practices to you think are
  - most effective;
  - least effective.

- Does the previous answer change if you contrast a child-centred with a subject-centred ethos?

- How might you act differently having considered the Fordingbridge case study?

Case study 2: Gallions Primary School

According to OFSTED, Gallions Primary 'is larger than the average primary school and the number of pupils is increasing as the school moves from having two classes in each year group to having three. The school is in an area of very high economic disadvantage and a high proportion of pupils are known to be eligible for free school meals. Pupils come from a wide variety of ethnic origins, the largest group being of Bangladeshi heritage. The next largest groups are White British and Black African. A very high number of pupils speak English as an additional language. The proportion of pupils with special educational needs and/or disabilities is higher than the national average. Most of these difficulties relate to autistic spectrum disorder, speech and language difficulties and behavioural, emotional and social difficulties. There are also pupils with physical difficulties. The school has the Artsmark Gold award.'

The key word that helps us understand Gallions is *engagement*. Seventy-five per cent of children arriving at the school's nursery do not or cannot speak. The children's attitude to learning is poor and if left unaddressed can lead to 'dysfunctional classrooms'. However, by creating a rich language environment, rooted in a creative arts curriculum where every child learns an instrument and there is an artist in residence, and where P4C is introduced from nursery onwards, children flourish and become part of a community.

For one member of staff the story began in the late 1990s. The school had just opened and the class teacher was despairing about the Year 4 children's behaviour to one another. She contacted an education charity who suggested using P4C. Initially sceptical, this teacher noted how behaviour began to change within three weeks. Children were beginning to listen to one another and in another two weeks were responding to one another. The children were able to contribute and engage and the class teacher attributed this to P4C giving children a voice that was validated by their peers.

Talking to current staff and children in the school it was noticeable to me that the language and philosophy of Aristotle is now deeply embedded in the school. An earlier section of this chapter discusses the idea of practical wisdom – a way of understanding that goes beyond the simple following of rules and procedures. Everyone I spoke to embodied certain key features of practical wisdom. There was evidence of *deliberation*, of *choice-making*, and of *discrimination*. The latter is often seen as a negative characteristic of modern living but in its positive sense it means making distinctions, between courses of actions or things, and choosing according to some scale of values. Children of all ages pointed out how P4C makes them think more, go beyond the surface and reason and question. Most importantly it helps them see people differently. Parents I spoke to told me of the impact of the school running P4C sessions for them as parents. One described a stop-and-search carried out by a policeman outside the family home. Before P4C the child's simplistic labelling of the person being searched as 'a bad man' would not have been challenged by the parent. Now, the parent reported, they had the courage to converse in a deep way with their child about choices and that it was possible to look deeper into issues that would normally be pushed to one side. This engagement was not only felt between parent and child but between children and the wider world.

Now aspirations are raised and children are able to see themselves in different ways. Seven-year-olds now believe that they might become engineers and architects; that they might transcend the mundane.

Reflecting on the case study

- What value is placed upon P4C by
  - children;
  - teachers;
  - management; and
  - other interested parties?

- To what extent is the experience of St Gallions transferable to other contexts?

- What techniques and practices do you think are
  - most effective;
  - least effective.

- How might the form of schooling (integrated 2–11 provision) impact on change management in your context?

- How might you act differently having considered the St Gallions case study?

 TRY THIS

Try this 1: Building the ethos

Working together in a group and for the group lies at the heart of community of inquiry approaches. Activities and games can build group ethos by making and rehearsing protected speaking turns as well as being worthwhile educational activities in their own right.

Activity 1: The name game

The group stands in a circle. The facilitator starts by saying 'My name is . . . and I like . . .'choosing something alliterative and illustrating with an action, e.g. 'My name is Darren and I like dogs', whilst making a patting action (from experience I can guarantee that someone will like either lollipops or kites!). The next person in the circle must state all the previous names and likes and conclude with their own contribution. Continue around the circle and encouraging actions only for prompts.

Should the facilitator go last to demonstrate their willingness to be considered as a peer in the community?

Activity 2: Creative naming

The group stands in a circle. Start by taking a mundane object, such as a scarf, and placing it in the middle of the circle. Model stepping out into the middle of the circle and using this sentence scaffold, 'This is not a . . . , it is a . . .' (skipping rope, fairy hammock, dried up rainbow and so on). Each contribution must build on the previous invention by using the sentence scaffold.

Did you notice the temptation to label or evaluate the children's responses? When might celebration be substituted for evaluation?

Activity 3: Sorting and naming

Place nine random objects at the centre of a circle. Children take turns to select three objects from the nine. The child must state a rule whereby of the three objects two are categorised as similar and one is different from the other two. As a variation allow the rest of the children to guess the rule before it is explained.

This is an excellent activity for rehearsing higher order thinking moves. Be sensitive to opportunities to acknowledge such thinking moves in subsequent discourse.

Activity 4: Stilling

Stilling is an exercise in mindfulness. Although very much an individual activity, shared discussion of children's experiences of stilling and guided visualisation can be very affirming. Start by sitting together in a circle. Make sure everyone is sitting comfortably and is relaxed with feet on the floor and hands in laps. Get the children to concentrate on noticing their breathing. Focus attention on diaphragm breathing where the breath enters deep into the lungs, pushing the diaphragm down and tummies out. Once inhaling and exhaling in a relaxed comfortable manner, start to draw attention to the body – starting from toes and feet, building up through the torso to the head. Finish by slowly coming back into the room, making eye contact and smiling.

In a world that arguably values extroversion, developing and appreciating introverted private activities may be a year-long project. How might you manage the situation when someone 'spoils' the activity for everyone else?

Try this 2: Responding to a stimulus

At the heart of a community of inquiry is a commitment to creating meaning together. The key process underpinning the inquiry is an intellectual curiosity, a predisposition to understand, query, consider and question. After a while children learn to go beyond the surface appearance of things and realise that there are certain types of questions that are rich grounds for discussion. These are philosophical questions and a good stimulus will provide opportunities to generate not one but many of these questions.

Activity 1: Generating questions

Present an interesting object, read a story, show a video clip, consider a painting, listen to some music. Neither discuss the stimulus as a group nor try to establish some definitive interpretation. Instead, in small groups get children to generate as many questions as possible about the stimulus. Each group is then to pass these questions on to another group. Next, each group works with the new questions they have been given and classifies them into sets or categories. Examples of categories might be questions involving senses, questions that can be answered using science, questions with 'easy' answers or questions that seem impossible to answer. Get groups to explain how they classified their questions.

Is there a 'best' way to order and classify questions?

Activity 2: Carousel questioning

Split class into two equal-sized groups. One group forms an inner ring (facing outwards) and the other group faces them, forming an outer ring facing inwards. Each pair generates a question (e.g. about a stimulus or the current topic). The outer ring then rotates one space clockwise. In these new pairings repeat the questioning process, this time generating a new question different from that generated before by either member of the pairing. Repeat until a variety of questions have been generated.

In what way does it matter if the inner ring rotates rather than the outer?

Activity 3: Question conversations

In pairs conduct a conversation where only questions count as a valid utterance. Any non-questions uttered count as a point against the speaker. After three points pairs split and winners play winners, losers play losers. Make children aware that rising intonation may not necessarily indicate that a question has been asked!

This will need modelling as the degree of self-reflection is considerable. It is worth considering what grammatical features of a question to look out for.

Activity 4: Diamond nine

In pairs or small groups generate nine questions in response to a stimulus. Write questions on separate cards or pieces of paper. Order questions in a diamond (five rows of 1, 2, 3, 2, 1 cards in a row). For younger children give an organising principle, e.g. top row = hardest to answer; bottom row = easiest to answer. Older children can create their own principle.

Are some organising principles better than others?

Activity 5: Fishbowl

The class decides on a list of questions, and then one group discusses and chooses the 'best' question whilst the remaining children sit around the group and watch. Comments can be offered at the end about the reasons used for choosing questions.

How might a 'philosophical' question differ from an 'empirical' one?

Activity 6: Snowballing

Starting in pairs decide on a question. Pairs form groups of four and choose one of the two questions giving reasons for rejecting one pair's question. The groups of four then double into groups of eight. Once consensus is reached the groups report back together in plenary.

Is it necessary to reach consensus on the substance of the question or is it acceptable to agree to disagree?

Activity 7: Surveying

In small groups use questions to create an interview schedule. Conduct surveys and discuss in plenary what types of question (e.g. open/closed) produce what types of response.

Even at a young age the ethics and etiquette of asking questions ought to be considered from the outset. What is private and what is public, and what may be asked about each, and how?

Activity 8: Election posters

Use questions to create visual information in the form of a poster. The children elect which question is to be discussed. These are then displayed on walls and then children tour the room viewing all the contributions.

What are the success criteria by which a question is judged?

Try this 3: Facilitating enquiries

The art of facilitation is not easy. It requires thinking and acting differently from conventional classroom practice, yet when incorporated into practice practitioners notice a transformation in classroom relationships. I have mentioned already the necessity of some form of training in order to create a holistic understanding of P4C. Nevertheless, the following activities are useful techniques to begin fostering understanding.

Activity 1: Sentence scaffolds

Using simple sentence scaffolds that emphasise relationships between participants can help children take ownership of the inquiry. Examples include, 'I agree/disagree with X because . . .' and 'I think/feel X and my reasons are . . .'

Does a scaffolded sentence promote critical thinking at the expense of creative collaborative, caring or other forms of thinking?

Activity 2: Turn-taking

When discussing together in the circle, children indicate they want to speak by a thumbs-up sign resting their hand on their knee. This stops any frantic hand-waving and primal 'ooks' whilst helping concentration by preventing tired arms. Similarly a talking object such as a shell can be passed around. Turn cards can be provided. These indicate how many more speaking turns you have left. A ball of wool can be passed from speaker to speaker to build a physical web describing the pattern of speaking turns. Alternatively speakers may be given the right to choose the next speaker whether they are indicating they want to be chosen or not. At any point the inquiry may wish to conduct a 'meta-discussion' about how the inquiry is being conducted.

Research is clear that it is easy to overlook certain groups of children despite the best will in the world. How does this activity help you and the children monitor (un) conscious patterns of discrimination?

Activity 3: Active listening techniques

How do you and the children know they are being listened to? Maintaining eye-contact, mirroring the speaker's body language, using paraphrase and summary, acknowledgement by nods and 'uh-huh' can all encourage speakers to elaborate upon their original contribution. Repeating the last few words of the speaker's previous sentence allows thought time and a fresh set of utterances:

'. . . so I think that all animals have minds because my cat knows how I am feeling' 'knows how you are feeling?' [Rising intonation mirroring how questions sound]

'Yes, because when I am sad she always comes over for stroking and this cheers me up.'

Are active listening techniques manipulative?

Activity 4: The power of silence

Silence is a rare commodity in the classroom, particularly the rich powerful silence that can occur in an inquiry. Often silence is associated with dominance and power; the teacher has enforced silence for no good reason except maintaining order or their sanity. Yet silence can be warm, comforting and profound. Where no-one is compelled to speak, or where a contribution has been offered that provokes thought and deliberation, then the facilitator needs to hold back from inviting more speech and show that they are comfortable with silence.

How much silence is enough? Should there be a signal to indicate that the silence is unhelpful and the facilitator ought to step in or should this be left to practical judgement?

SUMMARY

This chapter has explored what it means to think philosophically, and how philosophical thinking can be facilitated through the development of techniques described in this and other chapters. This is a practice that requires training and work with others in order for matters 'to come together' but it is possible to start using some of the suggestions from the Try this section. Philosophy for Children is a pedagogical programme that is participatory to its very core. The community of inquiry changes the relationships between teachers and children and demands different attitudes as well as skills and techniques. At its best, as we have seen in the two schools, it engages children, changes their behaviour and makes them think differently about the world. Not only that but it provides a sense of agency and a belief in the power of reason to make better worlds now and in the future.

FURTHER READING

The power of games and group activities to build ethos and group harmony cannot be underestimated. All the following provide a rich source and variety of activities that can build the group's effectiveness.

Brandes, D. and Phillips, H. (1979) *Gamesters' Handbook*. London: Hutchinson.
    The *Gamesters* series provide a whole raft of classroom suitable games.

Fisher, R. (1997) *Games for Thinking*. Oxford: Nash Pollock.
Fisher has produced a whole raft of supporting books using stories, games, and poems for thinking.

Rawlins, G. and Rich, J. (1985) *Look, Listen and Trust*. Basingstoke: Macmillan Education.
This resource is a set of drama-based activities that can help children become more accustomed to one another, more trusting whilst still being fun.

Stone, M. K. (1995) *Don't Just Do Something, Sit There: Developing Children's Spiritual Awareness*. Norwich: Religious and Moral Education Press.
This is an invaluable resource, often available from diocesan educational offices. It offers a programme of stilling and guided visualisation activities.

There are plenty of examples of scripts for stilling on the web, e.g. www.ely.anglican.org/education/schools/collective_worship/pdf/StillingExercises.pdf

For good general introductions to P4C in all its varieties see:

Fisher, R. (2003) *Teaching Thinking: Philosophical Enquiry in the Classroom*, 2nd edn. London: Continuum.
Fisher gives a rounded perspective on P4C and how it might be incorporated into practice.

Haynes, J. (2008) *Children as Philosophers: Learning Through Enquiry and Dialogue in the Primary Classroom*, 2nd edn. London: Routledge.
Haynes is long-established practitioner in P4C. She is well-known for her ground-breaking work with Karin Murris on the worth and validity of children's picture books as richly philosophical stimuli for inquiry.

Lipman, M. (2003) *Thinking in Education*, 2nd edn. Cambridge: Cambridge University Press.
Lipman wrote many books about P4C. *Thinking in Education* is a good examination of some of the deeper tensions and issues in education that P4C attempts to address and redress.

McCall, C. C. (2009) *Transforming Thinking: Philosophical Inquiry in the Primary and Secondary Classroom*. London: Routledge.
Of particular worth in McCall's account is her critical examination in Chapter six of the differences between different forms of enquiry with children.

Saran, R. and Neisser, B. (2004) *Enquiring Minds: Socratic Dialogue in Education*. Stoke on Trent: Trentham Books.
Socratic Dialogue tends to be more popular on continental Europe than in the UK. There is much of interest in the approach that stands in useful counterpoint to contemporary UK practice.

Splitter, L. J. and Sharp, A. M. (1995) *Teaching for Better Thinking: The Classroom Community of Inquiry*. Melbourne: ACER.
Ann Sharp joined with Matthew Lipman early in the development of P4C. Arguably she changed in significant ways certain emphases on how thinking and conduct in enquiry might be valued. The book she co-wrote with Lawrence Splitter is full of rich, practical material.

For books that relate philosophy for children to wider issues in thinking skills and childhood education see:

Kennedy, D. (2006) *The Well of Being: Childhood, Subjectivity and Education*. New York: SUNY. David Kennedy's book is notable for urging us to think more radically about the ethical implications for how we are to be with children. This is a more general book but fantastic for stimulating thinking about the ethos of our schools and our classrooms.

Johnson, S. and Siegel, H. (2010) *Teaching Thinking Skills*, 2nd edn. Key Debates in Educational Policy, edited by Christopher Winch. London: Continuum. Deriving from the Philosophy of Education Society of Great Britain's policy series, this book is a serious and sustained critique of current psychologistic models of thinking.

Quinn, V. (1997) *Critical Thinking in Young Minds*. London: David Fulton. Although not specifically concerned with P4C, Quinn's book is an excellent perspective on critical thinking from a holistic perspective.

Stables, A. (2008) *Childhood and the Philosophy of Education: An Anti-Aristotelian Perspective*. London: Continuum. The notion of what it is to be a child varies across time and space. In modern western cultures we have not always thought of children the way we do now. Nor are children viewed the same in all places of the world. Stables' book is an enormously important analysis of why it is that we view children the way we do in contemporary times.

SAPERE (2010) Society for Advancing Philosophical Enquiry and Reflection in Education, www.sapere.org.uk/ (accessed 27 April 2012). SAPERE have been active in UK education for over 20 years. Catherine McCall featured in a BBC documentary called *Socrates for Six-year-olds* highlighting the work she had been doing in America and Scotland. As a result of that programme a group of educators set up SAPERE, whose influence can be seen in the case studies mentioned earlier in the chapter.

Gallions Primary School's website is at www.gallions.newham.sch.uk/ The school has produced a DVD, *Thinking Allowed*, that is a step-by-step guide to the P4C approach.

REFERENCES

Brandes, D. and Phillips, H. (1979) *Gamesters' Handbook*. London: Hutchinson.
Fisher, R. (1997) *Games for Thinking*. Oxford: Nash Pollock.
Fisher, R. (2003) *Teaching Thinking: Philosophical Enquiry in the Classroom*, 2nd edn. London: Continuum.
Green, J. (2010) *Education, Professionalism and the Quest for Accountability: Hitting the Target but Missing the Point*. London: Routledge.
Harris, S. (2007) *The Governance of Education: How Neo-Liberalism is Transforming Policy and Practice*. London: Continuum.
Haynes, J. (2008) *Children as Philosophers: Learning through Enquiry and Dialogue in the Primary Classroom*, 2nd edn. London: Routledge.
Heilbronn, R. (2008) *Teacher Education and the Development of Practical Judgement*. London: Continuum.
Johnson, S. and Siegel, H. (2010) *Teaching Thinking Skills*, 2nd edn. Key Debates in Educational Policy, edited by Christopher Winch. London: Continuum.
Kennedy, D. (2006) *The Well of Being: Childhood, Subjectivity and Education*. New York: SUNY.
Lipman, M. (2003) *Thinking in Education*, 2nd edn. Cambridge: Cambridge University Press.

Lipman, M. (2008) *A Life Teaching Thinking*. Montclair, NJ: Institute for the Advancement of Philosophy for Children.

McCall, C. C. (2009) *Transforming Thinking: Philosophical Inquiry in the Primary and Secondary Classroom*. London: Routledge.

Olssen, M. (2010) *Liberalism, Neoliberalism, Social Democracy: Thin Communitarian Perspectives on Political Philosophy and Education*. London: Routledge.

Quinn, V. (1997) *Critical Thinking in Young Minds*. London: David Fulton.

Rawlins, G. and Rich, J. (1985) *Look, Listen and Trust*. Basingstoke: Macmillan Education.

SAPERE (2010) Society for Advancing Philosophical Enquiry and Reflection in Education, www.sapere.org.uk/ (accessed 27 April 2012).

Saran, R. and Neisser, B. (2004) *Enquiring Minds: Socratic Dialogue in Education*. Stoke on Trent: Trentham Books.

Splitter, L. J. and Sharp, A. M. (1995) The Practice of Philosophy in the Classroom, in *Teaching for Better Thinking: The Classroom Community of Inquiry*. Melbourne: ACER.

Stables, A. (2008) *Childhood and the Philosophy of Education: An Anti-Aristotelian Perspective*. London: Continuum.

Stone, M. K. (1995) *Don't Just Do Something, Sit There: Developing Children's Spiritual Awareness*. Norwich: Religious and Moral Education Press.

CHAPTER 11

TALKING AND LEARNING THROUGH LANGUAGE AND LITERACY

Carrie Ansell and Tor Foster

Thought is the blossom; language the bud;
action the fruit behind it.

Ralph Waldo Emerson, 1803–1882, American poet, essayist, philosopher

---

Chapter overview

The chapter will explore the principles and features of dialogic teaching and the context of talk in classrooms. Links will be made with key initiatives in the domain of talk from the National Oracy Project to developments in the nature of exploratory talk and interthinking. We will argue that talk is the foundation of literacy learning and that it is essential for teachers to create a classroom culture that puts children at the heart of learning. Finally we will examine the role of talk in bilingual learning and in reading, writing and spelling. Two case studies, where schools have embraced an early years' philosophy throughout the school, will be used to demonstrate how a focus on dialogue and listening can potentially transform literacy practices.

INTRODUCTION

We read an Ofsted report recently where a lesson was described as 'satisfactory'. The advice from the inspector was that the teacher should limit the opportunities the pupils had to discuss ideas so that they had longer to complete their writing. Now, without having witnessed this lesson, we can't make a judgement about the value of this advice, but it seems possible that the inspector may have been missing a trick.

Without the opportunity to talk through ideas, how could the children know what they wanted to say? How could they extend their thinking and refine their ideas, if not by listening and talking to each other? How could the teacher judge when and how to intervene to support the children's learning? It's also worth considering that in the world beyond school – the 'real' world – it will undoubtedly be oral skills that will be pre-eminent in affording access to successful lives and careers. Our argument here is not that writing isn't important, but that talk and active listening are the bedrock on which other literacy skills are built.

It is our belief that dialogic talk affords the greatest cognitive potential for learners, allowing children to exchange ideas and become joint enquirers. When children become 'agents of their own thinking' (Fisher, 2009) they are enabled to find their own voices. We imagine a setting in which the pedagogy of dialogic teaching is stimulating and engaging for all learners, resulting in increased classroom interaction and extended thinking opportunities. It is a place where children are truly 'thinking together' (Mercer and Dawes, 2008) creating a 'community of learners' (Cazden, 2001).

Classroom ethos is central to establishing successful dialogic teaching. What the teacher is aiming to set up is an environment in which there is a culture of questioning, probing and deep thinking. It is a place where it is understood that talk can be exploratory – a way of trying out or testing new ideas. The medium of talk is valued for its flexibility; it is seen as a way of 'thinking aloud'. Ideas can be revised, extended, improved or rejected. In such a classroom, risk-taking is encouraged, and mistakes are acknowledged and used for further dialogue. This could be intimidating to many children unless careful groundwork has taken place. All participants in the dialogue need to feel secure and valued in a setting that is respectful, trusting and inclusive.

The teacher, too, may feel threatened operating in such a democratic space, for it requires her to loosen the reins and be open to genuine collaborative endeavour, perhaps not knowing exactly where the learning will lead. Another concern the teacher might have is the difficulty of providing concrete evidence of children's learning if there is more talk and less writing. Where is the 'proof' to show to parents, governors or inspectors? How can she capture and record the essence of the pupils' learning so that she can validate judgements that demonstrate pupil progress?

In the Reggio Emilia approach to learning, teachers and children act as co-constructors of learning and talk together in meaningful relationships. The teacher's role is to facilitate talk and deepen understanding through considered questioning which opens up children's thinking. Teachers document key moments of children's talk to make visible their hypotheses, imagination and creativity. It is this pedagogy of listening and relationships that is the hallmark of Reggio Emilia. Teachers listen to the words and communication of children and try to provoke cognitive growth. The approach takes a socio-constructivist view of learning (Edwards et al., 2012). Children are encouraged to respond and express themselves using their 'hundred languages' through gestures, dramatic play, storytelling and emerging writing. In this way, dialogue, in Reggio terms, is used broadly and challenges our thinking of what dialogue is. Children can dialogue with spaces, materials and light (Filippini et al., 2008). Later on when we examine a case study school that has been inspired by this approach, you will see how the children and teachers are together 'in dialogue' with the city of Bath.

Of course, dialogic teaching is not specific to language and literacy; as a pedagogical tool it applies to all subject areas. But language is the medium through which thinking develops, and literacy is the subject where we specifically address children's ability to express their thoughts (both orally and in writing), reflect on their own ideas and those of others and, through debate and argument, refine their understandings. So, in teaching language and literacy, we want to adopt teaching approaches that encourage children to become reflective, confident and discerning speakers, readers and writers who recognise the power and the pleasure of words in wide-ranging contexts. It is vital, especially in a climate of easy access to information on the internet and media representation and misrepresentation, that children develop the skills of discrimination and reasoned argument. We believe they will do this best in a class where dialogue is valued.

In our case studies towards the end of this chapter we describe two schools where headteachers and their staff have taken bold steps towards achieving these aims.

DIALOGIC TALK IN LITERACY LEARNING

Examining the literature

During our early teaching careers in multicultural settings we had the good fortune to work collaboratively with teachers who were passionate about oracy in classrooms. One of the aims of the National Oracy Project, set up in 1987, was to promote the role of talk in thinking processes through active learning, and this culminated in the work of Kate Norman: Thinking Voices (1992). Perhaps the greatest impact of the National Oracy project was to influence the pedagogies of schools with children from diverse linguistic backgrounds. The project involved over half of England's local education authorities (Norman, 1992).

Why mention this seemingly dated national initiative? Is this still relevant for today's language and literacy teacher? The idea that talk is essential for children's thinking and learning, indeed that talk is the foundation of learning (Halliday, 1975), was transformational of practice at that time and continues to be influential today.

The 2012 draft English curriculum with its emphasis on reading and writing and prescriptive content and pedagogies, begged the question: What happened to these transformational practices that inspired creative approaches to classroom talk? Despite Robin Alexander's contribution to the initial consultation on the new curriculum, where he emphasised the importance of dialogue and classroom talk, there is little evidence of speaking and listening in the new programmes of study. Spoken language in the new English curriculum is primarily to be encouraged for the purposes of developing vocabulary, learning spellings, grammar, and reading and writing skills. Developing thinking as an important aspect of English in its own right has been subsumed, arguably due to the growing emphasis on learning that is measurable and easily assessable. Ironically, it has been shown that children who talk and actively engage with learning are more able to attain higher results in SATs (Mercer and Dawes, 2008).

Barnes and Todd (1977) coined the term 'school knowledge' and 'action knowledge' to distinguish between talk that is divorced from children's lives and talk that is relevant and meaningful to their lives. They suggested that learners, by being involved in learning through enquiry and using their 'action knowledge', would be more engaged in productive thinking. Their highly influential research suggested that when children are working together in groups, they are more likely to be engaged in open-ended discussion and reasoned argument. Barnes described such 'exploratory talk' as hesitant and incomplete as it enables the speaker to try out ideas, to hear how they sound, to see what others make of them and arrange information and ideas into different patterns (Barnes, cited in Mercer and Hodgkinson, 2008). Children may use exploratory talk in literacy, for example, when making sense of poetry or gaining insights into texts. Learners build on their existing knowledge to make meaning. In this way, literacy learning is social and talking may draw on children's popular culture. An example of this is when children engage in dialogue using the EXIT (Extended Interactions with Texts) model of interacting with non-fiction texts (Wray and Lewis, 1997).

Dialogic teaching

It was Sinclair and Coulthard (1975) who first described the common classroom interaction that became known as the 'three part exchange'. In this, there is an initiation (I), usually a question, followed by a response from the children (R) and finally a follow-up (F) or some feedback by the teacher. A very simple example of this in a literacy lesson could be the following exchange:

Teacher: Where do Danny and his father live?
Child: In a gypsy caravan.
Teacher: That's right.

It has been argued (Alexander, 2008) that for classroom talk to promote active participation and learning, there should be a move away from IRF exchanges towards dialogue. Alexander acknowledged that 'dialogic teaching' is work in progress, with its original concept continually evolving in response to evidence from research and practice. Dialogic teaching is underpinned by a Vygotskian approach to learning, which takes the view that language learning is a social process (Vygotsky, 1978). Children learn the spoken language with the support of adults, other children and the wider culture around them. The role of these 'others' with whom the children interact, is to scaffold (Wood et al., 1976) language learning through the use of carefully considered prompts, questions, modelling and resources.

Alexander draws a distinction between everyday language acquisition and interactions that engender learning for a 'specific cultural purpose'. An example of this in English could be the learning of a specific genre of spoken language, such as discussion and debate, where teachers might scaffold children's understanding and draw on their prior knowledge and home literacies. Ideally, in a reciprocal dialogue with children, teachers would familiarise them with all aspects of the genre, including vocabulary, grammar and discourse features of text. Teachers and children would also talk together about the linguistic and cultural conventions of discussion texts.

Bilingual learners

This notion of the difference between everyday language and language that has a specific cultural purpose is mirrored to an extent by Cummins' theory of language interdependence (Cummins, 2000). He distinguishes between basic and interpersonal communication skills and cognitive and academic language. Bilingual teaching has always emphasised the importance of dialogue and classroom talk that scaffolds language learning. The focus here, however, is on children drawing on their first language to support the acquisition of the second language, or what Cummins calls the 'CUP', or common underlying principle. To take the example given earlier a little further – if children are already familiar with the language of discussion in their first language, the theory is that they will have the cognitive and linguistic knowledge on which to 'hook' the second language. Cummins' theory explains why it is so important for children to continue to develop their first language alongside English as a second language, rather than be taught using a 'subtractive' model, which takes the view that the second language will eventually replace the first language. Recent bilingual learning theory has now adopted a more transformative 'third space' approach to learning English (Kelly, 2010) in which children's home language and culture can merge with that of the school to create new language and literacy.

Features of dialogic talk

Let's continue to focus for now on dialogic talk and teaching as expounded by Alexander (2008). The word 'dialogic', according to Alexander, replaces vague terminology such as 'interactive teaching' with its limited emphasis on developing pace and progression in learning. Of course, these aspects of teaching have a place in whole class teaching, but Alexander argues that it is the quality and dynamics of talk that are paramount. Dialogic teaching can occur within any organisational framework, such as pairs or groups, although there is a widespread misconception that it only refers to whole class teaching. Oral contributions, according to Alexander, need to be reflected upon, discussed and argued about and the dialogic element involves getting learners to do this (Alexander, 2008).

Dialogic talk should be:

- *collective*: teachers and children address learning tasks together, whether as a group or as a class, rather than in isolation;

- *reciprocal*: teachers and children listen to each other, share ideas and consider alternative perspectives;

- *supportive*: children articulate their ideas freely, without fear of embarrassment over 'wrong' answers, and they help each other to reach common understandings;

- *cumulative*: teachers and children build on their own and each other's ideas and chain them into coherent lines of thinking and enquiry;

- *purposeful*: teachers plan and facilitate dialogic teaching with particular educational goals in mind.

(Alexander, 2008)

The QCA Opening Up Talk CD (QCA, 2005) aimed to exemplify some of these features of dialogic talk. A clip of film showed a sustained argument between a teacher and some children in a Year 5 English lesson. It involved an exchange of ideas in which the teacher challenged the child's thinking and reasoning, through cumulative questioning and discussion. The teacher/child exchange that unfolded made uncomfortable viewing and listening for some teachers and you may argue that the style employed could inhibit children in offering their ideas. In many ways, the clip did not demonstrate fully how teachers could foster a 'community of enquiry' that begins by getting children to question a given stimulus or respond to a provocation by collaborating in thoughtful discussion (Wells, 2009). We lean towards the ideas of Wegerif (2010) who states that: 'Dialogues that do not promote the development of thinking should not be called educational at all.'

Exploratory talk and inter thinking

Mercer (2000) suggests that for both a teacher and learner to talk and learn effectively, they must create a shared communicative space known as the IDZ (intermental development zone). This is a further development on Vygotsky's idea of the zone of proximal development as it recognises that, although the talk that teachers and learners do together still means that the teacher is guiding the learner, both teacher *and* learner are involved together in a process that Mercer calls 'inter thinking'.

Mercer defined the kind of talk that helps learners to solve problems and develop a shared understanding as 'exploratory talk'. He argues that ground rules for talk are essential for this collective thinking and exploratory talk to occur.

Ground rules for exploratory talk:

- Partners engage critically but constructively with each other's ideas.

- Everyone participates.

- Tentative ideas are treated with respect.

- Ideas offered for joint consideration may be challenged.

- Opinions are sought and considered before decisions are jointly made.

- Knowledge is made publicly accountable (and so reasoning is visible in the talk).

- Challenges are justified and alternative ideas or understandings are offered.

(Mercer and Dawes, 2008)

Mercer's ground rules for talk would provide a useful starting point for teachers who want to establish talk for language and literacy. Expectations of what constitutes successful group talk will need to be made explicit, with the teacher discussing and modelling examples of exploratory talk. It would also provide a useful checklist for evaluating how well groups have worked together to develop understanding.

Classroom talk and social inclusion

Classroom talk is considered essential in engaging pupils in meaning-making and in developing pupils' understandings in language and literacy. Recent research into the effect that the social-economic status of pupils has on influencing teacher expectation, pedagogical practices and quality interactions in literacy is illuminating (Harris and Williams, 2012). In this study, the suggestion is that teachers may actually give more 'wait time' to affluent groups and that open questioning is more successful when children demonstrate that they have the 'cultural capital' (Bourdieu, 1977) required by teachers. The study shows that children's responses during book talk sessions with the teacher make visible the extent to which they know the rules of the literacy game and the expected discourse in this particular cultural context. Children from poorer social backgrounds may not make the expected responses, despite offering potentially valuable ideas that could be picked up, interpreted and validated by the teacher. It comes as no surprise that children from affluent backgrounds are more versed in dominant discourse patterns used in classrooms. Teachers need, therefore, to be aware of discourse patterns that have the potential to exclude learners from contributing to the dialogue.

Creative dialogues

Creative dialogue, as suggested by Fisher (2009), is underpinned by dialogic learning principles. According to Fisher, dialogue becomes creative when it allows for playful and divergent ideas. Creative dialogue is purposeful, but may veer off from a set agenda. Dialogic talk in literacy should put the learner at the heart of learning. Creative use of questioning and dialogic alternatives to questioning, such as providing a challenging statement or prompt, may stimulate curiosity and new ways of thinking. Creative talk allows children to 'possibility think' and become imaginative storytellers. Cremin (2009) has created a framework for creativity in literacy that fosters playful use of language and deep engagement in collaboration with authors, poets and storytellers. She asserts that creativity is more likely to develop in dialogic conditions. She also argues that personal oral stories deserve a central role in the curriculum and that teachers should allow children the time and space to tell their stories, which are key to their identity formation. Oral storytelling has been shown to have a marked impact on children's literacy (Grugeon and Gardner, 2000).

Book talk

Dialogic book talk (Whitehurst et al., 1988) is a language and literacy pedagogy that allows young children's rich dialogue to develop. It can also be developed successfully with families in order to bridge the link between home and school literacy. The idea is that children and adults genuinely listen to each other's responses to a text and expand on their thoughts, reinterpreting the text in the process. It is a way of enabling children to share books, connect with their own experiences and develop their language and literacy use (Whitehurst et al., 1988). Interestingly, multiple readings around a text were shown to be particularly effective in allowing for a context in which to ask meaningful questions. Perhaps the way forward in terms of enacting quality dialogue around children's texts would be to encourage teachers to get children to elaborate on their responses, even if some unexpected responses initially 'throw' the teacher off course. Skidmore (cited in Goodwin, 2001) called these opportunities 'critical turning points' in the unfolding discourse that can lead to higher levels of literate thinking. In this way, children can have the opportunity to explain their reasons behind their thinking, challenge other views about the text and ask questions of each other. Conversely, a limited view of reading comprehension activities around texts may reinforce the restricted access to inclusive critical thinking, appreciation and evaluation of texts that we previously discussed.

The 'Tell Me' approach

Chambers (2011) emphasises the importance of talk in reading contexts through asking particular kinds of questions. The approach originally stemmed from a quest to find an alternative to always asking a question beginning with 'Why?' Hence, the phrase 'Tell me . . .' emerged. Chambers suggested that there is also a strong correlation between the richness of the reading environment and the richness of the talk around texts. He made a useful distinction between 'formal talk', which is considered discussion around texts, and 'book gossip', which is chat between peers. He argued that teachers need to prepare carefully the questions they will ask around texts using a framework that divides questions into 'basic', 'general' or 'special'. A basic question would be: Is there anything you liked about this book? Was there anything that puzzled you? A general question may be: Have you read any other stories like this? Has anything that happens in this book ever happened to you? A special question may be: Where did the story happen? Who was narrating the story? How do we know? (See Chapter 7 for examples of these questions and how they can be applied to digital literacy.) The chapter on questioning has already emphasised the important role that the adult plays in asking open questions and giving 'wait time' to develop quality dialogue and extend children's imaginations.

Reciprocal teaching and reading

Dialogic talk has at its core the principles of reciprocal teaching (Palincsar and Brown, 1984). This is a powerful teaching technique that essentially involves a dialogue between learners and adults to enable joint construction of text meaning. Different members of a small group may assume the role of teacher. Reciprocal teaching was originally intended for pupils who had a gap between their decoding skills and comprehension and it comprises four steps: predicting, clarifying, questioning and comprehension. In reciprocal teaching, dialogue is the medium for exploring texts in depth. There is a high level of modelling and scaffolding from the teacher as she talks aloud the thinking processes involved in the four steps. Learners then follow the teacher's example, with the aim of their becoming active readers who are self-aware, thereby developing their meta-cognitive and thinking skills. In a sense, the children are learning about literacy with intent. Eventually a reader should apply the steps to their own independent reading.

The role of talk in writing

It is common practice to value the role of talk in preparing children for writing. Typically, a teacher might present a text to the class, talk through the conventions of the chosen text form, model aspects of the writing process, and draw on children's ideas to share with the class, perhaps recording them as a visual prompt. Success criteria, prepared by the teacher in advance or generated collaboratively with the class, might be used to provide additional support. A period of quiet writing follows and the draft or finished product might be self, peer or teacher evaluated in relation to the prescribed criteria.

It is our contention that talk has a much bigger role to play, if children are to be freed up to produce the 'vigorous, committed, honest and interesting writing' that the National Curriculum (1989) made reference to. Unfortunately, even then, it was recognised that capturing the essence of such writing so that it could be measured was a difficult task and so these words were omitted from the National Curriculum level descriptions.

If we are aiming to encourage honest and interesting writing, we want our pupils to find their own voices, not merely be skilled in imitating the voices of others and meeting pre-determined learning intentions and success criteria. Grainger (2005) refers to 'voice and verve' in writing and we believe that this more adventurous, playful and lively writing only becomes possible if dialogic teaching and learning underpins the process. Opportunities for talk should be fundamental to all parts of writing lessons; interactive discourse has a part to play before, during and after writing. Britton (1970: 29) described a situation where each piece of writing 'floats on a sea of talk', and it is that kind of classroom that we commend.

In supporting children in finding their own voices we need to encourage 'possibility thinking' (Craft, 2000). Initially, the children and the teacher will engage in generative talk where ideas, opinions and possibilities are discussed, played with and tried out in a 'conversational context' (Grainger, 2005) As mentioned earlier in this chapter, an essential precursor to working in such a context is the establishment of a trusting and respectful environment where writers put forward their tentative thoughts, secure in the knowledge that their ideas will be listened to, supported and valued.

At this stage, the teacher might draw on drama activities such as freeze frames, hot seating or short improvised scenes to allow children to explore in greater depth possibilities that arise from the text. This kind of physical engagement, where mind and body are working together in 'doing', provides a welcome extension to what can otherwise become a rather formulaic and predictable process in writing. Working in small groups, the children will listen to each other's views, hear alternative perspectives, further their own ideas and discuss ways forward. This process of selecting and refining ideas, to which drama can contribute, is an essential part of the compositional process, supporting writers in finding their unique and authentic voices.

Once the writing is underway, the dialogue about writing becomes more reflective and critical. Young writers learn from giving and receiving critical comments. It is an essential aspect of the creative process. Commenting on the writing of others allows them to adopt the role of reflective 'critical friends' and hearing the views of others helps them to write with an awareness of the reader – their audience. The teacher has a pivotal role here in modelling respectful, honest and supportive comments. She also has to ensure that opportunities are planned during the writing process for children to hear and respond to their own and others' writing. Initially, this could involve providing a framework to scaffold these constructive critical conversations. But, as children become inducted into the community of writers, acquiring a kind of 'guild knowledge' (Sadler, 1989: 129), fewer supportive props are needed. In addition to listening to the comments of their teacher and their peers, these writers are listening to their inner voices as they read, re-read and re-draft in response to their own and others' critical reflections.

The balance has shifted, from a situation where reflective critical comments on a finished piece of writing are part of the review process, to one where an on-going dialogue impacts on the writing when it is most useful – during the creative process. Rather than saving for 'next time' any learning that ensues from feedback from teacher and peers, the writer can take account of the comments as s/he crafts the piece.

Talk for spelling

Learning to spell is an essential aspect of developing writing skills, but so often it is taught in a lack-lustre way. Teaching strategies may include spelling lists, some spelling rules, 'look, cover, write, check', and then there is the weekly spelling test. Children either love it, because they have a good visual memory and they regularly score high marks, or they dread it, because it confirms their status as poor spellers. How can talk contribute to a classroom where children are more engaged by spelling and therefore more successful learners? Imagine a classroom where there is a buzz of excitement when a spelling pattern is identified, where links are made between known and unknown words, where children and teachers are fascinated by words, their meanings, their origins and their spellings. Imagine a school where the whole community is engaged in a joyful journey of discovery about words.

Tony Martin (2010) is a convincing advocate of talk for spelling in both Key Stage 1 and Key Stage 2. At the heart of the strategies and activities he suggests is the belief that learning is a social and collaborative activity, and that is as true for spelling as for any other aspect of English. The benefits of such talk, where children listen to each other and share their knowledge and understanding, leads to ideas being built upon collectively, creating 'a chain of thinking' (Alexander, 2008). Martin also illustrates how drama activities can become an integral part of spelling lessons, embedding children's learning about words using kinaesthetic approaches.

TWO CASE STUDIES

The following case studies have remarkable similarities in that both schools have taken early years' principles of practice and philosophy and have introduced these throughout the school. The challenge they face is to steer the fine path between accountability and measuring learning outcomes, and innovative practices that celebrate childhood and 'allow children to be children'.

Case study I: St John's C of E Primary School, Midsomer Norton

The school is a larger-than-average primary school where the proportion of children eligible for free school meals is below average. The vast majority of pupils are of White British heritage and the proportion with special educational needs and/or disabilities is below average.

Despite its lack of obvious difficulties or challenges, the school did not present the vibrant learning community that the headteacher was eager to foster. The senior management identified loss of learning time as an area on which the staff should focus. So the whole school began a journey towards a different, more exciting and engaging curriculum where every part of the day, including the dinner break, offered enriching opportunities for active learning.

The staff agreed that there was much to be learned from the Foundation Stage classes where children showed independence and a joy in active learning, and talk was the medium through which this took place. They decided to try to replicate this good practice throughout the school, using the EYFS six areas of learning as a basis for curriculum planning.

St John's adopted a form of curriculum planning where children were central to the process. Working with the 'plan, do, review' framework, the teachers give the children the task of coming up with the 'big questions' when planning their topics. Typically, the learning begins with a provocation or stimulus and then, through dialogue, the children generate the questions that provide the framework for the learning. This participation in the planning has given the children ownership, resulting in greater commitment to their learning. At the end of the topic, the learning is celebrated in a variety of ways – a book, a drama production, an event, an exhibition, a visit – and parents are often involved at this stage.

Another development at St Johns relates to the teaching of Communication, Language and Literacy. The school has been involved with The Write Team. As well as in-service training for teachers, The Write Team provided poets and writers who worked with classes to encourage high quality writing.

The school introduced a third innovation, whereby the outdoor space is divided into five zones where children choose to play at break and dinner time. Each zone relates to an area of the EYFS curriculum. So a child can choose between: 1) physical activities on the field; 2) smaller physical activities such as skipping ropes, hula hoops, mark making with chalks; 3) creative activities such as dressing up, puppets, role play; 4) small world play; 5) design and technology/science-based activities. Children, through negotiation with friends, decide each morning which zone to choose. They are encouraged to try everything. These zones are seen as providing forums for discussion – they are places with resources to encourage collaboration, decision-making and purposeful talk.

What the headteacher thinks

The headteacher is enthusiastic about what they have achieved through these fundamental changes to the curriculum. She believes that the children's dispositions have changed; they are more active, more engaged and more thoughtful learners. Before, it was the teachers who were doing all the hard work (and the talking), but now the children are working equally hard – they are actively involved and pupil talk is central to all their learning.

The headteacher believes that the adoption of 'The little book of Thunks' (Gilbert, 2007) throughout the school has had a significant impact on the children's learning. A Thunk is described by the author as 'a beguiling question about everyday things that stops you in your tracks and helps you start to look at the world in a whole new light'. The headteacher observed that the children are now much more prepared to listen, share ideas, argue, develop their thinking and, sometimes, change their minds. She says that previously these children would never attempt to 'go over the mountain', but now they are emboldened and they have a real desire to learn.

What the children think

All the children indicated that they felt empowered in their learning. They showed understanding of how talk had enabled them to develop their thinking and learning. They appreciated that sharing ideas was beneficial because, 'You can improve your ideas with other people's ideas.'

When asked specifically about how talk had impacted on their literacy skills, the children identified that, in reading, they had benefited from an increased vocabulary and a developed understanding of how story language works. But it was in developing their writing skills that the children were most enthusiastic about the value of talking and listening. The influence of the work of The Write Team was clearly evident – the children said they had been inspired. They were convinced of the benefits of collaborative talk for planning, redrafting, editing and evaluating their writing: 'I like talking about my writing with my friends. I can change things and improve them.' 'You can partner up and make a great story.'

What the teachers think

The teachers had 'signed up' to developing and changing their pedagogy. They had a shared vision of where they wanted to go. The curriculum was seen as a work in progress. But already several key principles had emerged:

- Everyone can succeed.

- Everything doesn't have to be written down.

- Children need to be inspired.

- Pupil voice will emerge if children realise the teacher is really listening.

- Talk should be purposeful and relate to first hand experiences.

The positive results that they have identified so far include:

- Children talk more and teachers talk less.
- Teachers are sometimes facilitators rather than leaders of learning.
- Children are engaged – they are no longer passive recipients.
- There is a greater bond between teachers and children – they are working together towards shared goals.
- Children are empowered and more independent learners.
- They have a more sophisticated understanding of how language works.
- Their writing skills have developed significantly.

Reflecting on case study I

- What are the strengths and possible difficulties in transforming a school's curriculum and pedagogy in this way?
- Which aspects might be most effective in your school?

Case study 2: St Andrew's C of E Primary School, Bath

The school is an average-sized primary school of approximately 180 children aged between 3 to 11 years. It is situated in the heart of the heritage city of Bath, a factor that is significant as the school uses the cultural centres of Bath to enrich its curriculum and the children's experiences. A large percentage of the children speak English as an additional language and more than 18 different languages are spoken. As the school is very diverse, the values of inclusion are hugely important. St Andrew's Primary feels like a 'village school in the city'; it is located near to the city park and its classrooms are light, airy spaces that allow children to access, and make full use of, the outdoor environment. The school aims to 'instil in children a love of learning and a love of life itself'.

St Andrew's Primary worked with 5x5x5= creativity (Bancroft et al., 2008) at *the egg* Children's Theatre in a project entitled 'Schools Without Walls' and this is the focus for this case study. All the adults interviewed talked about the project enabling the children to express themselves through their 'hundred languages' (Edwards et al., 2012), a concept developed by the Reggio Emilia approach to show how children can communicate and express themselves in multiple ways, not just through talk.

What the headteacher says

The headteacher wants her school to be an exciting, active learning environment, with inclusive values at its heart. She said that she wants the children to be playing, communicating and expressing themselves with all of their being. The school has initiated a number of projects that encourage talk such as 'Take One Picture', 'The

Story Making Project' and 'Thunks'. In 2009, when the school became involved with the 5x5x5=creativity project, the Primary Strategies were seemingly turning out curricula and children that were all the same. The school adopted the Quigley curriculum, a skills-based curriculum that aims to build a relevant and inspiring curriculum. Citizenship and listening to children's voices are crucial to the school too, with children working alongside the adults to build a strong sense of community.

Initially, artists worked with staff and children in their school and posed the question: 'What is school'? The outcome of their joint thinking was the 'schools without walls' project, which evolved into a two-year project of transformational learning. At the start of the project, a Year 5/6 class had a residency at *the egg* Theatre in Bath for 4 days a week for 7 weeks. There, they did all their learning, engaging with the theatre and 5x5x5=creativity staff and following through a range of projects. Provocations allowed children to play with the real and fantasy worlds that were evoked. Queen's Square in Bath became the children's daily playground. In the following year, a PGCE student teacher from Bath Spa University became involved. Children and staff began to negotiate with the city and make connections with spaces, similar to Reggio children who have 'dialogues with places' (Filippini et al., 2008).

The headteacher said the project has allowed children to become brave enough to communicate and ask questions. The children benefited from hearing other voices and speech patterns, not just their own teacher's. Children's dispositions to learning, in particular their collaborative talk and learning skills, grew throughout the project. The teachers also became far braver and more flexible in their approaches, enabling learners to become active agents who asked questions, challenging themselves and evidently enjoying their discussions and participatory learning.

What the teacher and student teacher and artist say

The learning at *the egg* has allowed the child's view of the world to be expressed, with the children becoming more creative, imaginative and 'truer'. The children have role played real life situations and rehearsed what they will say. Interestingly, the higher achieving children, who may have felt more secure in the classroom environment, perhaps felt de-skilled and had to find a new position. It could be that the experience was initially disorientating for their identity, which was built around doing well academically, rather than being socially and orally adept. Noticeably, one bilingual Polish speaker made huge leaps in progress in terms of her self-confidence, fluency and freedom of expression. The teacher felt that this must be because there is an immediate, meaningful context to all the talk at *the egg* Theatre. The adults listen more carefully to the children and relationships have become richer, with staff and children sharing their 'myriad versions of the truth'. The process 'shook up' the social dynamic and everyone now mixes in together, with a noticeable improvement in self-belief and learner identity. The future challenge is to notice when talk and learning might be slipping back into old ways back in the classroom. These teachers talked about being 'explorers of an uncharted world'.

The student teacher says that his practice has been transformed in that now he really listens to the children and elicits their ideas. He went from meticulously planning his lessons to giving children choice in their learning. He agreed that the children talk and learn for a real purpose that instantly gives meaning to the learning. He noticed that the gap has narrowed between those that used to speak a lot and those who did not.

What the 5x5x5=creativity artist says

The project has provided a space for children to 'think and dream and explore'. Their confidence as communicators has improved. Children with sensory impairment have learned to communicate through visualising their feelings in drawing and then putting this back into words. They are communicating 'the secret world inside them'. A recurring theme has been on reflecting, talking and thinking about the 'inner me' and the 'outer me'. An open, trusting relationship between the adults and children seems to be crucial for this to occur.

What the children say

All the children interviewed said they felt that they have more freedom to talk.

'It's just, well 'school without walls'; we are not locked in'. 'Our school is not as blocked up as some other schools.'

'I have learnt that I do not need to use speech to speak to people.'

'I speak a lot at *the egg* and have more friends.'

Reflecting on case study 2

- What would you do to ensure that talk and learning continued to be as inspiring in the everyday classroom environment?

- How could you take a creative enquiry approach to talking and learning into your own setting? What would the challenges be and in what ways could you overcome them?

 TRY THIS

All of the activities suggested in Chapter 10 (P4C) are further examples that will support purposeful and reciprocal communication.

Try this 1: Creating a classroom ethos where speech and the speaker are valued

Activity 1: Creating ground rules for effective discussion

The class needs to have a shared understanding of the kind of environment that best supports effective discussion. Involving the children in creating the ground rules will support a class ethos that is conducive to productive talk.

Agreed 'rules' might be something like this:

- We ensure that everyone gets the opportunity to speak.
- We listen to all ideas.
- We like to play with ideas and possibilities.
- We try to justify our thought and ideas by explaining why.
- We ask questions to find out, to make things clear and to expand on ideas.
- We can disagree.

Activity 2: We like this poem

In small groups, after browsing the poetry books in the class or library or online resources (poetry archive website), children choose a poem. They work on an oral performance of their poem for the rest of the class, possibly using movement and music. Children introduce their poem saying why they chose it and the audience is invited to respond to each performance.

What links can you make between activities 1 and 2?

Would you always start by establishing the ground rules?

Would the ground rules be the same throughout the school?

Try this 2: Encouraging children to develop effective questioning skills

Activity 1: Twenty questions

The teacher begins by saying, 'I'm thinking of a person (word, thing, book, event) and you have twenty questions to guess who or what it is.' Once the children have got the idea they can take on the role of the 'thinker'. With support and some recapping of information, children from Foundation Stage upwards can play this game.

Would this activity work best if the target word were related to a topic being studied by the class?

How can you ensure that the questions are asked by a range of children and everyone is involved?

How can you narrow the options if playing with younger children?

Activity 2: Would I lie to you? (An adaptation of the BBC TV programme)

The teacher and two additional adults (TAs, parents, headteacher) present to the class a story from their lives that they claim to be true. Only one is telling the truth. If no extra help is available the teacher could tell three stories, only one of which is true. The children, in small groups, discuss the questions they would like to put to each of the presenters. Through questioning, listening and reasoned discussion the children, in groups, make their decisions and then discover the truth. Older children could take on the roles of presenters, perhaps preparing their 'truth' or 'lie' for homework.

Do children develop their listening and questioning skills through playing these games?

Do these questioning skills transfer to other activities, for example when interviewing a visiting expert?

Try this 3: Creating a culture in the classroom that encourages problem solving in groups through dialogue

Activity 1: Re-create a poem

Choose a poem suited to the interests and ages of the children. Paste each line of the poem on a strip of card. In small groups (three or four) children work together to form a poem that makes sense. The interest lies in the discussion that occurs: What clues are the children using? How do they justify their choices? You may choose to appoint an observer for each group who reports back on the process. A variation of this activity would be to use a prose text split up into sentences. You could also provide blank strips so that words, phrases or lines could be added to the text.

Does this activity deepen children's understanding of texts?

How can you encourage the children to negotiate and, if necessary, compromise?

Activity 2: Odd one out

Four pictures are presented together on the IWB. Working in small groups the children have to decide which is the odd one out, offering justifications for their decisions. There is not necessarily a 'correct' answer. The chosen images could relate to texts that the children are familiar with from earlier language learning.

What kind of environment supports this activity where there isn't one right answer?

Do you think the class would become more adventurous in their learning generally as a result of engaging in this activity?

Activity 3: Sometimes, always, never

Children are presented with statements such as 'Teachers want you to be quiet'; 'Boys like fighting more than girls'; 'All living things need water'; 'If it's December, it's winter' . . . Their task is to reach an agreement in their group, deciding if the statement is sometimes, always or never true. If agreement can't be reached, then dissenting individuals are invited to justify their views.

Are there ways in which you could develop this activity into writing?

How could this activity be used to develop learning in a range of curriculum areas?

Activity 4: Explore the picture

Choose a picture (a painting, a photograph) which relates to a topic or theme that you are studying. You could use this framework to support the exploration.

- Observe: the children look in detail and 'say what they see'.

- Question: they pose questions that arise from their observations (Why? Where? Who? When? How?).

- Connect: they link these observations and questions to their current knowledge and experiences.

- Imagine: they envisage possibilities, motivations, reasons. They put themselves into the picture, empathising with the characters.

- Reflect: they mull over what they've discussed; they evaluate what's been said; they think about what this means and where they would like to go next.

This activity would work equally well with an artefact.

Does this framework support deeper discussion?

Try this 4: Establishing a classroom where alternative perspectives are recognised and valued

Activity 1: 'The good news is . . .'/ 'the bad news is . . .' or 'fortunately . . .'/ 'unfortunately . . .'

This works well in groups of five. One child starts with a positive statement and the next child follows with a statement that puts a negative slant on the situation. Example: 'The good news is tomorrow is Saturday . . .' 'The bad news is I have to tidy my room . . .' 'The good news is I get paid pocket money for tidying my room . . .'

Activity 2: Debates

To achieve a successful debate children will need a good deal of preparation. They need to understand the conventions – proposer, seconder etc. – and they need time to think through the arguments, and possible counter arguments.

This is best done in small groups. The teacher will need to offer a scaffolding framework, at least initially. With younger children issues of immediate personal concern (school- and home-related) will work best, whereas older children might attempt 'bigger' issues.

Activity 3: Who thinks what?

Offer a framework for a poem where consecutive verses begin: Teachers think . . . , Parents think . . . , Friends think . . . , I think . . . Each initial statement should be followed by three lines, each of which should offer a different idea. A whole class poem could be the result of this activity.

Can you identify a greater openness within the class? Are opinions expressed rationally and views substantiated?

SUMMARY

We have explored key initiatives and principles in implementing pedagogies of talk. We focused on what dialogic talk looks like in the classroom and we explored the teaching strategies that develop effective talk and learning in literacy. We have argued that exploratory, creative, reflective and evaluative talk affords the greatest cognitive potential for learners, allowing them to exchange ideas and become joint enquirers in the learning process. Implementing dialogic teaching results in increased classroom interaction and extended thinking opportunities The two case studies exemplify how stimulating and engaging teaching approaches can encourage children to become reflective, confident and discerning speakers, readers and writers who recognise the power and the pleasure of words. Finally, we offered some ideas for developing collaborative talk for a range of purposes in engaging and enjoyable contexts.

FURTHER READING

Websites

For information about Reggio Emilia inspired 5x5x5= creativity projects: Learning Without Walls: www.5x5x5creativity.org.uk/

For more on dialogic talk: www.robinalexander.org.uk/

To see more examples of Thunks: www.thunks.co.uk/

To explore research into dialogue in language and literacy and to read the UKLA response to the proposed English Curriculum (2012): www.ukla.org/

REFERENCES

Alexander, R. J. (2008) *Towards Dialogic Teaching: Rethinking Classroom Talk*, 4th edn. York: Dialogos.

Bancroft, S., Fawcett, M. and Hay, P. (2008) *Researching Children Researching the World: 5x5x5=creativity*. Stoke-on-Trent: Trentham Books.

Barnes, D. and Todd, F. (1977) *Communication and Learning in Small Groups*. London: Routledge.

Bourdieu, P. (1977) *Outline of a Theory of Practice*. Cambridge: Cambridge University Press.

Britton, J. (1970) *Language and Learning*. London: Penguin.

Cazden, C. B. (2001) *Classroom Discourse: The Language of Teaching and Learning*. Portsmouth, NH: Heinemann.

Chambers, A. (2011) *Tell Me: Children Reading and Talk*. Stroud: Thimble Press.

Craft, A. (2000) *Creativity Across the Curriculum: Framing and Developing Practice*. London: Routledge Falmer.

Cummins, J. (2000) *Language, Power and Pedagogy: Bilingual Children in the Crossfire*. Clevedon: Multilingual Matters.

Cremin, T., with Bearne, E., Dombey, H. and Lewis, M. (2009) *Teaching English Creatively*. Abingdon: Routledge.

Edwards, C., Gandini, L. and Forman, G. (2012) *The Hundred Languages of Children*, 3rd edn. Reggio Emilia: Reggio Children.

Filippini, T., Giudici, C. and Vecchi, V. (2008) *Dialogues with Places*. Reggio Emilia: Reggio Children.

Fisher, R. (2009) *Creative Dialogue: Talk for Thinking in the Classroom*. Abingdon: Routledge.

Gilbert, I. (2007) *The Little Book of Thunks*. Bancyfelin: Crown House Publishing Ltd.

Goodwin, P. (2001) *The Articulate Classroom Talking and Learning in the Primary School*. London: David Fulton.

Grainger, T., Goouch, K. and Lambirth, A. (eds) (2005) *Creativity and Writing*. London: Routledge.

Grugeon, E. and Gardner, P. (2000) *The Art of Storytelling for Teachers and Pupils*. London: David Fulton.

Halliday, M. A. K. (1975) *Learning How to Mean: Explorations in the Development of Language*. London: Edward Arnold.

Harris, D. and Williams, J. (2012) The association of classroom interactions, year group and social class. *British Educational Research Journal*, 38(3): 373–97.

Kelly, C. (2010) *Hidden Worlds: Young Children Learning Literacy in Multicultural Contexts*. Stoke-on-Trent: Trentham Books.

Martin, T. (2010) *Talk for Spelling*. London: UKLA.

Mercer, N. (2000) *Words and Minds; How We Use Language to Think Together*. Abingdon: Routledge.

Mercer, N. and Dawes, L. (2008) The value of exploratory talk, in N. Mercer and S. Hodgkinson (eds) (2008) *Exploring Talk in School*. London: SAGE.

Mercer, N. and Hodgkinson, S. (eds) (2008) *Exploring Talk in School*. London: Sage.

Norman, K. (1992) *Thinking Voices: The Work of the National Oracy Project*. London: Hodder & Stoughton.

Palincsar, A. S. and Brown, A. L. (1984) *Reciprocal Teaching of Comprehension Fostering and Monitoring Activities: Cognition and Instruction*. Hillsdale, NJ: Lawrence Erlbaum.

Sadler, R. (1989) *Formative Assessment and the Design of Instructional Systems*. Netherlands: Kluwer Academic Publishers.

Sinclair, J. and Coulthard, M. (1975) *Towards an Analysis of Discourse: The English Used by Teachers and Pupils*. London: Oxford University Press.

Vygotsky, L. (1978) *Mind in Society*. Cambridge, MA: Harvard University Press.

Wegerif, R. (2010) *Dialogue and Teaching Thinking with Technology: Opening, Expanding and Deepening The 'Inter-Face'*, in K. Littleton and C. Howe (eds) *Educational Dialogues: Understanding and Promoting Productive Interaction*. London: Routledge.

Wells, G. (2009) *The Meaning Makers*. Bristol: Multilingual Matters.

Whitehurst, G. J., Falco, F. L., Lonigan, C. J., Fischel, J. E., DeBaryshe, B. D., Valdez-Menchaca, M. C. and Caulfield, M. (1988) Accelerating language development through picture book reading. *Developmental Psychology*, 24: 552–9.

Wood, D., Bruner, J. and Ross, G. (1976) The role of tutoring in problem-solving. *Journal of Child Psychology and Child Psychiatry*, 17: 89–100.

Wray, D. and Lewis, M. (1997) *Extending Literacy: Children Reading and Writing Non-Fiction*. London: Routledge.

INDEX

Added to a page number 'f' denotes a figure.